THE
STRAIGHT
EIGHT
ENGINE

KEITH
RAY

THE STRAIGHT EIGHT ENGINE
Powering Premium Automobiles

KEITH RAY

Published 2020
ISBN: 978-1-85443-306-0

Printed by Interpress Ltd, Hungary
for the Publisher:
Dalton Watson Fine Books
Glyn and Jean Morris
Deerfield, IL 60015 USA
www.daltonwatson.com

TABLE *of* CONTENTS

PREFACE

Cars with straight eight engines have always fascinated me, an interest I can trace back to when I was seven years old. On Christmas of 1955 I was given as a present the *Observer's Book of Automobiles*. I still have this book, rather dog-eared by now as it has been greatly used. Even at that early age I had a fairly well-developed knowledge of cars, so when I saw a Bugatti listed as a 'current' model, the 101 Coach, I thought something was a little odd. I knew Bugatti did not make cars after the Second World War, but I must have filed this fact away somewhere in my brain under 'rather intriguing' and got on with whatever seven-year-old boys did at the time. It would not be for a further 20 years that I made sense of this, when I learned that a quantity of pre-war Bugatti 57 parts had been discovered in Molsheim, sufficient to build seven or eight 'new' cars, and that these had been slowly assembled into complete vehicles and sold as the Bugatti 101 Coach, clothed in extravagant coachwork. This modern coachwork concealed the fact that the first metre behind the radiator grille was just empty space because of the pre-war axle layout. I also discovered that the last of these cars had not been completed until 1965.

My next encounter with straight eights was when I was in my teens. My family lived in Cheshire, quite close to Manchester and Liverpool in an area popular with the 'nouveau riche' of the north west at the time, including many footballers and entertainers. In our town, parked discreetly out of sight, I sometimes noticed the most flamboyant car I had ever seen, which I assumed was a Figoni and Falaschi-bodied Delage straight eight and, I was told, belonged to a celebrity who was 'playing away'. I later discovered, when I summoned up the courage to take a closer look, that it was in fact a Delahaye, and so not a straight eight at all! But it was the most extravagant, and definitely not discreet, sky blue Figoni and Falaschi creation.

Roll forward a few more years, and having graduated from university and got married, my wife and I continued living in a flat in Cambridge just off Chesterton Road. Nearby was a private-hire limousine business which ran a small fleet of Daimler DE36s. I was fascinated by these silent giants, which glided past our flat scarcely making a sound, yet seemed so vast. Then, soon afterwards, a university friend acquired a Railton Special Sports, the super lightweight, 4-litre Hudson-powered, cycle-winged road rocket! It always left me speechless: a pre-war car which could show a clean pair of heels to almost all early 1970s cars of the time.

My last important encounter with straight eights, and the most poignant, only dates back a few years. My wife and I own a holiday apartment in Cornwall, part of a former Edwardian hotel. Seven or eight years ago the apartment above ours changed hands, and one day I met the new owner, Bryan Tyrrell, in the car park. I noticed he was wearing a Railton Owners Club T-shirt, so we got chatting about cars and found we had a mutual friend in the owner of the Railton Special Sports mentioned earlier. It turns out that Bryan had been Chairman of the Railton Owners Club, and we became good friends. I spent considerable time discussing the idea for this book with Bryan, and he shared a lot of information with me and gave me many useful contacts. Sadly, Bryan passed away after a long illness before he had a chance to see my draft manuscript.

I am pleased to see this book in print, and dedicate it partly to Bryan and our friendship, and partly to my patient wife who never complained about my spending many hours buried away in my study doing research and pouring over the manuscript into the early hours.

This book is something I had been wanting to write for a long time. It has given me a lot of pleasure, and a number of new friends, and I hope readers will also gain some pleasure from reading it. I have so many people to thank for their help.

Keith Ray
August 2020

OPPOSITE: The distinctive radiator of the 1924 Bugatti Type 30.

INTRODUCTION

The straight eight was very much an engine of its time. Although this engine format had been used in racing cars before the First World War, it was not until after the War that it found its way into road cars. From around 1920, until the mid- to late-fifties, this engine configuration was used by at least 90 car manufacturers worldwide. Whereas most other engine configurations, especially the straight four, straight six and V8, were present from the earliest days of motoring and continue to this day, the straight eight died out almost as suddenly as it emerged. There were several reasons for its demise, which will be covered later.

With one exception, the straight eight, together with the much rarer V16, is the longest engine that has been installed in cars. The sole exception was Gabriel Voisin's rather insane 27CV straight 12 built in 1934, a 4,660 cc sleeve valve oddity. The Voisin's extraordinary engine was so long it encroached into the passenger space. It is believed only two were made. Packard also built a straight 12 prototype engine in 1922, and although photographs of the engine survive it is not known for certain whether it was ever installed in a car chassis. The more sensible straight eight engine's length suited the fashion of the 1920s and 1930s, where a long bonnet equated to luxury, wealth, power and speed. Fashion changes after the Second World War were without doubt an important factor leading to its demise. Today the only use for the straight eight configuration is for marine diesel engines.

There were great regional differences between the roles fulfilled by the straight eight engines. It is likely that many European manufacturers were anxious to keep up with those in the United States where straight eights had become popular much earlier, albeit in most cases with fairly basic and straight-forward 'flathead' side valve units. In Britain and Europe straight eights were always rare and expensive beasts, often with sophisticated overhead camshafts, or at least overhead valves, and frequently clothed in expensive coachwork. The total production of straight eights in Britain was probably fewer than 3,000 units whilst in Europe, where they were more common, only around 40,000 were made. In contrast, in the United States, whilst there was a similar market sector

of expensive and sophisticated straight eights like Duesenberg, Cord, Auburn and Pierce Arrow, there was also a vast market for middle-range versions with simple 'flathead' side valve engines, and total production was in the many hundreds of thousands. Some manufacturers, like Packard and Studebaker, carried on with the straight eight well into the 1950s.

During its lifespan the straight eight was seen in many formats including side valve units, overhead valve, overhead inlet over side exhaust, single overhead cam, dual overhead cam and sleeve valve, and both normally aspirated and supercharged. It powered ordinary family saloons, luxury limousines, rakish open coupes, fast 'supercars', racing cars, as well as many other types of vehicles such as lorries, military vehicles, and fire tenders.

Along the way the straight eight also found its way into a number of the most unusual cars ever seen, including the Burney Streamline, a car designed by the man responsible for the R100 airship, the ZIS 101 Sport, a two- seater based on the massive ZIS limousine, the Bugatti 101 Coach, already mentioned, the Leyland Eight, the Rolls-Royce Phantom IV, and the spectacular 1955 Bugatti Type 251 Grand Prix car, with its pre-war straight eight mounted transversely behind the driver. Descriptions of all these cars can be found in the appropriate chapters.

At the same time, the engine format allowed some glamorous and beautiful cars to grace the roads, including Duesenberg, Isotta Fraschini, Pierce Arrow, Bugatti, Marmon, Delage and Auburn, which were often clothed in expensive coachwork from the world's top design houses.

In this book I have attempted to record every company which has made a straight eight, and to overview their models. Of course, it is not perfect, and I suspect quite a few manufacturers have 'slipped under my radar', especially tiny businesses which made just a handful of vehicles. Some manufacturers receive more attention than others, usually because of especially important technological input into car design. At the other end of the scale the information available on some now defunct manufacturers is so sparse that only a brief mention can be made.

The left side of the Mercedes-Benz 500K's 5-litre engine.

WHY THE STRAIGHT EIGHT?

The straight eight occupies a unique place in the history of motoring. Whereas straight fours, straight sixes, V8s and other formats have been around since the beginnings of the car and continue to this day, the straight eight first appeared in a serial production car in 1919, in the 5.9-litre Isotta Fraschini Tipo 8, and virtually died out suddenly just before the Second World War. Only a few models, such as the Rolls-Royce Phantom IV, the Daimler DE36, a handful of Packards, Hudsons and Pontiacs, and the Russian ZIL appeared after the War.

So why, throughout the 1920s and 1930s, did the straight eight become popular, and indeed in the early '30s outsell straight sixes for a while? A number of factors came into play during those 20 years.

Even before the First World War a handful of companies, such as Ballot, had been successful on the track with straight eight powered racing engines, and after the War others, including Bugatti and Alfa Romeo, followed suite. This was particularly true when Grand Prix cars were restricted to small engines, as in 1924 when the limit was 2-litres. The Bugatti Type 35, with a displacement of just 1,991 cc (121 cu in) from its eight-cylinder engine with a 60 mm (2.4 in) bore, and an 88 mm (3.5 in) stroke, could rev to 6,000 rpm thanks to lightweight reciprocating parts and its five ball bearing crankshaft. Many manufacturers sought to leverage this success by 'selling' the concept of the straight eight to the ordinary motorist as a 'must have' engine.

It was an era when long bonnets were seen as fashionable, and an indication of the owner's status. Long bonnets also suited the designs of the coachbuilders who built expensive bodywork to mount on expensive chassis, and they allowed plenty of room for a long straight eight engine. Whilst the appeal and benefits of multi-cylinders could equally be satisfied by a V format, especially a V8, such engines were much wider than straight eights which was potentially a problem. In cars with a chassis frame that had to be narrow at the front to allow a reasonable steering lock with semi-elliptic suspension, there was limited width for a vee engine. Today, with every new car having independent front suspension, and with the freedom offered by unitary

A sensational 1930 Duesenberg Model J.

construction, this benefit of the straight eight format has been negated.

In order to keep the length of the engine reasonable, most straight eights had bores considerably smaller than the stroke, and the long stroke of the typical straight eight of the period resulted in a machine that was flexible with high torque. Many straight eights could be driven from rest in top gear, which appealed to drivers not confident about changing gear in the days before synchromesh. This flexibility also allowed smooth running at low speeds, which suited the upper part of the market where many of the more expensive cars would be chauffeur-driven.

The smooth and quiet running of a straight eight was without doubt a good selling point in the car showroom.

11

Certain technological benefits were also claimed. For example, in 1921 Autocar magazine published an editorial expounding the virtues of the straight eight, including more even torque resulting in less strain on the gearbox, and requiring a much smaller flywheel as a result, allowing the engine to be placed lower in the chassis. The editorial also conjectured

improved acceleration, reduced tyre wear (although that benefit is a little dubious!) and less stress on the driveline.

Compared to the V configuration, the straight engine, especially with side valves, offered much better accessibility to spark plugs and other accessories,

and facilitated cylinder head removal for de-coking which was quite routine in those days. In addition, there was not the limitation of having two con rods on a common journal, essential if the benefits of the more compact dimensions of the vee engine were to be fully exploited.

Whilst it is true many straight fours in the 1920s and 1930s could be a little rough and unrefined, not helped by the absence of rubber engine mounts which would appear later, straight sixes were certainly a lot smoother, and in most cases could deliver the same degree of refinement as a straight eight, whilst avoiding many of the drawbacks of the latter.

Overall, aside from applications in racing, the spread of popularity of the straight eight in the 1920s and 1930s can mainly be put down to fashion, marketing and a degree of 'technological snobbery', rather than to any over-riding technological advantage or driver benefit.

Today the only use for the straight eight configuration is in the marine world, where the current fashion is for powering large container ships, tankers and cruise liners with a straight, low-speed diesel engine, often of quite massive proportions. For example, Wartsila, the manufacturers of the largest motive power unit of all time (which weighs 2,300 tonnes and generates 103,000 bhp), produces straight engines with all numbers of cylinders from four up to fourteen, including several 'eights'. In such applications the slow, and steady, engine speed negates many of the drawbacks of the long crank of the straight eight, whereas in car applications these dynamic drawbacks helped hasten the demise of this configuration.

Another classic German, a 1939 Horch 853 A.

13

TECHNICAL PROBLEMS WITH STRAIGHT EIGHT ENGINE DESIGN

Designing any automobile engine presents technical problems and often requires compromises to be made. In the case of the straight eight several of these problems are more challenging than in a shorter engine such as a 'four' or a 'six', and the compromises which have to be made are correspondingly greater. Sometimes they come down to simple economics, when the ideal solution would be too expensive. In other cases, particularly in the 1920s and 1930s when the straight eight was at the height of its popularity, the compromise was driven mainly by the contemporary limitations of technology.

The six areas where the biggest challenges arose were:
◆ Engine length
◆ Firing order
◆ Torsional vibration
◆ The number of main bearings
◆ Carburettors
◆ Inlet and exhaust manifold design

In practice, all these challenges interact, and the design of a long engine is complex. Today the only place where long straight engines are found is in the marine world, where diesel engines will typically run for hours or even days at a constant slow speed, often as low as 80-300 rpm. Under those conditions many of the problems faced by the car engine designer do not exist.

ENGINE LENGTH

With eight cylinders in a line, the straight eight will inevitably be a long engine. The only way to reduce this length is to have a small cylinder bore, and keep the spacing between the cylinders as tight as possible. The result of a small bore is that the stroke will be correspondingly long, which tends to limit engine speeds to around 3,000 to 4,000 rpm and increases cylinder wear. A long stroke does have the advantage that low speed torque is good, and many straight eights could be happily driven using top gear alone, although cooling issues can arise if the gap between cylinders is too small.

FIRING ORDER

With a four stroke straight eight there are four firings per revolution of the crankshaft, and getting these four, and the four of the next revolution, in the optimum order is important for a number of reasons. Of course, the total number of different firing patterns is enormous. The first firing can be in one of eight cylinders, the second firing in one of seven, the third in one of six... and so on. The total number of possible combinations is 'factorial 8', which is 40,320; but of these possible firing orders, only around five were commonly used, and perhaps only a further ten have ever been used.

A large number of these possible combinations can be immediately ruled out. For example, it would be extremely difficult to have neighbouring

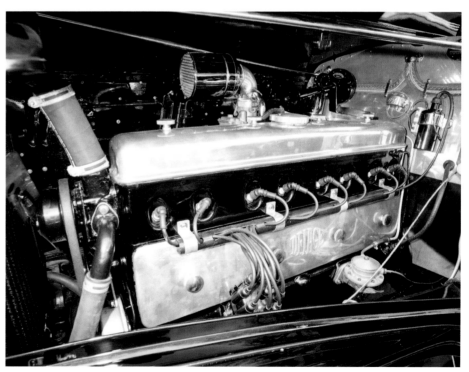

1936 Delage D8 100: elegant alloy covers enhance the engine bay.

cylinders firing one after the other, since this would potentially cause serious cooling and crankshaft flexing problems, as well as difficulty getting fuel in and exhaust out efficiently, unless each cylinder had its own exhaust pipe and its own carburettor. Some racing straight eights did have completely separate exhaust systems for each cylinder, but eight separate carburettors is simply not feasible. Anyone who has had to balance even two or three carburettors would appreciate how impractical it would be to balance eight! Fuel injection would have obviated this problem completely, but it was not available at that time when straight eights were in vogue. Similarly, it would not be a good idea if, for example, cylinder one is firing to compress cylinder eight as this would maximise the torsional twist on the crankshaft. So quite quickly the 40,320 possible firing orders are reduced to 20 or so which would work in practice. In this context 'work effectively' means:

◆ Maximum balance between cylinders to give smooth rotation
◆ Minimum torsional twisting and vibration
◆ Optimum cooling of the cylinder block
◆ Efficient input to all eight cylinders from just one or two carburettors
◆ Similarly efficient exhaust through a common exhaust 'rail'
◆ Minimum noise
◆ A pleasant engine sound, an important factor when many straight eights were expensive cars!

The engineers designing straight eights are often said to have followed one of two routes; the first was to think of the 'eight' as two 'fours' joined end to end, and the second was to think of the middle four-cylinders as a 'four' with a 'twin' (effectively a 'split' four) attached at each end. The designers with the 'two fours' mentality seem generally to have opted for either of the following firing orders:

(1) 1-6-2-5-8-3-7-4
(2) 1-5-2-6-3-7-4-8

Whilst the 'two-four-two' brigade tended to select one of the following:

(3) 1-5-3-7-4-8-2-6
(4) 1-7-3-8-4-6-2-5
(5) 1-5-2-6-4-8-3-7

As examples, Isotta Fraschini, Diana and Jordan used firing order (1), Beverley-Barnes used (4), and Bugatti (2). But Frontenac used a different order, 1-6-3-7-4-5-2-8, whilst Packard had its own system as did Panhard Levassor. There was clearly no agreement about the 'correct' order, and perhaps there never could be an 'ideal' sequence. As will be seen from the photographs throughout this book, many manufacturers stamped the firing order onto the block.

TORSIONAL VIBRATIONS

On a long engine, regardless of bearing support, torsional vibration or oscillation can prove problematical for both the crankshaft and the camshaft. In time this can lead to fatigue fracture of the crankshaft. Designers had three possible ways around this.

Firstly, they could make the crankshaft so stiff and strong that the torsional effects are minimal. But this makes the crank heavy and relatively expensive, and in many ways is a sledgehammer to crack a nut.

A second solution used for example, by Alfa Romeo, was to split the 'eight' into two 'fours', and take the final drive and cam drive from the middle of the engine. The crank vibration or oscillation is thereby effectively halved.

The third solution, used by many manufacturers, was to incorporate an active damper at the end of the crank to iron out the vibrations and oscillations.

THE NUMBER OF MAIN BEARINGS

Even with a small bore and a long stroke, and closely packed cylinders, any straight eight is going to be a long engine with a long crankshaft. Typically, the bore on a straight eight was around 70%-75% of the stroke, although the 1930s Pontiacs were unusually 'square' with a ratio of 91%. With a long crankshaft comes the issue of how many main bearings to use. The ideal number is nine, so that each big end is supported on both sides by a bearing. This was the pattern followed by Isotta Fraschini, Beverley-Barnes, Panhard Levassor and Packard amongst others. In fact, Wolseley went one better with ten main bearings because the drive to the ohc was in the centre of the block separating the two banks of four-cylinders.

Reducing the number below nine, whilst saving cost, risks a different kind of vibration occurring, the 'whipping' vibration of an unsupported crank. Hupmobile, Jordan, Marmon, Hillman and Locomobile chose to use five which did not seem to cause major issues, although engine speeds at the time were rarely in excess of 4,000 rpm, often a lot less. Surprisingly the earliest straight eight Bugattis managed with just three bearings, each set of four 'big ends' having no intermediate support. This seemed to work satisfactorily in European races where lots of corners moderated engine speeds, but was less than satisfactory on circuits in the United States which were typically high-speed ovals.

CARBURETTORS

If someone were to design and build a straight eight today, carburettion would not be an issue at all as they would use fuel injection which can deliver the right amount of fuel to every cylinder every time, whether the engine is a 'four', a 'six', an 'eight', an in-line, a V or any other cylinder format. When the straight eight was in vogue in the 1920s and '30s, fuel injection was unheard of for motor cars and the only fuelling answer was the carburettor. It is easy to hypothesise about a 'perfect' straight eight, where each cylinder has its own, identical, independent exhaust and its own, identical, independent inlet manifold and separate carburettor. In theory that sounds great, but balancing, and keeping balanced, eight carburettors would be virtually impossible. In the 1920s, '30s and '40s, most engines used just one or two carburettors and relied on careful manifold design to ensure no major problems. The issue is quite simple. If there are eight cylinders drawing fuel mixture from just one or two carburettors, it is inevitable that some cylinders draw mixture along

a much longer route than others, and almost by definition that mixture will be different. At low speeds and modest power, as in most road cars of the time, this would not be a big issue. But during the 1950s and '60s such issues became much more significant, helping to contribute to the death of the straight eight.

INLET AND EXHAUST MANIFOLD DESIGN

This in an area where firing order is highly relevant. Whilst some racing and fast road cars with straight eight engines had separate long exhaust pipes for each cylinder, for example the Triumph Dolomite, sometimes finally coming together in a large 'box', for the vast majority of cars this would have been both far too expensive and too bulky. But placing an exhaust manifold close to the cylinder itself meant that neighbouring cylinders firing at the same time, or very soon afterwards, could cause back-pressure problems. Similarly on the inlet side, if cylinders equidistant from the carburettor fire at the same time then a better balance will be achieved. Increasing the carburettors to two or four helps mitigate these issues, but the downside is the necessity to keep multiple carburettors properly balanced at all times.

These six areas of design issues all interact, and in reality, nearly all straight eight engine designs are a big compromise. Fortunately, as engine speeds were generally relatively low, these compromises could be lived with fairly easily in practice.

THE BIRTH
OF THE
STRAIGHT EIGHT
AUTOMOBILE

It is often difficult if not impossible to identify the true 'first' in most areas of technology, largely because 'first' can have many different meanings. For example, do we mean the first concept (which may be just an engineering drawing), the first prototype, the first patent application, the first patent awarded, the first serial production (even if it were a failure), the first successful serial production, or the first mass production? Also, it is common for parallel but independent developments to take place, such that more than one 'first' can appear at almost exactly the same time.

Before the First World War there was quite a lot of limited scale activity around the concept of a straight eight engine, almost all of it focused on racing and record breaking, and most based on two four-cylinder engines effectively working in tandem. The earliest incarnation of what today we might call a straight eight was possibly in 1903 when the French company of CGV (Charron, Girardot et Voigt), which had been a retailer of cars such as Panhards, built a 8,168 cc (498 cu in) 40 HP 'T head' engine with eight cylinders of 100 mm (3.9 in) bore and 130 mm (5.1 in) stroke (ratio 77%). This was in effect two of the previous year's 20 HP engines sitting on a common crankcase. This 'eight' produced a modest 12 bhp (6.7 kW) at 250 rpm rising to 52 bhp (38.9 kW) at 800 rpm. Quoting the low speed power output here is significant because this car had no ratio-changing gears, the belief being that provided the engine was large enough changing gear would be unnecessary. The next season's CGV had a simple planetary gear to give a starting ratio, a running ratio and a reverse gear. One drawback of the design was that the engine occupied about half the wheelbase of the vehicle, not an important drawback for a racing car but a real handicap for other applications. But CGV was not to be long lived, as it went out of business in 1906.

Also in 1903 the Winton Motor Carriage Company of Cleveland, Ohio built a straight eight racer, again with two four-cylinder units joined in tandem, but in this case steeply angled to the right side giving an ultra-low profile. The eight cylinders were each separately jacketed and were fed from a single

1903 CGV straight eight.

carburettor. In 1904 the engine was slightly enlarged to 16,894 cc (1,031 cu in) giving 65 mph at 700 rpm, and a recorded top speed of 92 mph. Like the first CGV, this car had no choice of gear ratio.

Another American straight eight appeared in 1903 in the form of an air-cooled engine from the Premier Motor Manufacturing Company based in Indianapolis. This ohv 6,155 cc (376 cu in) engine, like the two previous vehicles, used two 'fours' on a common crankcase and a single crankshaft. It was a much more 'square' engine with a bore of 95 mm (3.75 in) and a stroke of 108 mm (4.25 in) giving a ratio of 88% compared to 77% for the CGV.

The first 'pure' straight eight, as opposed to twin tandem fours, is generally recognised as the Dufaux, manufactured by C H Dufaux et Cie of Geneva. The aim was to enter the 1904 Gordon Bennett Race. The design was a 12,763 cc (779 cu in) side valve unit with a bore of 125 mm (4.9 in) and a stroke of 130 mm (5.1 in) giving a bore/stroke ratio of a high 96%. It was claimed to produce

1904 Dufaux brothers' racer.

Bellamy eight.

around 120 bhp at 1300 rpm, a modest 9.4 bhp per litre. Unfortunately, the car failed to start in either the 1904 or 1905 Gordon Bennett Race.

For 1906 the Dufaux brothers produced a larger 'eight' of 14,726 cc (899 cu in) and competed both with this and the earlier car. The 14.7-litre car entered the 1907 French Grand Prix but did not finish. This same year the Dufaux brothers stopped making motor cars.

Dufaux had a tenuous link with Rolls-Royce. In 1904, whilst the Dufaux brothers were also making four-cylinder road cars, Rolls-Royce ordered a trial run of five cars intending to stop selling Panhards and switch to Minervas, Dufauxs and their own cars. The order from Dufaux was running very late when one four-cylinder 150 HP vehicle was successfully shipped to compete in the 1905 Brighton speed trials. The car was a dismal failure and the order was cancelled.

Additionally, in 1904, a most remarkable French straight eight saw the light of day. Built by a Monsieur Bellamy, this car had a massive 38,507 cc (2,350 cu in) side valve engine which was, unusually, exactly 'square' with bore and stroke of 183 mm (7.2 in). Each of its eight cylinders was a separate casting. The massive engine produced around 165 bhp (123 kW) and like the early CGV had no facility for changing gear ratios, apart from changing the chain drive sprockets. It was claimed to be capable of 115 mph using its single gear.

Another twin tandem four appeared in 1904 when Herbert L. Bowden, a Waltham Massachusetts based industrialist, acquired a Mercedes 60 which he had lengthened so it could accommodate a second engine, which came from a power boat. Strictly this can scarcely be called a straight eight as the two separate engines were only properly reunited at the final drive unit. The car was, however, fast achieving 105 mph over a measured mile.

A similar twin tandem four approach was taken by Alfred Vanderbilt in 1905 when a stretched chassis was equipped with a pair of 10.5-litre Fiat engines. It was claimed to produce 250 bhp, but the original Fiat 'fours' only produced around 60 bhp each, so a combined output around 120 bhp seems more probable. The car was a dismal failure.

1905 Vanderbilt racer.

Between 1905 and the First World War a small number of other twin tandem four 'eights' appeared, including:

- ◆ The Maxwell-Briscoe in the US which was entered for the 1906 Vanderbilt Cup
- ◆ The 1907-1909 Osterfield in the UK, a 4,964 cc (303 cu in) road car
- ◆ The Laurin-Klement, a 4,877 cc (297 cu in) of which two were manufactured in Prague in 1907
- ◆ The Porthos, a 10,857 cc (663 cu in) French offering also seen in 1907
- ◆ The 14,866 cc (907 cu in) Weigel of which two were entered in the 1907 French Grand Prix

It is interesting that in the 1907 French Grand Prix there were four different makes of straight eight, all twin tandem fours. But this changed quickly as new regulations limiting total piston surface area came into force in 1908 which greatly favoured long stroke four-cylinder engines.

Possibly the last straight eight to appear before the War was the Palladium made by Palladium Autocars Ltd in Kensington, London. The company had started making 'fours' using Chapuis-Dornier engines but also listed a 20/28 HP side valve 'eight' of 3,451 cc (211 cu in), but it is not known if any were in fact sold.

Before the outbreak of war there were probably only around 30-40 straight eights in the world, and just a handful of proper road cars. During the First World War little happened in the automobile industry and much of the industry was given over to war production. It was only after the war that proper straight eights began to appear, perhaps most significantly with new models from Isotta Fraschini and Duesenberg in 1919. The 1920s, 1930s and the first few years of 1940s would become the 'golden era' of the straight eight.

THE
STRAIGHT EIGHT:
A KISS
OF DEATH?

Several 'authorities' have suggested that adopting a straight eight engine format has triggered the demise of many car manufacturers. Indeed, some have suggested that even the launching of a straight six by a company familiar only with straight fours had a similar end result. Cecil Clutton in his *The Vintage Motor Car Pocket Book* pointed out an apparent correlation between the launch of a 'six' and a company's entry into administration. In his later book, Lost Causes, Lord Montagu of Beaulieu recognised this link but postulated that it was much more evident when looking at the launch of a straight eight. He wrote 'The straight eight stalks like some sinister skeleton through the story of the Lost Causes'.

The truth is a little more complex than simply launching a straight eight model. The real problem could have been that many were launched at a bad time. The Great Depression, lasting from 1929 to 1939, was the worst economic downturn in history, yet many new straight eight models were introduced during this period. Not only were many manufacturers stepping into an unfamiliar area of automotive engineering, they were doing so when the market for their products was shrinking rapidly, and in some cases disappearing altogether. Also some manufacturers were simply stepping outside the area their loyal customers were familiar with, and would not buy the new models. A prime example of this must be Hillman, a company with a sound reputation for solid but not exciting side valve fours and sixes. The decision to launch a luxury ohv straight eight in 1928 must have been rather surprising to Hillman's customers. Also, stepping into a new area of technology caused the launch of the car to be delayed until 1929, the height of the Great Depression. The Hillman Straight 8 was in reality doomed even before it appeared. Soon afterwards the company was taken over by the Rootes Group.

RIGHT: 1932 Duesenberg Model J: on the later Model Js, the exhaust manifold is two separate sections for the front and rear groups of four cylinders.

The list of 'straight eight casualties' is long, and includes:

AMILCAR

The company's C8 straight eight in 1928 was a disaster, proving unreliable which aggravated the company's financial pressures. The business changed ownership twice and it did not re-emerge after the Second World War.

ARROL-ASTER

Relying solely on straight eights, Arrol-Aster was never successful and went into receivership in 1929, finally closing in 1931.

BELSIZE

The company had been in receivership since 1923, and tried to launch a 2496 cc straight eight in 1924/5 as a possible rescue plan, but it ceased trading in 1925. Launching a straight eight as a 'rescue plan' looks, in retrospect, a rather crazy idea.

DUESENBERG

The business relied on straight eights like the J and SJ, but these became less

popular in the later 1930s during the Great Depression, and this contributed to the financial failure of Duesenberg's owner, Cord, which collapsed in 1937.

HAMPTON

One of the most foolish ventures into the world of the straight eight must be Hampton. Having repeatedly gone into receivership, their idea of a 'rescue plan' was to launch an up-market straight eight called the Empire Sportsman in 1931, which was, in reality, just a 1931 Röhr 8 Type RA 10/55

from Germany bolted together in the US. Did Hampton not know that Röhr itself had bounced back from bankruptcy just the year before?

These are just some examples, but there are many others. It was not so much the case that launching a straight eight was the 'kiss of death', rather that the appeal of expensive straight eights waned in the late 1930s during the economic downturn, and the companies which looked to the straight eight as a saviour could not survive.

HILLMAN

As mentioned earlier, the launch of a straight eight by Hillman precipitated the acquisition by the Rootes Group.

LANCHESTER

The company's last design as an independent business was the 1928 4436 cc straight eight. Only 126 were made, the Great Depression killing demand. Lanchester became part of BSA (British Small Arms) in 1930, being purchased for £26,000, a fraction of its real value.

LOCOMOBILE

After being acquired by Durant Motors in 1922, Locomobile launched the JR-8, the Model 70 and the Model 8-80/8-88, all straight eights. But the company was already in trouble and these new models were just more nails in the coffin.

1939 Lanchester 32: the 'business' side of the Daimler engine.

WOLSELEY

The introduction of the ambitious 21/60 ohv model, which was expensive, contributed to the collapse of Wolseley in 1926 with debts of £2 million. The business was bought by William Morris in February 1927 for £730,000, money from his own pocket.

SUNBEAM

The company's launch of two straight eights in 1926 and 1927 did little to prevent substantial losses leading to the sale to the Rootes brothers in 1934.

Sunbeam straight eight twin cam engine.

THE MANUFACTURERS OF STRAIGHT EIGHT AUTOMOBILE ENGINES

The main body of this book covers 92 manufacturers and users of straight eight engines It is almost certain that there were other manufacturers of straight eights that are not covered, but the author believes the list to be reasonably comprehensive. Should more come to light, especially from readers, these will be included in a second edition.

Of the 92 companies:

- ◆ 68 manufactured both their own engines and complete cars.

- ◆ 4 manufactured cars using engines of their own design but assembled by a specialist engine company.
  - • Graham-Paige designed its own engines but had them built by Continental
  - • Locomobile similarly had its engines assembled by Continental
  - • Duesenberg engines were designed in-house but manufactured by Lycoming
  - • La Salle engines were made by Oldsmobile

- ◆ 6 used engines supplied by other car makers.
  - • Railton and Brough Superior used Hudson engines
  - • Jensen used engines made, amongst others, by Nash
  - • Burney employed Beverley-Barnes engines
  - • Hampton used engines supplied by Röhr
  - • Hartz used Miller engines

- ◆ 14 automobile makers used engines supplied by large proprietary engine manufacturers:
  - • Eight used Continental engines (Diana, Dupont, Elcar, Jordan, Moon, Peerless, Ruxton and Windsor)
  - • Six used engines sourced from Lycoming (Auburn, Cord, Gardner, Kissel, McFarlan and Roamer)

Apart from Continental and Lycoming, there were many other proprietary specialist engine manufacturers such as Wisconsin, Hercules and Rutenber,

but virtually all of these did not make straight eight engines. One other, Henry Meadows in the UK, did make straight eights for Jensen, but the number supplied was extremely small.

Given that most companies produced both engines and cars, it seems logical to format the book around the automobile makers. Included here are overviews of Lycoming and Continental, the two main specialist engine manufacturers who provided 'off the shelf' power units to many automobile

companies. Some manufacturers, such as Alfa Romeo, Bugatti, Packard, Duesenberg and Mercedes-Benz, are given much more coverage than others. Extra coverage has been given where:

◆ The engines are of special technological interest, such as twin overhead cams, four valves were cylinder, sleeve valves or supercharging

◆ The scale of production was large, for example, Packard

◆ Sound information is available. It would have been preferable to give greater coverage to some marques, but for several now defunct manufacturers information has been difficult to find.

The geographical distribution of the manufacturers is interesting:
◆ 43 in the United States
◆ 19 in the United Kingdom
◆ 11 in France
◆ 7 in Italy
◆ 6 in Germany
◆ 2 in Austria
◆ 2 in Belgium
◆ 1 in Czechoslovakia (as it then was)
◆ 1 in Russia

It was to be expected that most would be in the US, but finding the UK in second place was a surprise. All the UK straight eights were up-market models, and none was produced in large volumes. While France was in third place, many of the 11 manufacturers are little known today. Although Germany only ranks fifth, it was responsible for some important and impressive vehicles, such as Horch and Mercedes-Benz.

There is, of course, some debate over nationality; for example, Ettore Bugatti was Italian, but the business started in Molsheim, which at the time was in Germany, although today it is part of France. It's been counted here as a French company.

CONTINENTAL (US)

Continental and Lycoming were the two dominant providers of 'off the shelf' straight eight engines to the US automobile industry. Unlike Lycoming, which began as a manufacturer of sewing machines, Continental was from the outset an engine manufacturer. Also, unlike Lycoming, Continental did manufacture complete automobiles, although only for a short period in 1933-1934, as the venture was not a success. However, both Continental and Lycoming would end up as almost exclusively manufacturers of aero engines after the straight eight 'era' came to an end.

The Continental story began in 1903 when the Autocar Equipment Company was founded by Ross Hudson, an engineering student who set up an engine shop in Chicago. He built one prototype engine, a four-cylinder L-head, which

One of Continental's factories where they produced a range of 'off the shelf' engines for manufacturers including Dupont, Ruxton and Peerless.

A Continental engine on display at an automobile show, where its reliability, ruggedness and simplicity were the key marketing attributes.

was exhibited at the 1903 Chicago Automobile show. The show attracted enough orders for Hudson to set up full production facilities, which were fully operational by 1905. The first substantial order was from Studebaker which ordered 100 units, but quickly increased the order to 1,000. The company name was changed to Continental Motor and Manufacturing in 1905 when it was realised the Autocar name was already being used by a truck company in Ardmore, Pennsylvania.

By 1911 the company was also making a six-cylinder L-head engine, the Model 6-C, followed in 1913 by the Model 54, by which time Continental claimed to be the world's largest manufacturer of six cylinder engines. These engines were produced in large numbers with a range of bores and strokes, and then sold 'off the shelf' to any automobile manufacturer who needed them. The range quickly expanded to include straight eight engines.

With its eight-cylinder engines, Continental followed a similar strategy to Lycoming and Packard, having a simple standard L-head design offered with just two stroke options, but a range of bores to give a variety of displacements and power outputs. The variant with a 114.3 mm (4.5 in) stroke was available with bores ranging from 77.2 mm (3.0 in), giving a displacement of 4,273 cc (260.9 cu in), to 86 mm (3.38 in) with a displacement of 5,279 cc (322 cu in). On rare occasions, Continental made a bespoke variant of the standard design. For example, a 3,940 cc (240.4 cu in) variant with a bore of 76.2 mm (3.0 in) and a stroke of 108 mm (4.25 in) was produced exclusively for Diana.

In addition to the 'off the shelf' engines, Continental also built engines under licence for automobile makers. Locomobile's in-house designed engine, a 3,260 cc (198.9 cu in) unit with a bore of 68 mm (2.69 in), a stroke of 102 mm (4.0 in), and a single Stromberg carburettor, was made by Continental. Similarly, Graham-Paige subcontracted engine manufacture to the business.

In 1933 Continental started production of the Continental Beacon automobile. This was a bad mistake which almost bankrupted the business. In late 1933 and 1934 three automobiles were offered, the four-cylinder Beacon, the six-cylinder L-head Flyer and the six-cylinder Ace. In reality these cars were essentially rebadged DeVauxes aimed at exploiting the Continental name. The venture was not a success, with 6,500 sold in 1933 but just 1,000 in 1934.

LYCOMING (US)

Lycoming began life in 1845 as a manufacturer of sewing machines and diversified widely over the next few decades until the 1907 'Bankers' Panic' brought a halt to the company's expansion. In 1908 the business was bought

by a local banking group, which sought more profitable business outlets, and hit upon the idea of making automobile engines. Initially Lycoming focused on four-cylinder engines, and achieved some success becoming a major supplier of 'off the shelf' engines to America's growing automobile industry, delivering 60,000 units a year by 1920.

The next logical step would have been to expand into the six-cylinder market in direct competition with Continental, but in 1924 the company took the bold decision to introduce a series of L-head straight eight engines, beginning

1927 Auburn Advertisement.

with the Model H and Model 2H, the latter engines being bought by Auburn from 1925, once it had become part of E. L. Cord's business empire. The company did develop straight sixes, but by 1926 it was concentrating almost exclusively on straight eights.

Lycoming's history became closely entwined with that of the Cord Corporation. As well as Auburn, Cord purchased both Duesenberg and Lycoming in 1927. In addition to supplying the engines for Auburn, Lycoming also built the engines Duesenberg had designed for its cars. When Cord launched a range of cars under its own name in 1929, it was inevitable that the vehicles would also be Lycoming-powered. Up until 1937, Lycoming supplied engines to Cord, Auburn and Duesenberg, as well as to Gardner, Kissel, McFarlan and Roamer. But by 1937 the Depression killed off the demand for these up-market automobiles, and E. L. Cord's automobile businesses collapsed. From 1937 Lycoming switched entirely to the design and construction of aero engines.

With its straight eights, Lycoming followed a similar strategy to Packard. The engine design remained throughout very simple, a basic side valve unit which was only ever offered with a choice of two stroke lengths, 114 mm (4.5 in) and 120 mm (4.7 in). A wide range of displacements was offered by changing the bore, a quite simple process on such a basic engine. The 114 mm (4.5 in) stroke engine was produced with a range of bores from 75 mm (3.0 in) to 83 mm (3.3 in) giving displacements from 4,040 cc (246 cu in) to 4,894 cc (298 cu in). The longer stroke engines had bores ranging from 70 mm (2.8 in) to 84 mm (3.3 in) giving displacements from 3,699 cc (226 cu in) to 5,317 cc (325 cu in).

This degree of simplification allowed a high degree of interchangeability of parts, whilst allowing the engine specification to be tailored closely to the customers' own specific requirements. The limited design changes also helped to ensure Lycoming's engine were reliable.

Unlike Continental, which in 1933 launched the Continental Beacon almost bankrupting the company, Lycoming never produced a complete automobile.

ENGINE DIMENSIONS: A NOTE ABOUT ACCURACY AND PRECISION

Throughout this book engine dimensions are given in both metric units, standard across Europe, and imperial units which are still generally used in North America. In many cases the metric measurement has been derived from the imperial unit using a conversion factor, and conversely in other cases the imperial measurement has been derived from the metric unit. The metric to imperial conversion is straight-forward. However, converting imperial to metric can cause problems because of precision.

For example, in many instances, engine displacement is quoted in external sources just as a whole number, such as 240 cu in. An exact 240 cu in corresponds to 3,932 cc. However, because the imperial measurement given as a whole number lacks precision, it could embrace a range of exact volume from 239.500 to 240.499; with the conversion factor of 16.39 (one cubic inch equals 16.39 cubic centimetres) the '240 cu in' could be anything from 3925 cc to 3950 cc, a difference of 25 cc. This can make it difficult to determine whether two similar engines are actually the same. When the displacement in cu in is quoted with one decimal place, the problem is greatly reduced.

To further explain, based on the imperial measurement and a conversion rate of 16.39 Ruxton used a Continental engine with a displacement of 4,408 cc. Moon used a similar engine of 4,403 cc whilst Jordan had a 4,402 cc power plant. It is almost certain these engines were identical, and the variation is simply the result of limited precision.

It is important to be aware of this issue when comparing engines together.

ALFA ROMEO
(ITALY)

Alfa Romeo Automobiles S.p.A was founded in 1910 in Milan by a Frenchman, Alexandre Darracq. Originally it was just A.L.F.A. or Anonima Lombarda Fabbrica Automobili. From 1931 to 1953, which covers the period when the company was involved with straight eights, it was owned by the Italian state holding company Istituto per la Ricostruzione Industriale, before it later became part of the Fiat group.

From 1910 until 1920 it produced four- and six -cylinder cars for both road and track use. A highly significant vehicle was the 1914 Alfa 40/60, which began an Alfa tradition for dual overhead camshafts. This car was also advanced in having four valves per cylinder. Of particular importance was the 6C series (6C indicating six-cylinders), starting with the 6C1500 in 1927 and progressing through 6C1750, 6C1900 to the 6C 2300. The 6C series introduced some glamorous coachwork which would become a hallmark of the road cars. Then in 1931, alongside the 6C series, Alfa started adding straight eight models to its range, and these would become amongst the most desirable sporting cars of the 1930s.

It is interesting to track the Alfa straight eights by means of their chronology.

1931-34: The first straight eight, the 8C2300, was launched in 1931, and would remain in production until 1934. The 16 valve 2,336 cc (142.6 cu in) engine featured an alloy block and head, and double overhead camshafts with the drive to the cam located between cylinders 4 and 5; so in effect there were two four-cylinder twin cam units on a common crankcase, an arrangement

adopted to minimise torsional vibration of the shafts. The block had bores of 65 mm (2.6in) and the stroke was 88 mm (3.5in), giving a ratio of 74% and a compression ratio of 6.6:1. The engine was fed by a single Memini SI36 carburettor via a Roots-type supercharger. Power output was 178 bhp (133 kW) at 5,400 rpm, allowing a top speed of 106 mph. Around 188 8C2300s were made for road use.

1931: Sports racing versions of the 8C2300 were produced in 1931, achieving success at Le Mans, the Mille Miglia, Spa and Monza. Often these models are referred to by the name of a circuit where they achieved success.

1932: This year the Tipo B (P3) for Grand Prix use was launched. It replaced the Tipo A, Alfa's first single seat racer, which had twin six-cylinder engines, but which proved to be unreliable. The Tipo B had a similar engine to the 8C2300, with the same 65 mm (2.6in) bore but with a longer stroke, 100 mm (3.94in) up from 88 mm (3.5in) giving a bore:stroke ratio of 65% and a displacement of 2,650 cc (161.7 cu in). The Tipo B featured twin superchargers giving 190-255 bhp (141.7-190.2 kW) at 5,400 rpm allowing a top speed in excess of 140 mph.

1933: For the 8C2600 (Monza), the company reverted to the original 88 mm (3.5in) stroke, but the block was bored out to 68 mm (2.7in) giving a bore:stroke ratio of 77% and an increased displacement of 2,557 cc (156.0 cu in) for the 1933 racing season. Fed from a single Memini carburettor via a Roots-type supercharger, the output ranged from 180 bhp (134 kW) to 215 bhp (160

TOP LEFT: Longitudinal section of the Alfa Romeo P2 engine, a refined version of the Fiat 405. The crankshaft ran in ten roller bearings. The con rods also ran on rollers.

TOP RIGHT: Cross sectional view of the Alfa Romeo engine used in the P2 Grand Prix car.

BOTTOM LEFT: A longitudinal section of the 8C 2300 engine showing details of the central valve gear train.

BOTTOM RIGHT: Transverse section of the Alfa Romeo 8C 2300 engine where the supercharger was located. There was a lot of water jacketing, except under the valves.

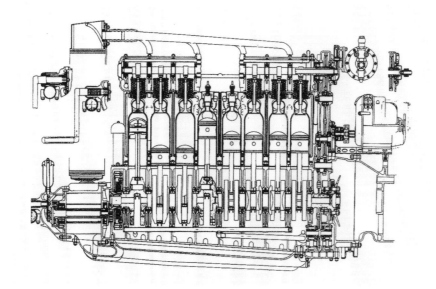

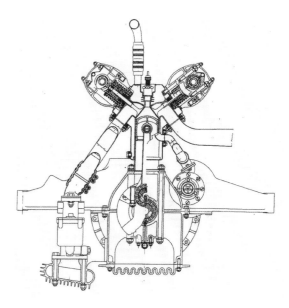

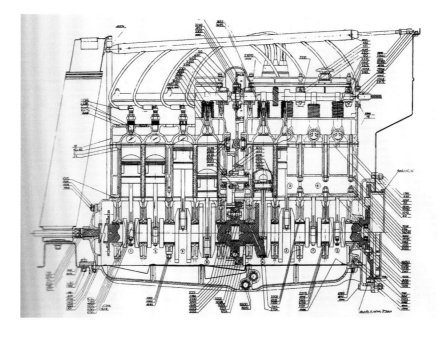

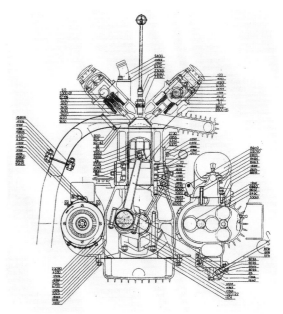

kW). The car was good for 135 mph and was said to achieve 0-60 mph in under seven seconds. In total 188 were produced.

1935: The mighty Bimotore appeared. With two eight-cylinder 3,165 cc (193 cu in) engines, one in front of the driver and the other behind, it produced 540 bhp (403 kW) from its 6.3-litres (386 cu in). Whilst incredibly fast in a straight line, it was difficult to handle, especially in the corners. Just two were built.

1935: At the same time, the 8C 35 Type C, of which just 6 were made, was introduced. The 3,822 cc (233.2 cu in) engine in this model shared no castings with any of the earlier 'eights'. The bore was 78.0 mm (3.1in) and the stroke was 100 mm (3.9in) giving a bore:stroke ratio of 78%. With two Roots-type superchargers, and an 8.0:1 compression ratio, it produced 330 bhp (246 kW) at 5,500 rpm, and 320 lb ft (434 Nm) of torque.

1935-39: 1935 also saw the introduction of the second main straight eight variant, the 8C 2900, still with 16 valves and dohc. With a bore of 68 mm (2.68in) and a stroke of 100 mm (3.94in) the bore:stroke ratio decreased to 68% and displacement increased to 2,905 cc (177.2 cu in). With two Zenith carburettors, a supercharger and a 6.5:1 compression ratio, it produced 180 bhp (134 kW) at 5,200 rpm. Like the earlier 8C2300, it was designed for both road and track use.

1935: The 8C 2900A was designed for sports car racing, and featured a de-tuned version of the racing engine from the 8C 35 Type C. With two Roots-type superchargers and a 6.5:1 compression ratio it produced 220 bhp (160 kW) at 5,300 rpm. Ten of this model were built.

1937: This year saw a further de-tuned version, the 8C 2900B, with a lower compression ratio of 5.75:1. Power was down to 180 bhp (133 kW). The de-tuned version was deemed more tractable and practical for road use.

1938: The Tipo 308 was a Grand Prix car made for the 3-litre class introduced in 1938. Only four were made. The 2,991 cc (182 cu in) engine, derived from the 8C 2900, produced 295 bhp (220 kW) at 6,000 rpm. Unfortunately, as with the later twelve-cylinder 12C and sixteen-cylinder 16C, the Tipo 308 was not very successful.

1938: The 8C 2900B Mille Miglia had 225 bhp (168 kW) from its twin supercharged 2,991 cc (182 cu in) engine. Just four were made. In addition, there was a single 8C 2900B Le Mans Speciale.

1938-1949: The 158 Alfetta (meaning little Alfa) would be a mainstay on the racing circuit for 11 years. Its small 1,479 cc (90.3 cu in) engine, with a single Roots-type supercharger, delivered 190 bhp (142 kW). A later version for Formula 1 could produce 350 bhp (261 kW) at 8,500 rpm.

1950-53: After the war, the 158 evolved into the 159 with a two-stage supercharger giving 425 bhp (317 kW) at 9,300 rpm. But the dated engine, running on a rich mixture in order to burn methanol, struggled to achieve more than 1.5 miles per gallon, whereas contemporary competitors like the Talbot Lago could achieve 9 mpg.

ALFA ROMEO EIGHT MODELS

MODEL		8C 2300	8C 2600	8C 35 Type C	8C 2900	8C 2900 A	8C 2900 B	8C 2900 MM
Year introduced		1931	1933	1935	1935	1935	1937	1938
Displacement	cc	2,336	2,557	3,822	2,905	2,905	2,905	2,991
	cu in	142.6	156	233.2	177.2	177.2	177.2	182
Power output	bhp (max)	178	215	330	180	220	180	225
	kW	133	160	246	134	160	133	168
	@ rpm	5,400	5,400	5,500	5,200	5,300	5,200	5,200
Specific output	bhp/litre	76.2	84.1	86.3	62.0	75.7	62.0	75.2
	bhp/cu in	1.25	1.38	1.42	1.02	1.24	1.02	1.24
	kW/litre	56.9	62.6	64.4	46.1	55.1	45.8	56.2
	kW/cu in	0.93	1.03	1.05	0.76	0.90	0.75	0.92
Compression ratio		6.6:1	6.5:1	8.0:1	6.5:1	6.5:1	5.75:1	
Bore	mm	65	68	78	68	68	68	68
	inches	2.6	2.7	3.1	2.68	2.68	2.68	2.68
Stroke	mm	88	88	100	100	100	100	100
	inches	3.5	3.5	3.9	3.94	3.94	3.94	3.94
Bore:stroke ratio		74%	77%	78%	68%	68%	68%	68%
Valve gear		dohc 16v	dohc 16v	dohc 16v	dohc 16v	dohc 16v	dohc 16v	dohc 16v
Carburettor		1xMemini s/c	1xMemini s/c	1xMemini 2xs/c	2xZenith s/c	2xZenith 2xs/c	2xZenith 2xs/c	2xZenith 2xs/c
Number made		188	188	6	10	10	33	4

ABOVE: 1932 Alfa Romeo 8C 2300 Spyder, the ex-works Le Mans car. **OPPOSITE:** The inlet side of the Le Mans 8C 2300 Spyder's engine showing the elegant finned inlet manifold and the central drive for the camshaft.

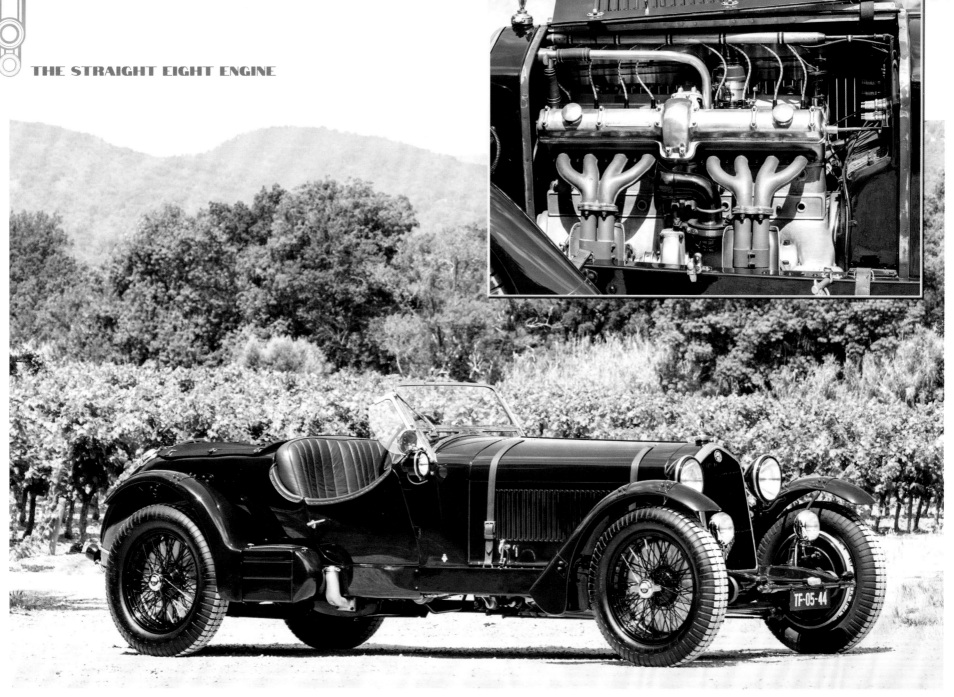

THESE TWO PAGES: 1935 Alfa Romeo 8C 2300, one of the last 8C 2300s which was Alfa's first straight eight, introduced in 1931. Inset shows engine exhaust side, and opposite is the engine inlet side.

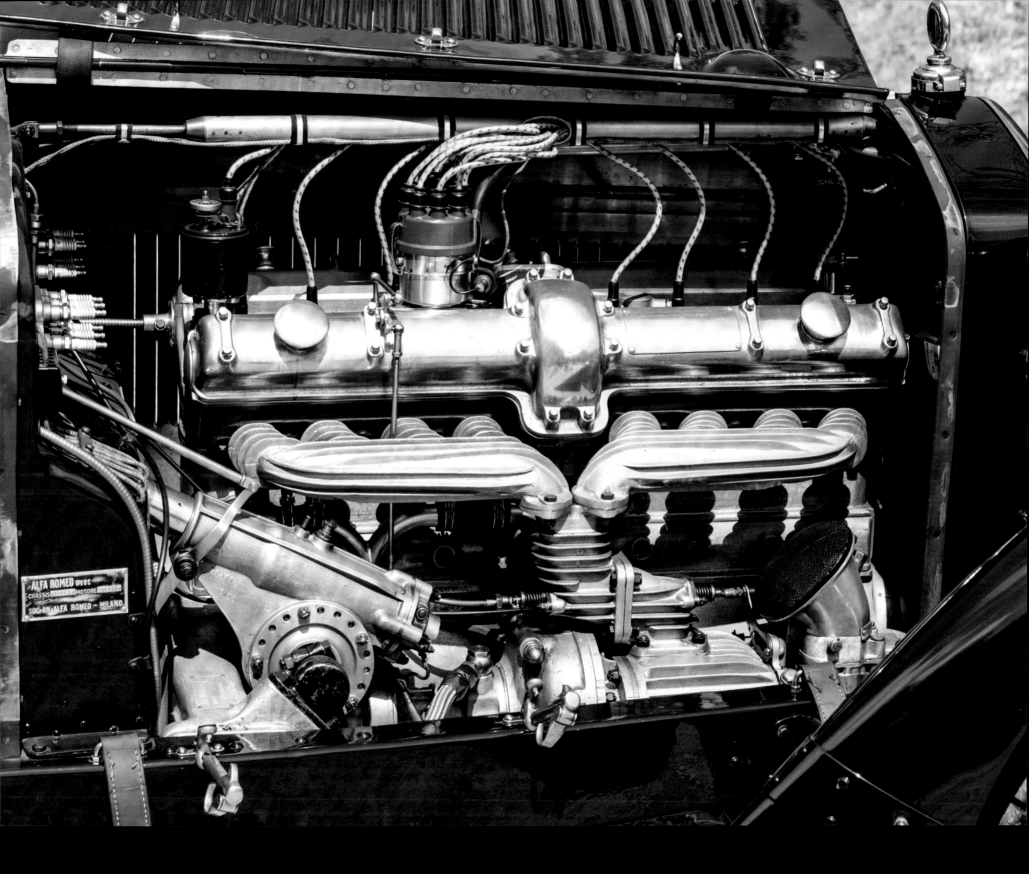

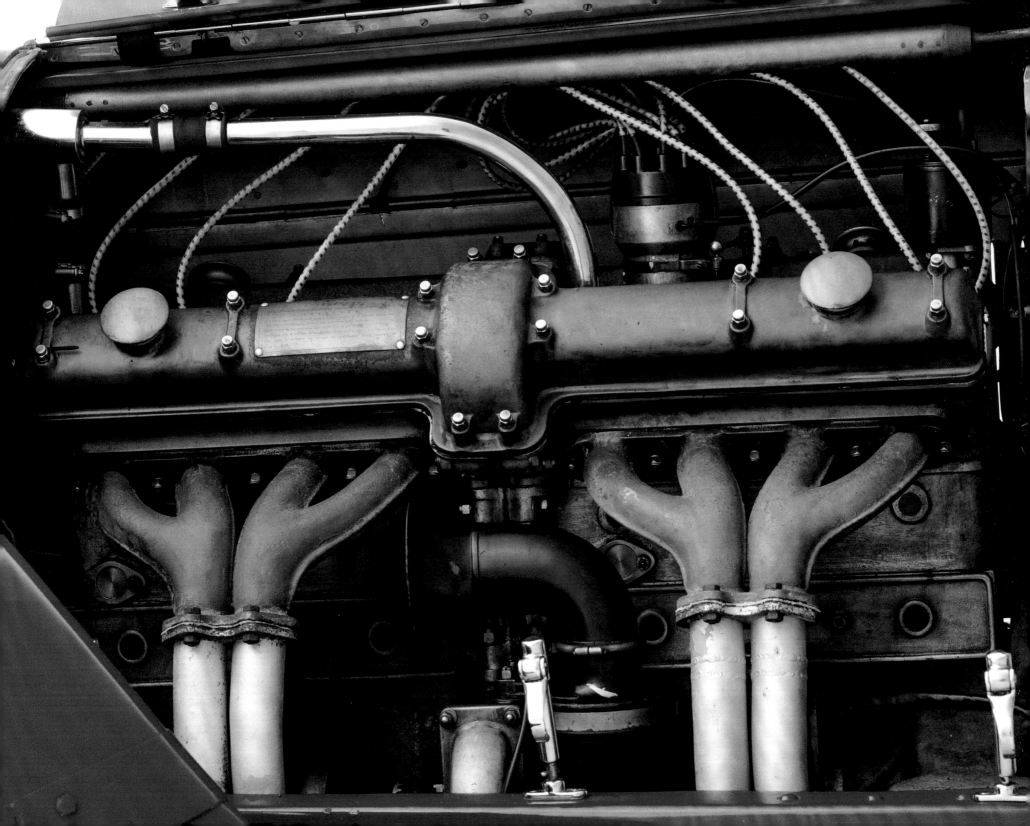

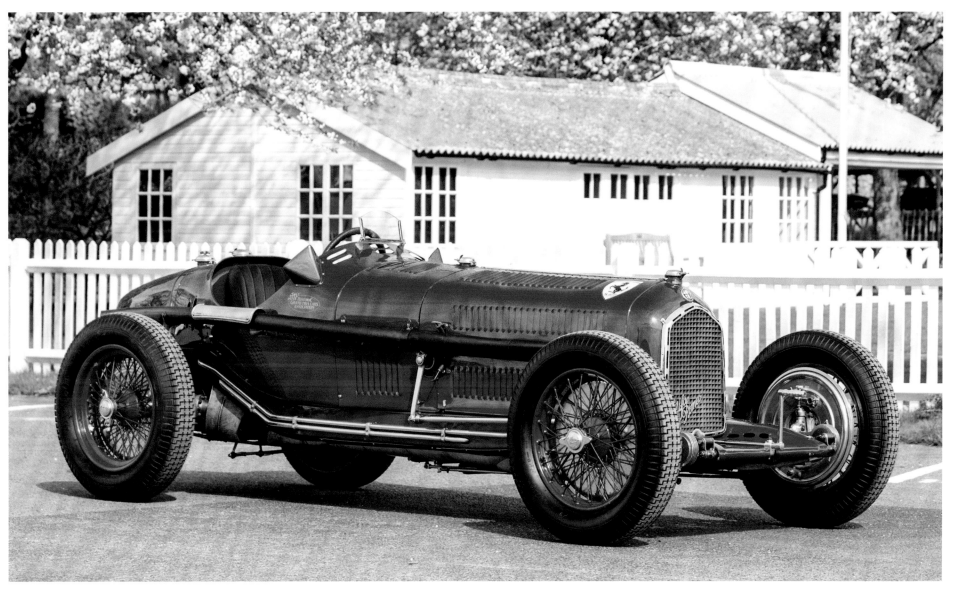

ABOVE: A design classic, the 1934 Alfa Romeo Tipo B Grand Prix. Note the massive brake drums. **OPPOSITE:** The exhaust side of the Spyder's engine showing the four exhaust pipes leading from the 'siamesed' stubs.

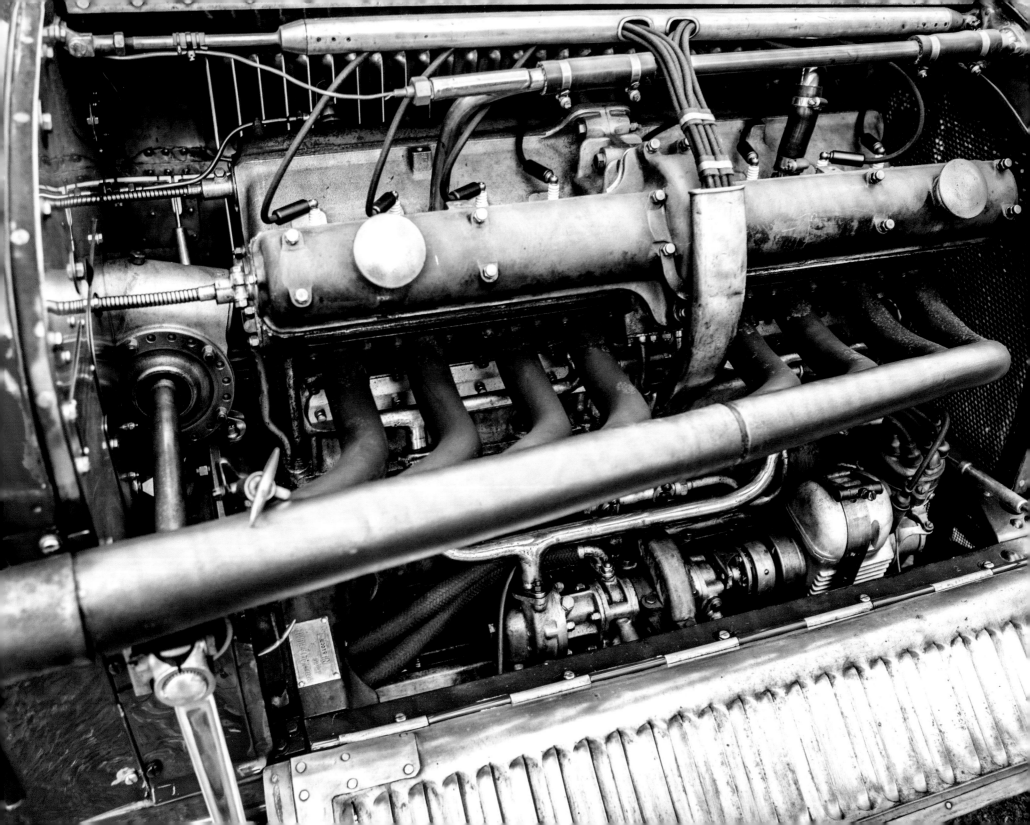

THESE TWO PAGES: The 1934 Alfa Romeo Tipo B GP engine features an elegant exhaust system. The above image shows the forced induction arrangement.

THESE TWO PAGES: Alfa Romeo Bimotore, taken in 2008 at the Torino Esposizioni.

THESE TWO PAGES: Alfa Romeo 8C-35, taken at the 2013 Quail Motorsport Gathering, in Monterey, California.

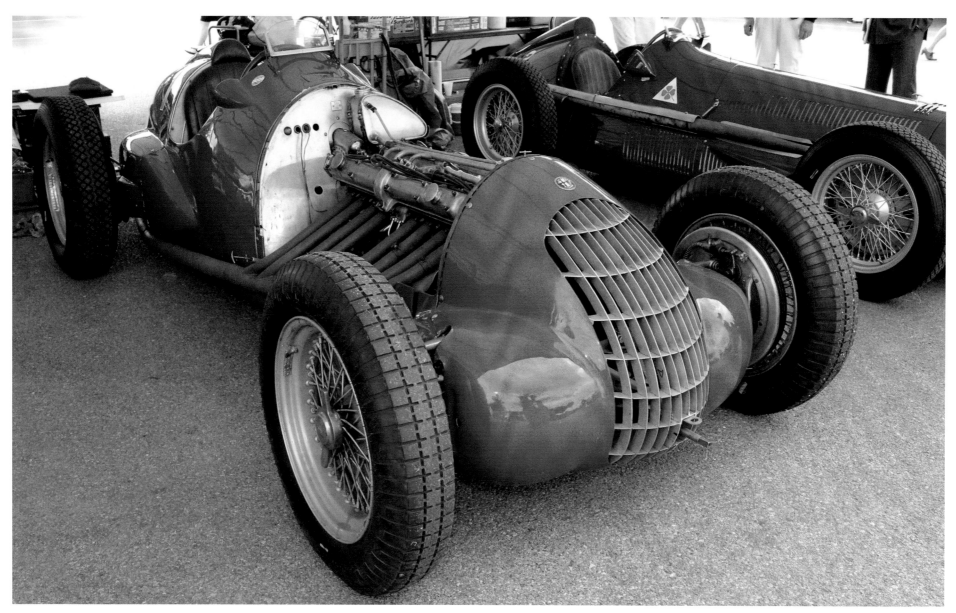

THESE TWO PAGES: Alfa Romeo 308C, taken at the 2010 Goodwood Revival.

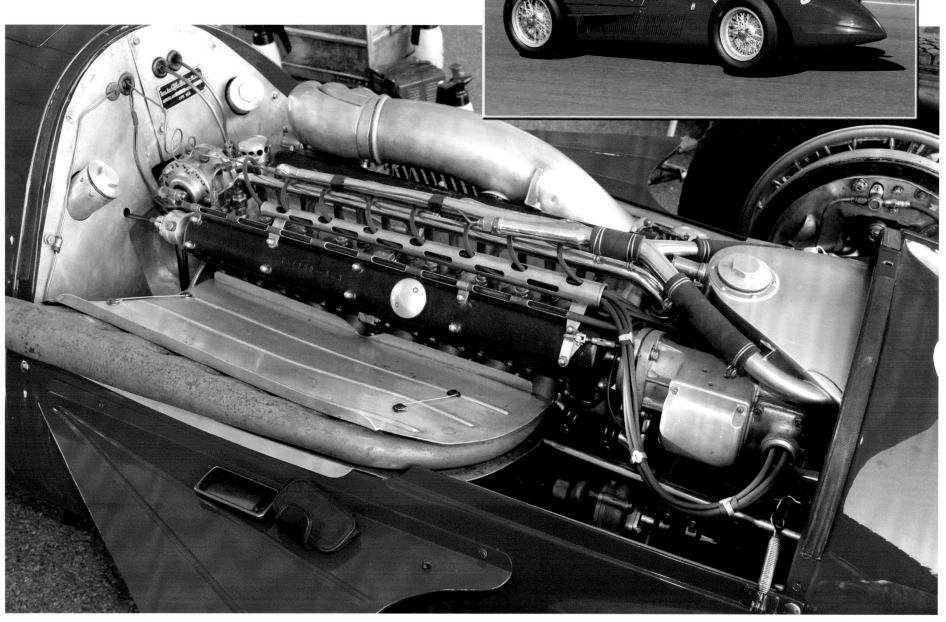

Alfa Romeo Tipo 159 Alfetta, taken at the 2011 Goodwood Revival.

Alfa Romeo Tipo 159 Alfetta, taken at the 2010 Techno Classica in Essen, Germany.

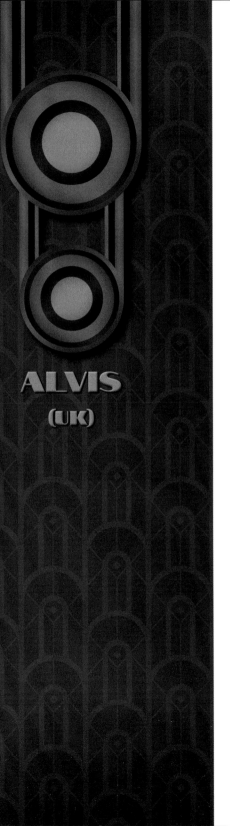

ALVIS
(UK)

The name Alvis has always been associated with quality workmanship and superior performance, mainly with medium to large-sized luxury saloons. Alvis dates back to 1919 when the original company, T. G. John and Company, was founded by Thomas George John. It began life making stationary engines and motor scooters. Geoffrey de Freville joined the company in 1920 and designed their first car engine, a four-cylinder side valve unit with aluminium pistons and pressure rather than splash lubrication, unusual in

1920. The first car, the 10/30, was a great success, evolving into the 12/50 by 1923, this design remaining in production until 1932. Alvis branched out into six-cylinder models in 1927 with the 14/75, and this engine became the basis for a succession of luxury models until the Second World War. Post-war the company continued with luxury sporting saloons, such as the TC, TD, TE and

TF models, under various ownership, until car production ceased in 1967. The high price of such hand-built models, twice that of the top of the range Mk2 Jaguar, helped herald the end of the marque.

Alvis's first venture into straight eights was in 1926 with a Grand Prix engine. This had horizontally opposed valves, which had been used before on Lanchesters and on Harry Ricardo's tank engine. It offered certain advantages in terms of combustion chamber design. The engine, by all accounts, worked well, but for the 1927 Grand Prix season it was completely redesigned with valves angled at 90 degrees.

In 1929 a road car, the 8/15 Ulster TT, was planned. Its engine was to be essentially the same as the 1927 Grand Prix car, with dohc, 2 valves per cylinder, 55 mm (2.2 in) bore and 78.5 mm (3.1 in) stroke, giving a displacement of 1,491 cc (91 cu in) and a bore:stroke ratio of 70%. With a single SU carburettor, the unit delivered 125 bhp (93 kW) enabling a top speed of 105 mph. One difference from the 1927 GP car was the sump; on the GP car it had been a dry sump, but for the road car the extra height allowed a wet sump. The car was also notable for having front wheel drive.

The production quantity is not clear. It is believed that six were built in 1929 and a further four in 1930, although some sources claim two more were built. There were also some 'specials' produced using this engine, notably the Barson Special.

ABOVE: A contemporary view of the engine of the 1926 Alvis Grand Prix car from the nearside rear.

OPPOSITE: A contemporary view from the nearside front of the engine of the 1926 Alvis GP car showing the cam covers of the horizontally opposed valves.

A view of the 1926 Alvis Grand Prix car showing the differential, inboard brakes and twin quarter elliptic springs.

A contemporary photograph, from the 23 July, 1926 edition of *Autocar* magazine, showing the engine with the rocker covers removed.

For the 1927 Grand Prix season, the valve gear for the Alvis was redesigned from horizontal to 90 degree 'Vee'. Above left is a view of the engine from the front right, and above right, the same engine from the left side rear.

A contemporary front three-quarter view of the 1927 Grand Prix car showing the prominent differential.

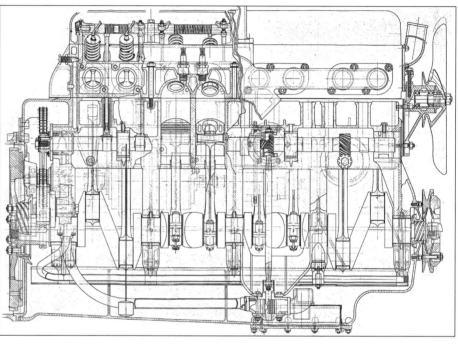

ABOVE AND RIGHT: 1929 Alvis TT car engine during an engine-out restoration, showing the shallow dry sump and the FWD unit and the same engine from the rear showing the 90-degree twin cam arrangement.

FAR RIGHT (BOTH): Longitudinal and cross section cutaway drawings of the of the 1927 Grand Prix engine, clearly showing the 90-degree 'Vee' valve arrangement.

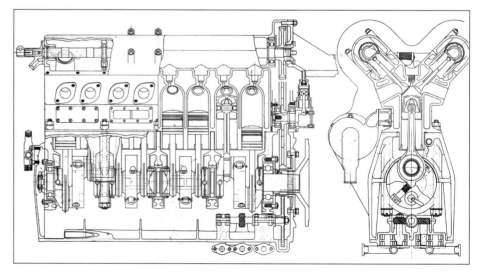

ABOVE: For the 1929 Grand Prix season the differential was concealed. **RIGHT:** 1930 was the last year of the Alvis straight eight in the form of this 1930 TT car.

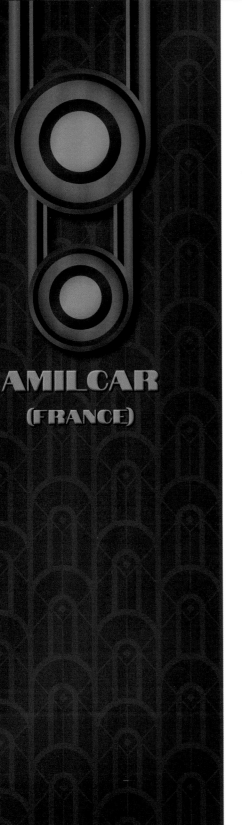

AMILCAR
(FRANCE)

Amilcar was founded in 1921 by Joseph Lamy and Emile Akar. In the early years Amilcar exclusively made small cars, its first being a cycle car, similar to the pre-First World War Le Zebre, and shown at the 1921 Paris Motor Show. The company benefited from a low tax rate on cars weighing no more than 350 kg, carrying no more than two people, and with an engine not exceeding 1,100 cc (67 cu in). In 1922 it successfully expanded into the light car market with the 4-cylinder 903 cc (55 cu in) Amilcar CC, adding two variants, the C4 and CS, in 1924. A CGS Grand Sport model was added in 1924, and this evolved into the sportier CGSS Grand Sport Surbaisse. Amilcar also entered motor sport in the mid-1920s with a supercharged dohc six-cylinder model, with advanced roller bearing crankshaft. The model range was extended in 1928 with the M-Type with a 1,200 cc (73 cu in) side valve engine. This was quite a successful model which lasted through M2, M3 and M4 variants until 1935.

Then, in 1928 the company moved outside its area of expertise of light cars and launched a small-engined straight eight model, the C8, in two variants, a 1,980 cc (120.8 cu in) 11CV and a 2,326 cc (141.9 cu in) 13 CV. The two engines were similar, both having a single overhead camshaft, two valves per cylinder, five main bearings, and both fed from a single Solex carburettor. The 11CV had a bore of 63 mm (2.48 in) and a stroke of 80 mm (3.15 in), whilst the 13CV had a 66 mm (2.6 in) bore and a 85 mm (3.35 in) stroke.

The 11 CV C8 was produced in three variants, a 2-door, 2/3-seat 'faux cabriolet' fixed head coupe, a 4-door, 4/5-seat saloon and a 2-door, 4-seat fixed head coupe. The 13 CV came as a four-door 4-seat fixed head coupe, a 2-door, 2/3 seat 'faux cabriolet', and a 2-seat roadster.

Both eight-cylinder C8 models proved unreliable and only around 350 were sold. Sales were not helped by the fact that Amilcar had a 'small car' image, whereas the company planned the C8 to compete against cars like the Delage D8. The car had been conceived in a period of rising incomes, but was launched into an over-supplied market sector during a time of economic problems. The company entered a period of financial difficulties and changed hands a couple of times before finally ceasing production at the outbreak of war.

The C8 is now extremely rare, and even photographs of the car are hard to find. But a 13CV example emerged in the famous Baillon Collection 'barn find'. The car is complete but in need of extensive restoration.

A contemporary photograph of a 1932 two-door 13CV Amilcar.

AMILCAR EIGHT MODELS

Model		11CV	13CV
Year introduced		1928	1928
Displacement	cc	1,980	2,326
	cu in	120.8	141.9
Power output	bhp (max)	49	58
	kW	36	43
Specific output	bhp/litre	24.7	24.9
	bhp/cu in	0.41	0.41
	kW/litre	18.2	18.5
	kW/cu in	0.30	0.30
Bore	mm	63	66
	inches	2.48	2.60
Stroke	mm	80	85
	inches	3.15	3.35
Bore:stroke ratio		79%	78%
Valve gear		sohc 16v	sohc 16v
Carburettor		1xSolex	1xSolex
Main bearings		5	5

THIS PAGE: The 1932 Amilcar 13CV from the famous 'barn find' Baillon Collection, one of the very few 13CVs known to survive. Shown (right) is the exhaust side of the 2.3-litre (142 cu in) 13CV engine, calling for some significant restoration.

THESE TWO PAGES: This Amilcar C8S is an earlier version built in 1928. It has 2.33-litres, 58hp @ 4000rpm and reaches 120kph. The photograph was taken at the 2017 Collingrove Vintage Hillclimb near Angaston in the Barossa Valley, South Australia.

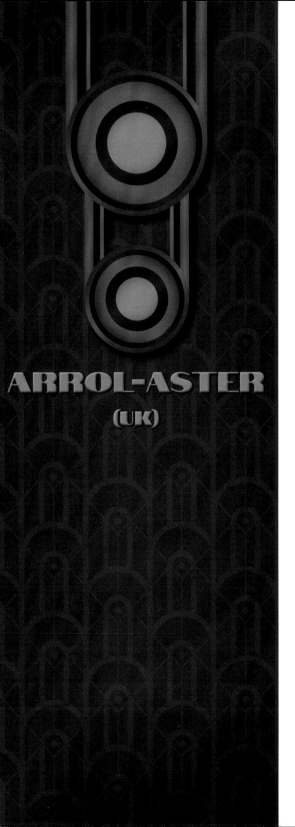

ARROL-ASTER

(UK)

A rrol-Aster was founded in 1927 when the Scottish company Arrol-Johnston merged with the English Aster company. Upon the merger the Wembley works of Aster were closed and the business moved to Dumfries in Scotland. Arrol-Aster cars, many of which used sleeve valves, were expensive and sales were poor, resulting in receivership in 1929 and final closure in 1931 after just four years.

Models were marketed under three separate names: Arrol-Johnston, Aster and Arrol-Aster, and the range consisted of:

◆ 1927-1930 Aster 21/60 3,042 cc Straight 6 Overhead valve

◆ 1927-1930 Aster 24/70 3,460 cc Straight 6 Sleeve valve

◆ 1927-1929 Arrol-Johnston 15/40 2,413 cc Straight 4 Overhead valve

◆ 1927-1930 Arrol-Aster 17/50 2,370 cc Straight 6 Sleeve valve

◆ 1927-1930 Arrol-Aster 23/70 3,293 cc Straight 8 Sleeve valve

The 3,293 cc (201 cu in) eight-cylinder engine had a bore of 67.5 mm (2.66 in) and a stroke of 110 mm (4.33 in), giving a bore:stroke ratio of a fairly low 61%. The 23/70 used a Burt-McCollum design of single sleeve valves similar to the Knight sleeve valve engine. The rest of the car was similar to the six-cylinder 17/50. Between 1927 and 1930 only around 80 of the 23/70 model were produced as saloons, four-seat convertibles and five-seat coupes. The 3,293 cc sleeve valve engine was said to be fragile and prone to disintegrating if taken over 3,400 rpm. The options list included a supercharger and a free-wheel. In total around eighty Arrol-Asters were produced across all the specifications, and only two are known to survive, one 23/70 and one 17/50.

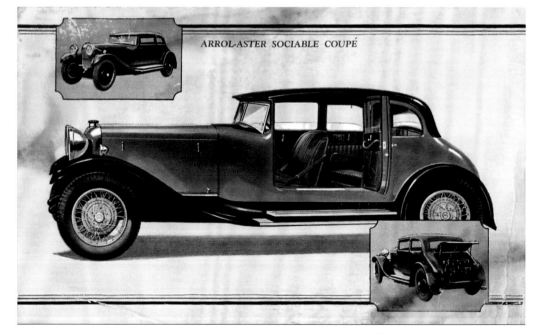

ARROL-ASTER SOCIABLE COUPÉ

A contemporary advertisement for the 1927 Arrol-Aster 23/70 Sociable Coupe.

The Auburn Automobile Company (AAC) was founded in 1903 by Frank and Morris Eckhart in Auburn, Indiana. In 1924 E. L. Cord became general manager, having been hired by a group of Chicago investors who had bought AAC from the Eckhart family. Without doubt he saved the business at a time when production had fallen to just six cars a day. Cord improved the reputation of Auburn by building a range of upmarket cars with extravagant bodywork, powered by 'off the shelf' Lycoming straight eight engines. Along with Cords and Duesenbergs, the Auburn defined a clear market sector of upmarket, sporty, powerful, fast and rather rakish vehicles, especially when in speedster form.

Auburn's first straight eight appeared in 1925, and the models evolved as follows:

◆ 1925 The Eight-in-Line with a 4.5-litre Lycoming S8

◆ 1926 The Eight-in-Line was renamed the 8-88 and the capacity was increased to 4,894 cc (298 cu in) delivering 68 bhp (50.3 kW)

◆ 1927 The engine was upgraded to 115 bhp (85.1 kW) and the car was renamed the 8-88 115

◆ 1929 Further upgrades upped the output to 120 bhp (88.8 kW), and the name became the 8-88 120. A 4,040 cc 8-90 was also introduced

◆ 1930 Power increased to 125 bhp (92.5 kW)

◆ 1934 The famous Speedster 851 was launched for the 1935 year

◆ 1936 The Speedster 852 appeared

The journey ended in 1937 with the bankruptcy of AAC.

The specifications of the various Lycoming engines were similar, and the different models are summarized in the table. All were flathead side valve units, with an aluminium head, two valves per cylinder operated by a block mounted camshaft, five main bearings and all used a single carburettor.

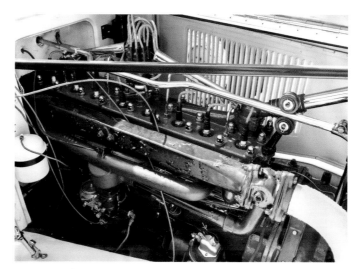

The inlet/exhaust right side of the simple flathead 4.9-litre (298 cu in) Lycoming engine in the 1928 Auburn 8-88 115S.

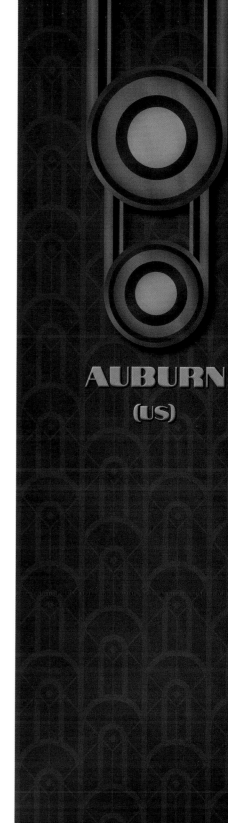

AUBURN

(US)

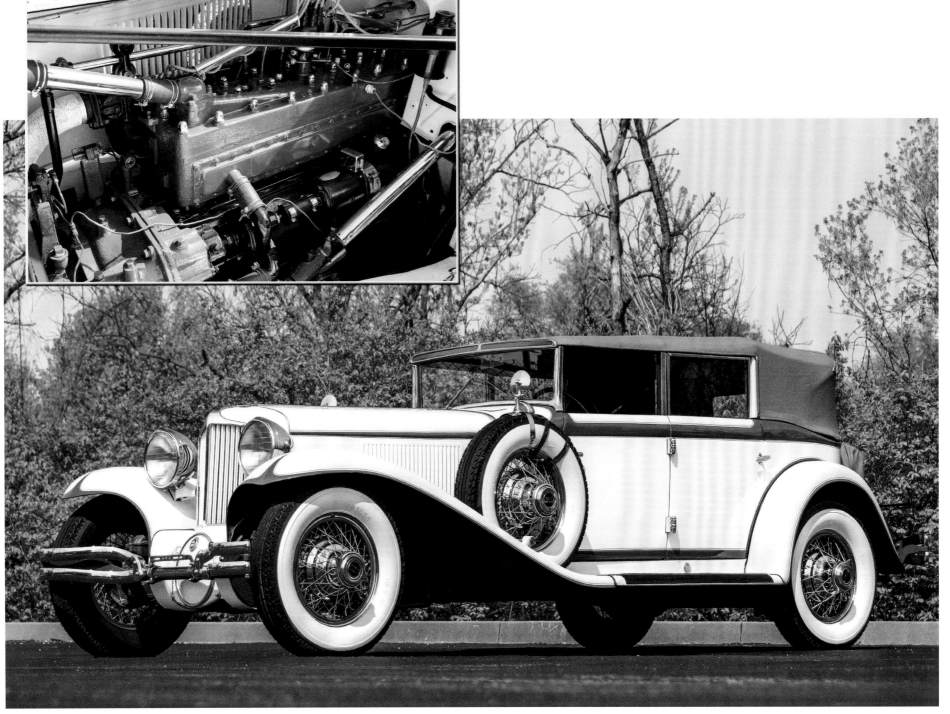

A superbly stylish 1928 Auburn 8-88 115S, and inset, the tidy ignition wiring solution on the flathead Lycoming engine.

AUBURN EIGHT MODELS

Model		Eight-in-Line	8-88	8-88 115	8-90	8-88 120	851	852
Year introduced		1925	1926	1927	1927	1929	1934	1936
Displacement	cc	4,575	4,894	4,894	4,040	4,894	4,575	4,575
	cu in	276.1	298	298	246	298	279.2	279.2
Power output	bhp (max)		68	115	90	125	150	115
	kW		50.3	85.1	66.6	92.5	111	86
	@ rpm		3,600	3,600	3,600	3,600	4,000	3,600
Specific output	bhp/litre		13.9	23.5	22.3	25.5	32.8	25.1
	bhp/cu in		0.23	0.39	0.37	0.42	0.54	0.41
	kW/litre		10.3	17.4	16.5	18.9	24.3	18.8
	kW/cu in		0.17	0.29	0.27	0.31	0.40	0.31
Compression ratio		4.5:1	4.5:1	5.25:1	5.25:1	5.25:1	6.5:1	6.5:1
Bore	mm	79.8	82.6	82.6	75	82.5	77.7	77.7
	inches	3.14	3.25	3.25	2.95	3.25	3.1	3.1
Stroke	mm	114.3	114.3	114.3	114.3	114.3	120.6	120.6
	inches	4.5:1	4.5:1	4.5	4.5	4.5	4.8	4.8
Bore:stroke ratio		70%	72%	72%	66%	72%	64%	64%
Valve gear		s/v 16v	s/v 16v	s/v 16v	s/v 16v	s/v 16v	s/v 16v	s/v 16v
Carburettor		1xSchebler	1xSchebler	1xSchebler	1xSchebler	1xSchebler	1xStromberg s/c	1xStromberg
No of main bearings		5	5	5	5	5	5	5

A supremely elegant 1931 Auburn 8-98 Boattail two-seater, the 'playboy's dream'! Inset is the 'business side' of the four litre Lycoming engine.
OPPOSITE: The right side of engine showing a Purolator oil filter stating, 'THIS CANISTER MUST BE REPLACED EVERY 8000 MILES', and chassis lubrication reservoir.

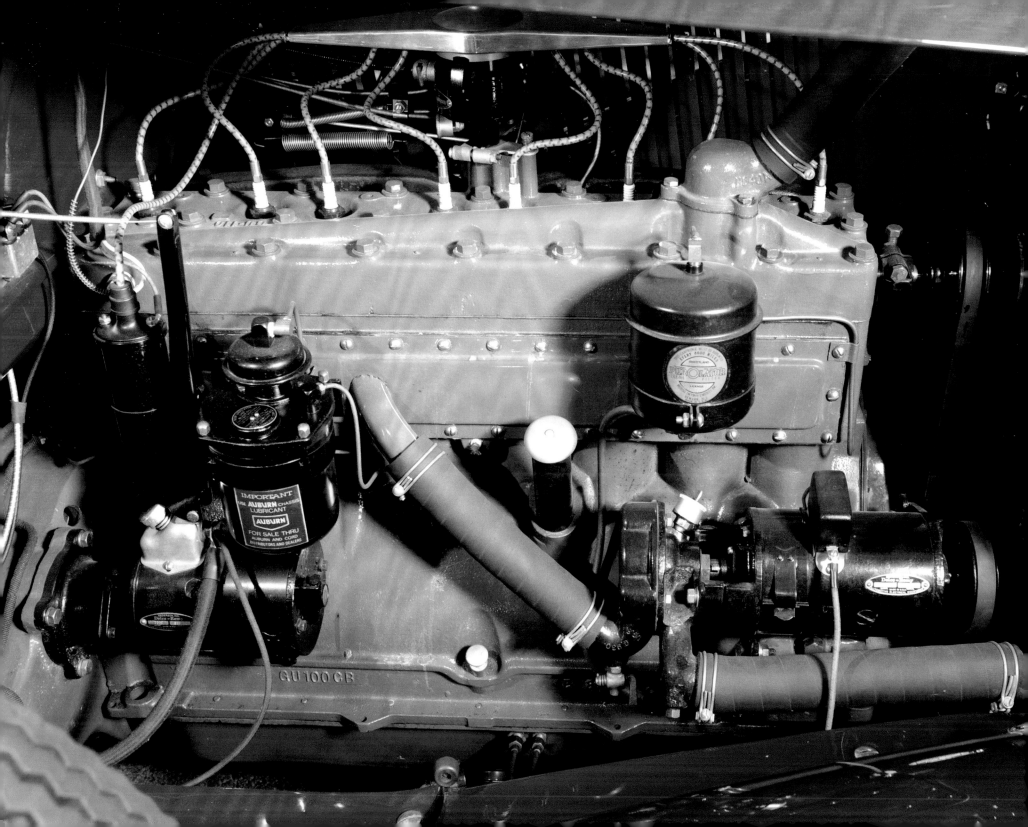

A 1935 Auburn 851 Speedster. **OPPOSITE:** The right-hand side of the engine in the 851 Speedster is dominated by a pair of impressive horns! **INSET:** The 'business side' of the engine showing its massive air filter.

The company Audi Automobilwerke Gmbh Zwickau was incorporated on 25 April 1910, by August Horch. Horch had first started motorcar manufacturing in 1899 with a company under his own name, A. Horch & Cie. In 1904 this evolved into August Horch & Cie Motorwagenwerke AG, but after conflicts with the chief financial officer, August left to set up a separate business called August Horch Automobilwerke Gmbh. However, he was sued by his former business for trademark infringement, and was forced to adopt a new name. The name Audi was chosen as it derived from the Latin 'audire', meaning to listen; the word 'horch' in German means 'hear', so the new name was deemed highly appropriate.

Between 1927 and 1932 Audi produced two straight eight models, one using an engine of its own design and a second using a Rickenbacker engine.

The first of the two straight eight models was the Type R Imperator, which replaced the earlier six-cylinder Type M. The Type M had been considered too expensive and hence was difficult to sell, so for the Type R, the overhead valves were dropped in favour of side valves, the light metal cylinder head was dropped, a three-speed gearbox replaced the four-speed, and the brakes reverted to being mechanical rather than hydraulic. Although more efficient and less expensive than the Type M, the new car found few buyers, just 145 leaving the factory over the three years of production. Although production of the Type R ceased in 1929, it was still listed for sale until 1933. The engine had a bore of 80mm (3.1 in) and a stroke of 122mm (4.8 in) giving a capacity of

4,872 cc (297 cu in), and it delivered 74 kW (99 bhp) at 3,300 rpm. This enabled a top speed of 120 km/h (75 mph). However the sales volume was so low it looked like Audi might not survive, but then in 1928 the company was given a lifeline when it was bought by Jorgen Skafte Rasmussen, a Danish entrepreneur.

Just the previous year Rasmussen had purchased the

manufacturing plant of the failed American Rickenbacker company and had shipped all the equipment to Germany. His plan had been to build versions of Rickenbacker's engines to sell on to other German car manufacturers. Even though the engines were not expensive, he failed to secure any orders and decided instead to use the engines in a new Audi model, the Type SS Zwickau. The engine was a 5,130 cc (313 cu in) unit with a bore of 82.6 mm (3.3 in) and a stroke of 120.7 mm (4.8 in) which delivered 74 kW (99 bhp) at 3,000 rpm. The performance was similar to that of the Type R, with a top speed of 120 km/h (75 mph). The car found more buyers than the Imperator, with 457 examples leaving the factory by 1932, but the sales figures were not encouraging enough for Audi to continue with straight eight models. Audi would not launch another eight cylinder engined car until 1988, although of course that was to be a V8.

THIS PAGE: THE 4,872 cc (297 cu in) straight eight in the 1929 Audi Type R Imperator. This was the last year that model was made before it was replaced by the SS 'Zwickau'.

OPPOSITE: A 1929 Audi SS 'Zwickau' in the Audi Museum collection, and the 5,130 cc (313 cu in) Rickenbacker engine. The radiator badge is the coat of arms of Zwickau, where the car was manufactured.

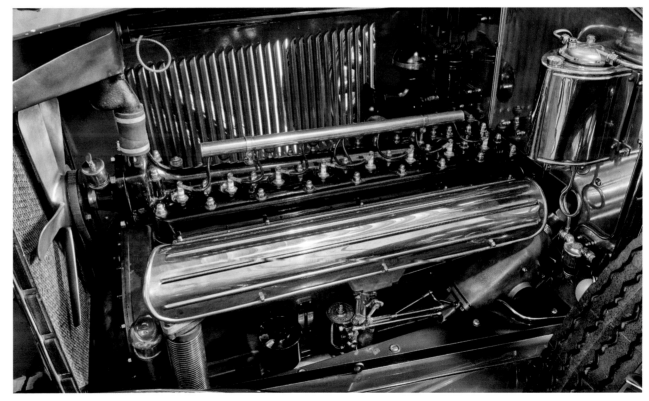

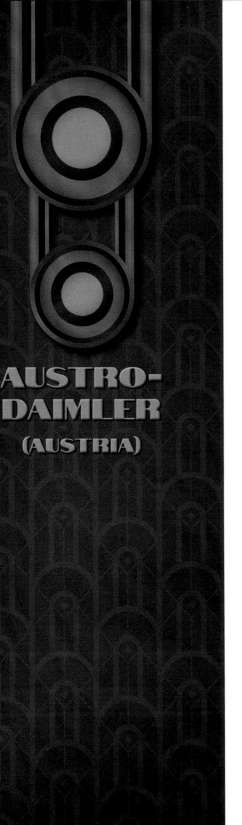

AUSTRO-DAIMLER
(AUSTRIA)

Austro-Daimler dates back to the beginning of motoring. In 1890 Eduard Bierenz was appointed as Austrian retailer for German parent company Daimler Benz. He was so successful he began manufacturing Daimler Benz-style automobiles himself and in 1899 the Austro-Daimler Company was formed. The company went through difficult times in the 1920s, but in 1928 it launched what would be its greatest car, the six-cylinder ohc ADR available in 2,540 cc (155 cu in), 2,650 cc (162 cu in) and 2,994 cc (183 cu in) versions.

Then in 1931 a highly expensive luxury vehicle, the ADR Alpine 8, was launched. It had an eight-cylinder 4,624 cc (282 cu in) engine with a bore of 80 mm (3.1 in) and stroke of 115 mm (4.5 in) with 2 valves per cylinder and a single overhead cam, and featured twin spark plugs in each of the eight cylinders. The engine delivered 120 bhp (89 kW) which enabled the car to reach around 95 mph (153 km/h). This car was probably too grand and expensive for the time, and only sold in limited numbers. It certainly did little to prevent the company going under in 1934.

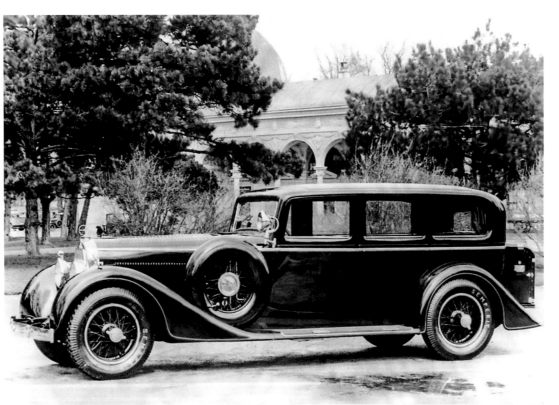

LEFT: A magazine photograph of a 1932 Austro-Daimler ADR8, the company's most expensive model, sold only in limited numbers.

OPPOSITE: The engine of the 1932 Austro-Daimler ADR8, showing the twin spark plugs and plain cover for the single overhead camshaft.

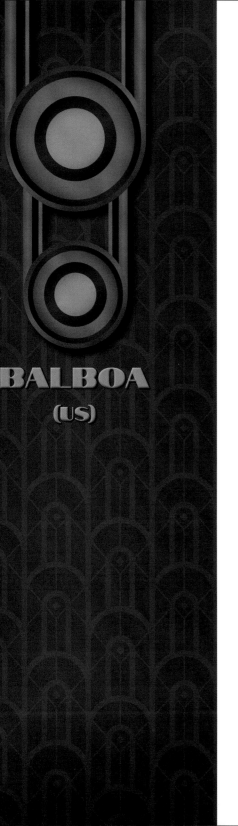

BALBOA
(US)

Balboa is possibly the least well-known straight eight manufacturer in this book. Its origins are complex and not entirely clear. Around 1920 two car companies started quite independently at about the same time. These were Ace in Ypsilanti and Kessler in Detroit, both in the state of Michigan. Although both cars looked conventional, they had unusual features. The Ace used rotary valves in its 'four' designed by Fred Guy, whilst Kessler used a rotary valve integrated supercharger in their Kess-Line cars. This engine was designed by Martin Kessler, an engineer and company founder. When Kessler introduced a supercharged straight eight ohc 100 bhp engine, vice president William Radford took credit for it.

At Ace there were also problems, and Fred Guy and president Otto Heinz left to form a new company to further develop Guy's rotary valve engine. Neither the Ace nor the Kess-Line were successful. Only twelve Kess-Lines straight eights were made before the company failed, and around 256 Ace cars were produced, mostly after Guy and Heinz had left, but these cars had conventional engines.

By 1924 Heinz had got rid of Guy and his engine design, and Heinz (from Ace) and Radford (from Kessler) combined to form a new company, Balboa, to use a 178 cu in 100 bhp (75 kW) straight eight similar to that in the Kess-Lines car. But the engine was a failure and was soon replaced by a Continental L-head. Soon afterwards Balboa folded.

A complicated story. Just one Balboa engine is known to survive.

THESE TWO PAGES: A real rarity. The engine from a 1925 Balboa, the only known surviving example, with its unusual fan with just two blades. The supercharged 100 bhp engine from the 1925 Balboa is so rare it certainly deserves a second photograph!

BALLOT
(FRANCE)

Most of Ballot's experience with straight eights was gained on the racing circuit before a straight eight road car was launched in 1927.

René Thomas had won the 1914 Indianapolis 500 in a Delage. During the First World War he dreamt of repeating this success in 1919, the first to be held after the war. Thomas approached Ernest Ballot with the idea of building a suitable car, even though at that time Ballot had never built a car. In just 102 days Ballot designed and produced not just one car, but a team of three. After some initial disappointment the cars performed well in the 1921 Italian Grand Prix, coming first and second. The engine, with a bore of 74 mm (2.9 in) and a stroke of 140 mm (5.5 in), giving a bore:stroke ratio of 69%, came just marginally under the 300 cu in limit. The engine was essentially two 'fours' joined end to end with the planes of the two 'four' cranks set at 90 degrees to each other. Novel for the time, the ohc and all the valve gear was enclosed under a cover.

For the 1920 3-litre formula a new team of cars was produced, these being essentially scaled down 1919 cars.

In 1921, Ballot started manufacturing road-going cars. The first was the four-cylinder 2LS, with a 1,994 cc (121.7 cu in) engine, twin overhead cams and four valves per cylinder. In 1923 the Ballot 2LT, and a sporting 2LTS version, appeared. From 1927 the 'fours' were replaced by a straight eight, the RH of 2,974 cc (181.5 cu in). This had a bore of 66 mm (2.6 in) and a stroke of 105 mm

Start of the 1929 French Grand Prix with Ballot taking the lead off the grid.

The Ballot Grand Prix engine, showing the twin cam covers and the two carburettors, each feeding a bank of four cylinders.

(4.13 in), two Zenith carburettors and delivered 76 bhp (57 kW) at 3,500 rpm. Later the RH3 of 3,049 cc (186.1 cu in) appeared. But in 1931 the company was taken over by Hispano Suiza, and the Ballot business went into rapid decline, finally closing in 1932.

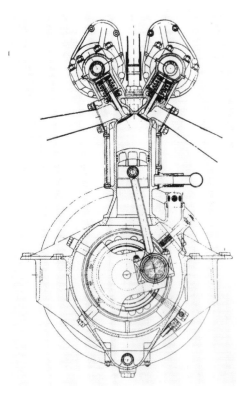

Transverse cross section of the 3-litre Ballot engine.

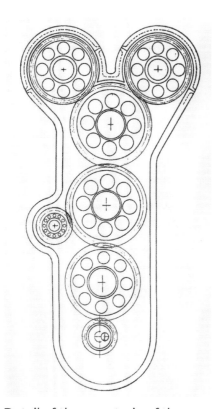

Detail of the gear train of the 3-litre Ballot engine. All the gears ran in ball bearings.

1921 Italian Grand Prix: a dramatic painting of a Ballot holding the lead. Artist Frederick Gordon Crosby (1885-1943).

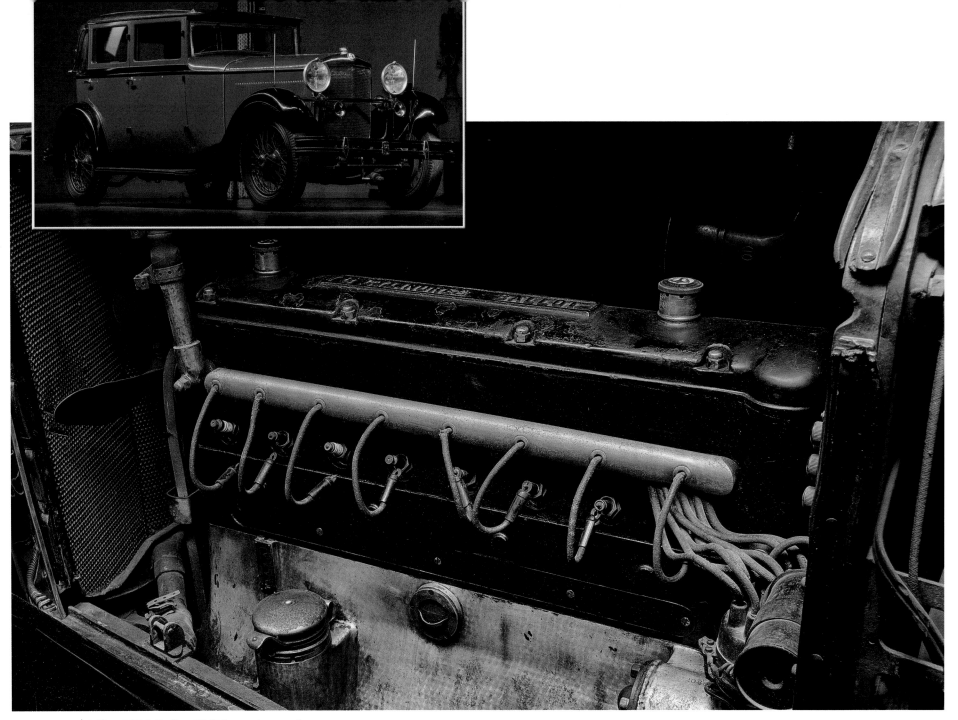

THIS PAGE: A fine 1930 Ballot RH3 four-door saloon.

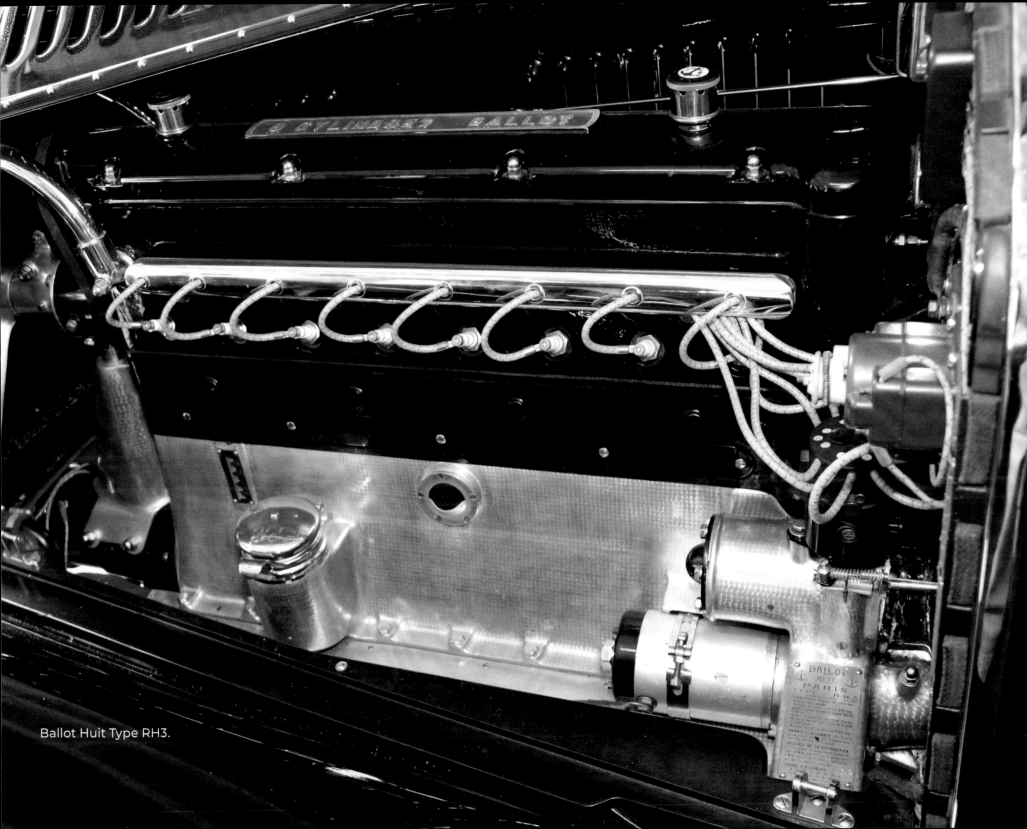

Ballot Huit Type RH3.

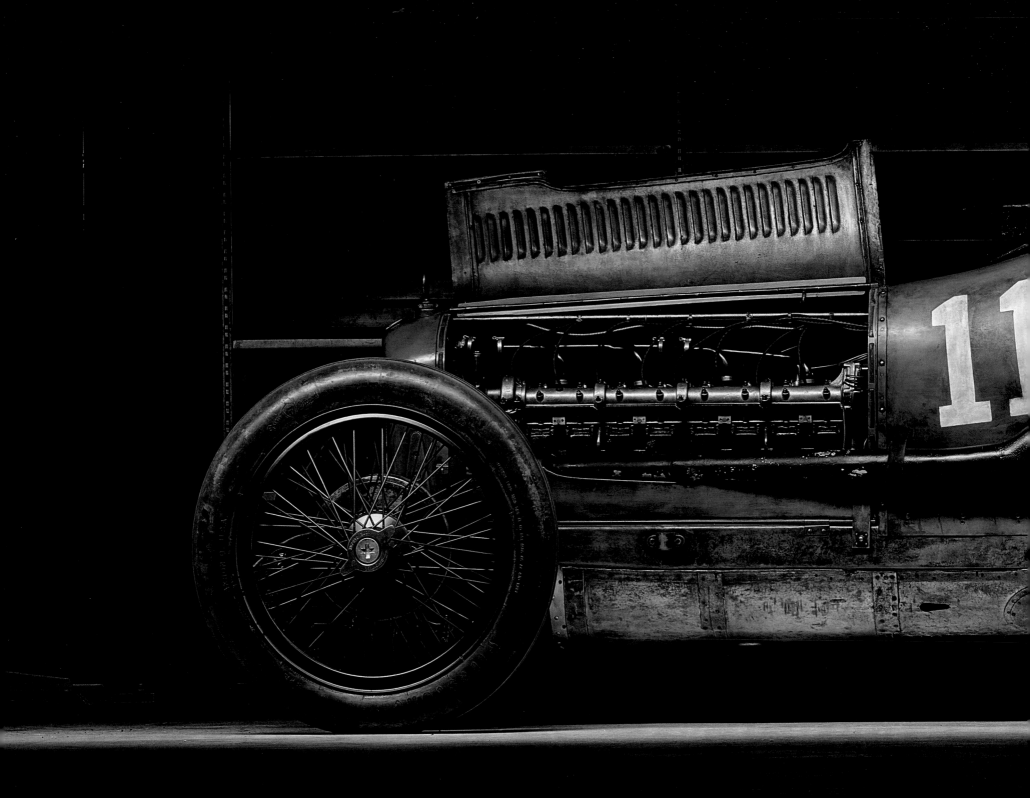

Ballot 3.8 LC.

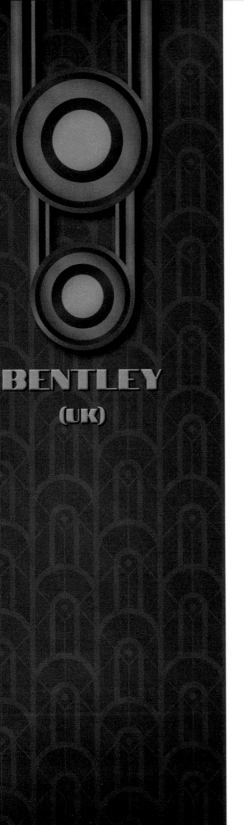

BENTLEY
(UK)

There was a one-off prototype straight eight Bentley, generally known as the 'Scalded Cat' on account of its scintillating performance, which was a Mark V Bentley fitted with the 6.3-litre (384 cu in) straight eight Rolls-Royce engine which would become known as the B81. It was capable of over 100 mph, and is said to have been capable of climbing Porlock Hill in Somerset, UK in top gear. Porlock Hill is the steepest main road in the country, with gradients up to one-in-four, or 25%. The 'Scalded Cat' was popularly said to be the inspiration for the Phantom IV, although the only real link is probably the engine. It is covered under the Rolls-Royce entry.

The car shown here was inspired by the Scalded Cats, but is based on a Mark VI rather than a Mark V chassis. However it uses a straight eight engine very similar to the original.

everley-Barnes as an automobile manufacturer is almost unique in that it only ever made straight eight models. Production was limited, and between 1923 and 1930 only around fourteen cars left the factory. The cars were expensive, the Sports model costing £1,150 (£67,540 in 2020 values) and the Saloon £1,350 (£79,300 in 2020 values). The company started as Lenaerts and Dolphens, but changed its name to Beverley Works Ltd in 1928.

In all five models were produced. In 1923 the first model, the 24/80, appeared powered by a 3,958 cc (241 cu in) sohc engine. Two years later the larger 30/90 was introduced, with a 4,825 cc (294 cu in) sohc unit. Then between 1927 and the demise of the company three smaller dohc cars were made, the 2.5-litre (2,736 cc or 167 cu in), the 18hp (2,440 cc or 149 cu in) and the 22/90 (2,956 cc or 180 cu in). Of the fourteen made, five were the 24/80, three the 30/90 and the remaining six were a mixture of the three smaller dohc models. Today just two survive.

The 30/90 engine is interesting in that it was also used in the early Burney Streamline cars, although it was later dropped because of reliability issues, possibly the result of inadequate cooling in its rear location. This 4,825 cc (294 cu in) unit had a sohc, two plugs per cylinder, and aluminium pistons. With 90 bhp (67 kW) on tap at 2,700 rpm it was good for 70 mph.

Having a range of five expensive models with just 14 cars produced was a certain recipe for failure.

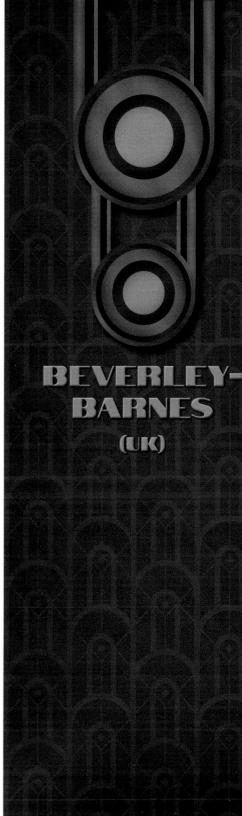

BEVERLEY-BARNES

(UK)

The 1925 Beverley-Barnes 30/90. A 4.8-litre straight eight it was the company's largest and most expensive model. Only three were made and this is the sole survivor.

The left-hand side of the 1925 30/90 Beverley-Barnes engine showing the twin plugs.

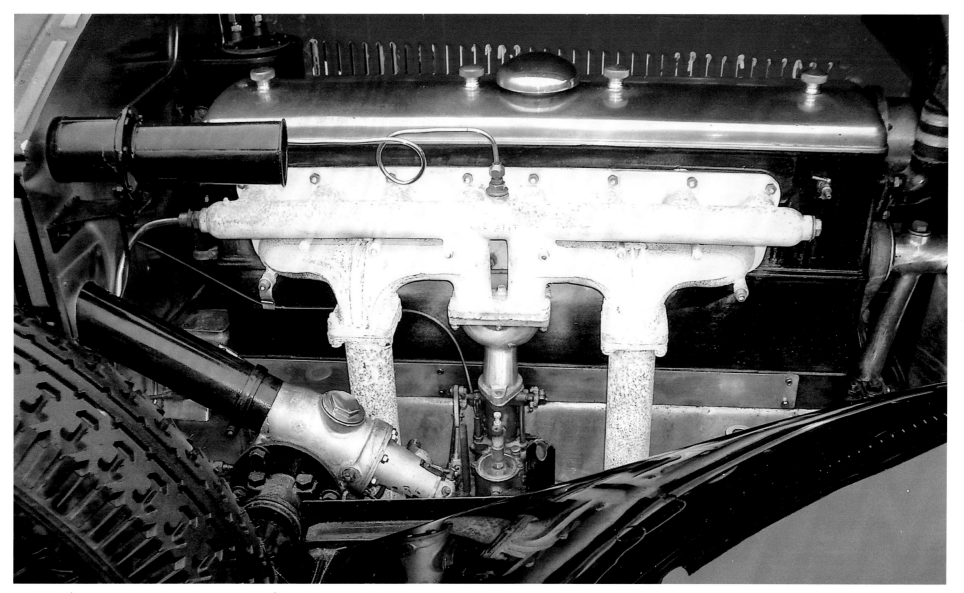

The inlet/exhaust right side of the 1925 30/90 Beverley-Barnes engine, showing the polished cover for the sohc. The same engine was used in the first Burney Streamline cars.

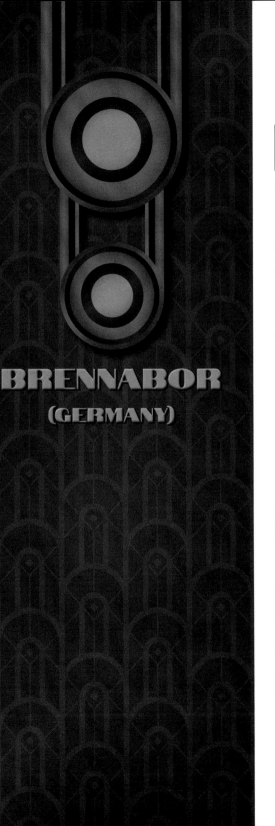

BRENNABOR
(GERMANY)

During the mid-1920s Brennabor was the largest automobile manufacturer in Germany, and even by 1928 it was still in second place to Opel. Yet today it is largely unknown by most people. Like so many car companies its demise was largely the result of not having the right vehicles to weather the recessionary period in the 1930s.

The company was founded by the three Reichstein brothers in 1871. From 1892 it became a major manufacturer of bicycles, and then in 1901 it branched out into motorcycles. 1903 saw the company producing three and four wheeled automobiles, and in 1919 the Type P, aimed at the upper middle class, was launched. By 1921 they were producing on a large scale following many of the mass production principles of Henry Ford.

In 1929 the company launched the Juwel 6, which became a moderate success with around 3,000 being sold. In order to complement the Juwel 6, the company launched the Juwel 8 14/60 in 1930. This featured a 3,417 cc (208.5 cu in) side valve straight eight, with a bore of 74 mm (2.9 in) and a stroke of 100 mm (3.9 in). With a compression ratio of 5.4:1 it delivered 60 bhp (44 kW) at 3,200 rpm. It could attain 62 mph.

The company only sold around 100 Juwel 8s. It did not have smaller, less expensive models to help it survive the economic woes of the 1930s, and car production ceased in 1933. In 1941 the whole plant was dismantled.

Photographs of the Juwel 8 are fairly rare, and it has not been possible to find an image of the engine.

1930 Brennabor Juwel 8: Only 100 of this top-of-the-range model were made, and it is not known if any survive. Even photographs are very rare, and this is one of the few known.

George Brough beside his personal 1935 Brough Superior.

Although better known as a manufacturer of motorcycles, of which he built around 3,000, George Brough also made approximately 100 cars between 1935 and 1938. In many ways very similar to Railtons, the Brough Superior cars used Hudson engines and Hudson chassis.

The first car was the '4-litre' which used a 4,170 cc (254.5 cu in) straight eight side valve Hudson engine, with a bore of 76.2 mm (3.0 in) and a stroke of 114.3 mm (4.5 in) giving a bore:stroke ratio of 67%. With a compression ratio of 6.5:1 it delivered 125 bhp (93 kW) at 4,000 rpm, enough to give it excellent performance, a 0-60 time of under 10 seconds putting it in the 'supercar' category in the 1930s. Nineteen 4-litre models were produced.

Unfortunately Hudson stopped supplying the eight cylinder engine and chassis in 1936, so subsequent cars used a 3455 cc (210.9 cu in) six-cylinder Hudson engine instead. In standard form this delivered 107 bhp (80 kW), but an optional supercharger increased this to 140 bhp (100 kW). Around 80 of the 3.5-litre model were made.

As a final fling, there was a 'XII' made in 1938 using a 4,387 cc (267.7 cu in) V12 Lincoln Zephyr engine installed in a chassis designed by Brough. This car was a one-off which still survives.

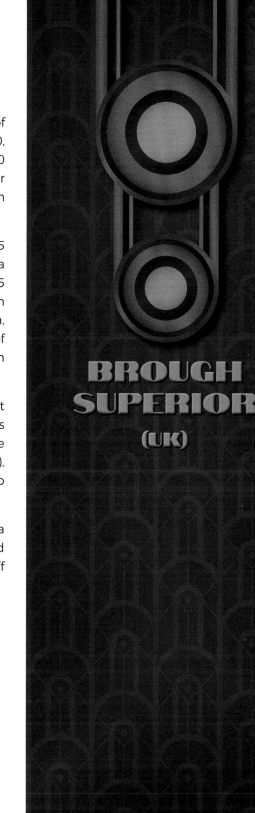

BROUGH SUPERIOR

(UK)

ABOVE: In the 1935 Brough Superior, the humble 4.2-litre Hudson 'flathead' hides under the large but fake ohc cover! **OPPOSITE:** A 1935 Brough Superior 4.2-litre, one of the classic Anglo-American hybrids of the 1930s. **OPPOSITE INSET:** In the 1935 Brough Superior 4.2-litre, the pipe from the left side air filter arches over the fake cam cover to reach the single carburettor, whilst the spark plug leads enter the fake cover through a rather shiny chrome plated tube.

BUGATTI
(FRANCE)

Bugatti is given much greater coverage than most manufacturers in this book because it produced so many different engine designs, around 37 distinct types in total. Although Chrysler produced well over 50 engine variants, and Packard 58 variants with over 400 distinct models, they were basically variations of a single design. Also Bugatti was always at the leading edge of technology, with overhead cams from the outset, whereas Chrysler and Packard retained a 'flathead' side valve format throughout.

The Bugatti Company was founded in 1910, and until the First World War it focused exclusively on four-cylinder cars. The first, the Type 10, was just a prototype, which led to the Type 13, an advanced car at the time with four valves per cylinder, one of the first of this type. The Type 13 began a series running through Types 15, 17, 22 and 23. After the war, the design was resurrected as the Type 13 Brescia in both racing and touring form.

Bugatti had planned to construct a straight eight 3-litre car for Grand Prix racing to be known as the Type 28. But this never left the prototype stage as the racing governing body announced that Grand Prix cars would be limited to just two litres. Along the lines of the 3-litre, Bugatti started work on a smaller straight eight using two blocks of four-cylinders. The vertical valves were operated by a single overhead camshaft, and whereas the 3-litre would have had nine crankshaft bearings, the new 2-litre, known as the 29/30, had just three. This turned out to be a weak spot in the design, and it was not a great success. Its successor reverted to nine bearings. Power output for the 29/30 ranged from 75 bhp (56 kW) to 100 bhp (74 kW), making it fast, but it was not very reliable.

From 1922 onwards, the straight eight format became a vital part of Bugatti's repertoire, resulting in many of the company's most iconic models. Unravelling all the different 'Types' is complicated; throughout the rest of the company's existence there were basically six different series of straight eights:

- ◆ The Type 30
- ◆ The Type 35
- ◆ The Type 46/50
- ◆ The Type 51
- ◆ The Type 57
- ◆ The Type 41 (not a series, but unique)
- ◆ plus several interesting prototypes.

THE TYPE 30 SERIES

The Type 30 Series was the first series of straight eight cars, which grew out of the Type 29/30 and became the basis of the Type 35 Series racing cars. The Type 30 and Type 35 Series were produced in parallel.

TYPE 30 (1922-26): The first in the Series, this was a road-going version of Type 29/30, with a 1,991 cc (121 cu in) sohc 3 valve engine, and a three bearing crankshaft. Around 600 were made. It was a success and paved the way for the Type 35 racer.

OPPOSITE: The 1924 Bugatti Type 30 was the first of the straight eights with its two-litre sohc engine.

The inlet side of the 1924 Type 30 engine showing the twin carbs, very boxy sohc cover but neat wiring solution.

The exhaust side of the 1924 Type 30 engine showing the two sets of four exhausts.

TYPE 38 (1926): This used the engine from Type 35A racing car, a 1,991 cc (121 cu in) 3 valve unit of 60 mm (2.4 in) bore and 88 mm (3.5 in) stroke, giving a bore:stroke ratio of 68%. It delivered 60 bhp (45 kW) and was capable of 75mph.

TYPE 38A (1927): A Type 38 with the addition of the supercharger from the Type 37A. Just 39 were made.

TYPE 43 (1927-1931): Another evolution of the basic straight eight Type 30 platform, this used the supercharged 2,262 cc (138 cu in) 3 valve engine from the Type 35B, with bore of 60 mm (2.4 in) and stroke of 100 mm (3.9 in)

giving a lower bore:stroke ratio of 60%. With 120hp (89 kW) it could achieve 0-60 in 12 seconds and reach 110mph. In total 160 were produced.

TYPE 43A (1931-1932): The roadster version of the Type 43.

TYPE 44 (1927-1930): The most numerous of the range. Its 2,991 cc (182 cu in) 3 valve, sohc, nine bearing engine with its single Schebler carburettor delivered 80 bhp (59 kW). 1095 were made.

TYPE 49 (1930-1934): The last of the Series used a 3,257 cc (199 cu in) engine of 72 mm (2.8 in) bore and 100 mm (3.9 in) stroke with 3 valves per cylinder. 470 were made.

The 1928 Bugatti Type 43 Grand Sport, an evolution of the 35. The Type 43 used a super-charger to deliver 120 bhp and 0-60 in twelve seconds.

DALTON WATSON FINE BOOKS

COACHBUILDING/DESIGN

Title	Author	Price
Ballot (2-Volume Set) – 2020 Cugnot Award Winner	Daniel Cabart and Gautam Sen	Regular: $350; Leather: $1500
Berlinetta '60s: Exceptional Italian Coupés of the Sixties	Xavier de Nombel and Christian Descombes	$95
The Bertone Collection	Gautam Sen and Michael Robinson	$155
Gaston Grümmer: The Art of Carrosserie (2-Volume Set)	Philippe-Gaston Grümmer and Laurent Friry	$89
Marcello Gandini: Maestro of Design (2-Volume Set)	Gautam Sen	Signed/Numbered: $125
Park Ward: The Innovative Coachbuilder 1919-1939 (3-Volume Set)	Gautam Sen	Regular: $295; Signed/Numbered: $350
The Kellner Affair: Matters of Life and Death (3-Volume Set)	Malcolm Tucker	Regular: $375; Custom Leather: $1600
	Peter Larsen with Ben Erickson	Regular: $445; Leather: $1950

GENERAL AUTOMOTIVE/RACING

Title	Author	Price
Around the Circuit: Racing Car Transporters and Support Vehicles at Work	David Cross	$89
Augie Pabst: Behind the Wheel	Robert Birmingham	Regular: $79; Signed/Numbered: $99
Bahamas Speed Weeks	Terry O'Neil	$155
Cobra Pilote: The Ed Hugus Story	Robert D. Walker	$89
Colin Crabbe: Thrill of the Chase	Autobiography	Signed/Numbered: $125
Concours d'Elegance: Dream Cars and Lovely Ladies	Patrick Lesueur, Translated by David Burgess-Wise	$69
Cunningham: The Passion, The Cars, The Legacy (2-Volume Set)	Richard Harman	Regular: $350; Leather: $1200
Ferrari 333 SP: A Pictorial History 1993-2003	Terry O'Neil	$95
Imagine! Automobile Concept Art from the 1930s to the 1980s	Patrick Kelley	Regular: $350; Signed/Numbered: $135
Inside the Paddock: Racing Transporters at Work	David Cross with Bjørn Kjer	$135
Kirk F White: Don't Wash Mine	Kirk F White, Autobiography	$95
Meister Bräuser: Harry Heuer's Championship Racing Team	Tom Schultz	Regular: $95; Signed/Numbered: $125
Mid-Atlantic Sports Car Races 1953-1962	Terry O'Neil	Signed/Numbered: $155
Mille Miglia 1947-1956: Orizzonte Perduto - Lost Horizon	Carlo Dolcini	Regular: $195; Leather: $435
Pebble Beach Concours d'Elegance: The Art of the Poster	Robert Devlin, Kandace Hawkinson	Regular: $69; Silk: $295
Sports Car Racing in the South: Vol. I 1957-1958, Vol. II 1959-1960, Vol. III 1961-1962	Willem Oosthoek	Vol I: $125; Vol II: $155; Vol III (Signed/Numbered): $155
The Golden Days of Thompson Speedway and Raceway 1945-1977	Terry O'Neil	Signed/Numbered: $195
The Straight Eight Engine: Powering Premium Automobiles	Keith Ray	$95
Watkins Glen: The Street Years 1948-1952	Philippe Defechereux	$49

BRITISH CARS

Title	Author	Price
Bentley Motors: On the Road	Bernard L. King	$165
Bentley: Fifty Years of the Marque	Johnnie Green/Hageman, King, Bennett	$92
Making a Marque: Rolls-Royce Motor Car Promotion 1904-1940	Peter Moss and Richard Roberts	$125
Rolls-Royce: Silver Wraith	Martin Bennett	$125
Rolls-Royce: The Classic Elegance	Lawrence Dalton/Bernard L. King	$85
The Goodwood Phantom Drophead Coupe	Malcolm Tucker	$125
The Rolls-Royce Phantom II Continental	André Blaize	Regular: $395; Leather: $1750
The Silver Ghost: A Supernatural Car	Jonathan Harley	$69
Why Not? The Story of The Honourable Charles Stuart Rolls	David Baines	$89
Jaguar E-Type Six-Cylinder Originality Guide	Dr. Thomas F. Haddock & Dr. Michael C. Mueller	Regular: $95; Signed/Numbered: $135
Vintage Jaguar Keyrings, 1955-1980	Morrill 'Bud' Marston	$125

FRENCH CARS

Title	Author	Price
Amilcar	Gilles Fournier/David Burgess-Wise	$175
Crossing the Sands: The Sahara Desert Trek to Timbuktu	Ariane Audouin-Dubreuil/Ingrid MacGill	$65
Eighty Years of Citroën in the UK	John Reynolds	Regular: $70; Special Edition: $450

GERMAN CARS

Title	Author	Price
Gulf 917	Jay Gillotti	Regular: $150; Leather (2-vol): $1500
Mercedes-Benz 300 SL: The Car of the Century	Hans Kleissl and Harry Niemann	$ 50
Porsche by Mailander	Karl Ludvigsen	$ 50
Rudolf Uhlenhaut: Engineer and Gentleman	Wolfgang Scheller and Thomas Pollak	$89
The Incredible Blitzen Benz	Karl Ludvigsen	$69

ITALIAN CARS

Title	Author	Price
De Tomaso: From Buenos Aires to Modena	Dr. Daniele Pozzi	$79
Maserati 300S (Revised, 2-volume set)	Walter Bäumer	Regular: $270; Leather: $1500
Maserati A6G 2000 Zagato	Walter Bäumer	$55
Maserati Tipo 60 and 61: The Magnificent Front-engined Birdcages	Michel Bollée and Willem Oosthoek	$50
Maserati Tipo 63, 64, 65: Birdcage to Supercage	Willem Oosthoek	Regular: $140; Special Edition: $550

ICON / GENERAL INTEREST

Title	Author	Price
Steve McQueen: A Tribute to the King of Cool	Marshall Terrill	Special Edition: $95
Steve McQueen: *Le Mans* in the Rearview Mirror	Don Nunley with Marshall Terrill	$79
Steve McQueen: In His Own Words	Marshall Terrill	$95
Steve McQueen: The Last Mile Revisited	Barbara McQueen and Marshall Terrill	$49

ORDER FROM: Dalton Watson Fine Books / www.daltonwatson.com / info@daltonwatson.com / +1 847 945 0568

DALTON WATSON FINE BOOKS

Dalton Watson Fine Books
Glyn and Jean Morris
www.daltonwatson.com
+1 847 945 0568
info@daltonwatson.com

NEW RELEASES 2020

STEVE McQUEEN: In His Own Words

Marshall Terrill

Drawn from more than five decades of media coverage, memorabilia and detailed research, **Steve McQueen: In His Own Words**, serves up the most credible and thought-provoking insights spoken by Steve McQueen: more than 450 quotations directly from 'The King of Cool' covering such topics as fame, cinema, money, sex, racing, popular culture, and a forward-thinking approach on the environment. Accompanying the quotes are more than 500 photographs, personal documents, and memorabilia, many of which are seen here for the first time. They illustrate McQueen's early life and movie career, as well as his passion for automobiles, motorcycles and antique planes.

504 pages | 547 photographs
$95

THE STRAIGHT EIGHT ENGINE
Powering Premium Automobiles

Keith Ray

This is the first book specifically about automobiles with straight eight engines that have become amongst the most sought-after, collectible, and valuable vehicles of all time. In Britain and Europe, the straight eight was always a rare, expensive car, but in the United States, the engine also found its way into the mainstream 'mid-range' market in basic side-valve form. First appearing in a road car in the 1920s, the engine grew quickly in popularity, and flourished throughout the 1930s and the early 1940s, but by the 1950s only a small handful were available. Within these pages is a comprehensive survey of all the different cars and the many styles of engines that were produced.

404 pages | 479 photographs
$95

MERCEDES-BENZ 300 SL: THE CAR OF THE CENTURY

Hans Kleissl and Harry Niemann

For over 60 years, no other car has moved the lovers of classic cars more than the 300 SL. For Daimler-Benz AG, this car is an icon that with the magical suffix "SL", for Super Leicht or Super Light, has continued to this day to be used on Mercedes-Benz sports cars. Hans Kleissl, recognized worldwide as one of the top 300 SL experts, and the former Daimler historian Harry Neumann have produced a book that captures the magic of the world surrounding this car. The events, photographs and fascinating technology, all illustrated within these pages, explain the mystique that inspires people to this day.

374 pages | 403 photographs
$150

MAKING A MARQUE
Rolls-Royce Motor Car Promotion 1904–1940

Peter Moss and Richard Roberts

The promotional history of Rolls-Royce Motor Cars from the company's beginnings in 1904 to the outbreak of World War II has been exhaustively researched and documented in these pages. The book covers the story of the constant battle for recognition on both sides of the Atlantic and the different approaches used in each market, highlighting the outstanding variety and quality of Rolls-Royce's illustrated advertising, from publicity for success in races and trials, through advertising in important magazines and influential newspapers, to beautifully produced pamphlets and catalogues. The unique Rolls-Royce style illustrated here, promises enthusiasts a feast for the eyes and hours of entertaining reading.

464 pages | 932 photographs
$125

INSIDE THE PADDOCK: RACING TRANSPORTERS AT WORK

David Cross with Bjorn Kjer

For some years, David Cross was intrigued by the many ways that racing cars reached the paddock at a race meeting and was disappointed to find no specific guidance or literature on what appeared to be an important facet of motorsport. He decided to remedy this omission and his detailed research has resulted in the publication of this unique book. **Inside the Paddock – Racing Car Transporters at Work** contains nearly 550 images, many unpublished hitherto, which are enhanced and embellished by well-researched and informative captions.

REPRINTED IN LIMITED QUANTITY

392 pages | 546 photographs
$135

2012 OCTANE BOOK OF THE YEAR

DON'T WASH MINE

Kirk F White autobiography

Filled with fabulous and entertaining tales, **Don't Wash Mine** chronicles Kirk White's fascinating journey through the golden age of motorsports and car collecting. From running a Ferrari dealership in Philadelphia to fielding some of the most memorable competition vehicles of the time through his eponymous racing stable, White crossed paths with iconic figures such as Roger Penske, Brock Yates, Mark Donohue and Dan Gurney. The founder of the modern collector car auction industry, White left an indelible impression on automotive enthusiasts around the world and collected stories of a life well lived that are sure to delight readers of every age and interest.

400 pages | 450 photographs
$95

The neat exhaust side of the Type 43 engine showing the 2x four-cylinder concept. **INSET:** The inlet side showing the supercharger and inlet manifold.

97

A 1932 Bugatti Type 49 shown opposite. The Type 49 was the last of the Type 30 series. **INSET**: the exhaust side of the Type 49 engine with its elegant 2x four exhaust design. Above, the inlet side of the 3257cc engine in the Type 49, showing the twin plugs and neat wiring.

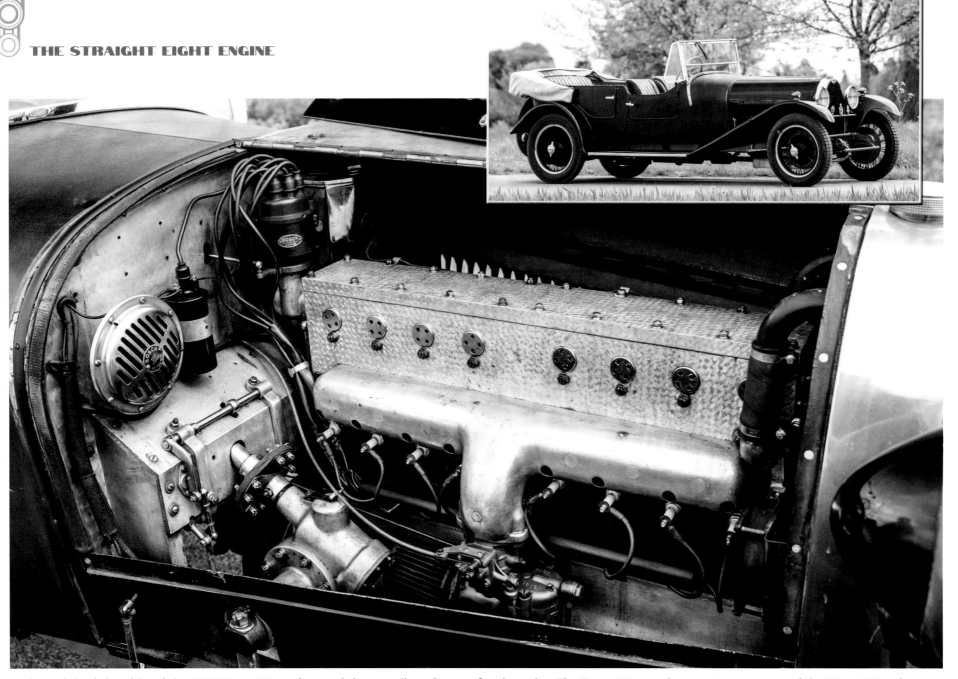

A view of the inlet side of the 1928 Type 44 engine and the very 'boxy' cover for the sohc. The Type 44 was the most numerous of the Type 30 series, 1,095 being delivered. This is a 1928 example.

The left (exhaust) side of the Type 44 engine showing again the 2x four-cylinder thinking for the exhausts.

THE TYPE 35 SERIES

Produced largely in parallel with the Type 30 Series, the Type 35s were the racing variants.

TYPE 35 (1924): A 1,991 cc (121 cu in) 3 valve sohc engine evolved from the Type 29/30, with a bore of 60 mm (2.4 in) and a stroke of 88 mm (3.5 in) was used. It had a five ball-bearing crankshaft which could rev up to 6,000 rpm and deliver 90 bhp (67 kW). Top speed was a genuine 110 mph. Total production was 96. There was a rare de-bored version with a reduced displacement of 1,494 cc (59 cu in).

TYPE 35A (1926): A less expensive version of the Type 35, with just three

bearings on the crankshaft and coil ignition like the Type 30. Power was down from 90 bhp (67 kW) to 70 bhp. (52 kW). Total production was 139.

TYPE 35C (1926): A Type 35 with the addition of a Roots supercharger and a single Zenith carburettor. This delivered a healthy 120-130 bhp (89-97 kW). Production totalled 50.

TYPE 35T (1926): Produced specifically for the Targa Florio, the 35T had an increased capacity of 2,262 cc (138 cu in) with a longer stroke of 100 mm (3.9 in). Just thirteen of these were produced as GP regulations started limiting engine size to two litres.

A 1925 Bugatti Type 35 Grand Prix, a genuine 110 mph car, with its two-litre sohc engine. **OPPOSITE:** The left-hand, exhaust, side of the engine.
INSET: The right-hand inlet side showing the twin Solex carburettors, the very neat wiring and the flexible coupling on the steering column.

TYPE 35B (1927): The final version of the Type 35 series. It used the same engine as the 35T but with the addition of a supercharger and produced 120-130 bhp (89-92 kW). Production was 45 units.

TYPE 39: Linked to the Type 35 series was the Type 39, similar to the Type 35C except for a smaller engine, the stroke being reduced from 88 mm to 66 mm (2.6 in) giving a capacity of 1,493 cc (91 cu in) and an almost square engine with a bore:stroke ratio of 91%. It had a mix of plain and ball bearings on the crankshaft. Production totalled 10 units. There was one odd version produced with a lower 1,092 cc (67 cu in) displacement, achieved by reducing the bore to 51.3 mm (2.0 in) using a liner. At 136.5 cc (8.3 cu in) per cylinder this was one of the smallest straight eights of the period.

THE TYPE 46/50 SERIES

Type 46 Series and later Type 50 Series were large enclosed touring cars produced in the 1930s. There was also a Type 50B racing version. The Type 46/50 series often carried extremely elegant coachwork by leading design houses.

TYPE 46 (1929-1936): A 5,359 cc (327 cu in) 3 valve sohc engine of 81 mm (3.2 in) bore and 130 mm (5.1 in) stroke, with one Smith-Barriquand carburettor, was installed. It was a large car with a chassis weight of 1134kg. The three speed gearbox was combined with the differential on the live rear axle, which gave a rather harsh ride. Production totalled around 400.

TYPE 46S: A supercharged version of the Type 46, with a Roots supercharger delivering 160 bhp (118 kW). It was not a success, with just 18 being made.

RIGHT: The 1931 Bugatti Type 46 was a large enclosed touring car with a 5.4-litre sohc engine. **TOP:** The inlet (right) side of the 1931 Type 46 engine showing the twin plugs and single Smith-Barriquand carburettor.

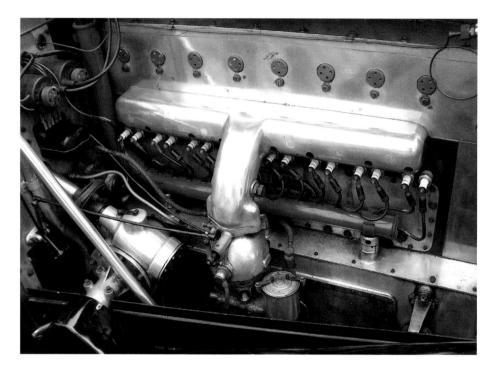

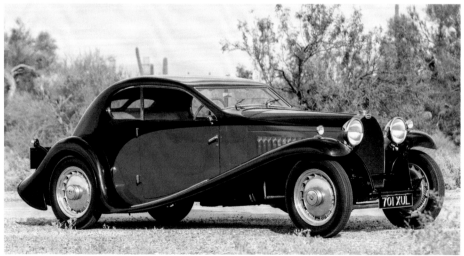

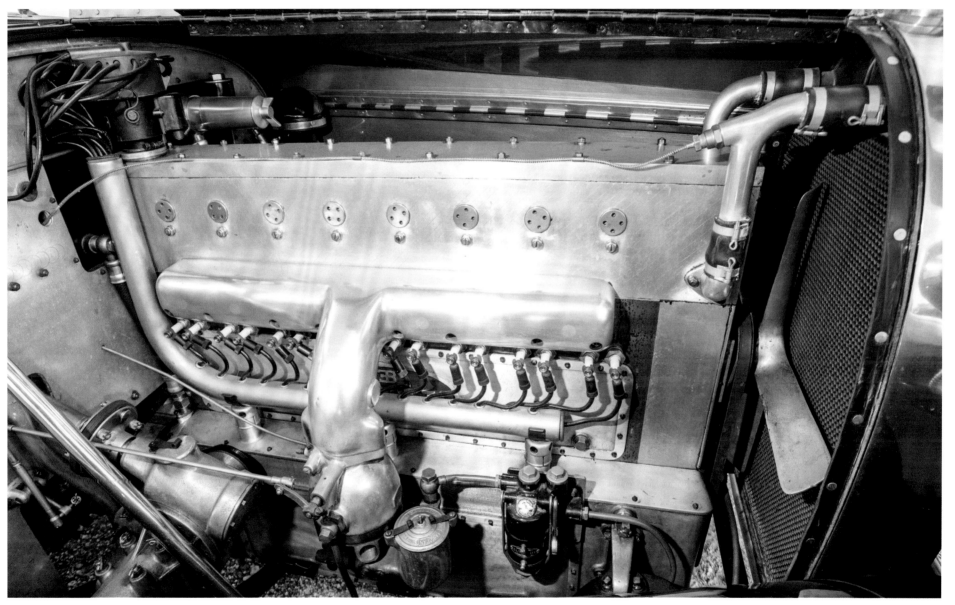

A broader view of the Type 46 engine, showing how effectively the 5.4-litre engine fills the bonnet space.

TYPE 50 (1930-1935): A shorter, sporting version of the Type 46 with a smaller 4,972 cc (303 cu in) engine, but now with dohc and 2 valves per cylinder. It delivered 225 bhp (167 kW). Including the Type 50T, production totalled 65.

TYPE 50T (TOURING): A saloon version of Type 50, the car had the same 138 inch wheelbase of the Type 46 but shared the 4,972 cc engine of Type 50. Tuned more for torque, with power down from 225 bhp to 200 bhp (148 kW), the engine had a bore of 86 mm (3.4 in) and a stroke of 107 mm (4.2 in), giving a high bore:stroke ratio of 80%. It had two valves per cylinder operated by dual overhead camshafts.

TYPE 50B (1937-1939): A racing version of the Type 50 with a 4,972 cc 2 valve supercharged engine delivering a healthy 470 bhp (348 kW).

THE TYPE 51 SERIES

These cars replaced the Type 35 Series as Bugatti's premier racing cars for the 1930s. But the Types 51, 53, 54 and 59 could not compete with the German state-backed Auto Union and Mercedes-Benz teams, and were not a great success.

TYPE 51 AND 51A (1931): A 2,262 cc (138 cu in) dohc evolution of the supercharged sohc of the Type 35B was used. The engine delivered 160bhp (118 kW). Total production was 40.

TYPE 54 (1932): A larger 4,972 cc (303 cu in) dohc engine delivering 300bhp (222 kW). Production was 4 or 5.

TYPE 59: Bugatti's final race car of the 1930s had an enlarged 3,257 cc (199 cu in) version of Type 57 engine, delivering 250 bhp (185 kW), in a Type 54 chassis. The engine was lowered to improve cornering stability. Production was 8.

TYPE 55 (1932-35): The road-going version of the Type 51, its 2,262 cc (138 cu in) supercharged engine was slightly de-tuned by reducing the compression ratio delivering 130bhp (96 kW) at 5,500 rpm. Total production was 38.

TYPE 53 (1932): A four wheel drive version with the 4,972 cc engine from the Type 50 road car in a Type 51 chassis. The engine delivered 300bhp (222 kW) with its Roots supercharger. Because of the front wheel drive train, it used independent front suspension, the only time this was ever approved by Ettore Bugatti. Production was a mere two or three.

A 1932 Bugatti Type 55 Super Sports which was the road going version of the Type 51, with a slightly detuned supercharged 2.2-litre engine.

OPPOSITE: The neat exhaust (left) side of the Type 55 Super Sports engine showing the twin cam head and 2x four exhaust setup.

THE TYPE 57 SERIES

This was a completely new design created by Jean Bugatti, son of Ettore, and built between 1934 to 1940. 710 Type 57s were manufactured. The Type 57 used a dohc 3,257 cc (199 cu in) engine based on that in the Type 49 with six main bearings. There were basically two variants, the 57 and the 57S/SC. Oddly the car reappeared in 1951 as the 101, using up remaining parts from before the war. The last model was sold as late as 1965!

TYPE 57 (1934-1940): A touring car with the 3,257 cc (198.7 cu in) engine from the Type 59 GP cars. With 135bhp (100 kW) it could achieve 95mph. Hydraulic brakes were used from 1938. Total production was 630.

TYPE 57T: A tuned version of the Type 57 giving a top speed of 115 mph.

TYPE 57C (1937-1940): A racing version of the Type 57, it used the

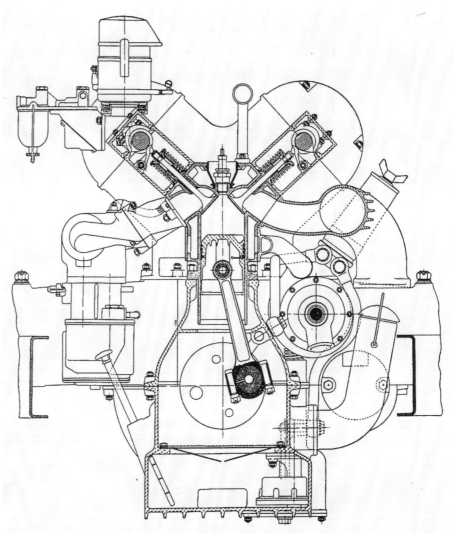

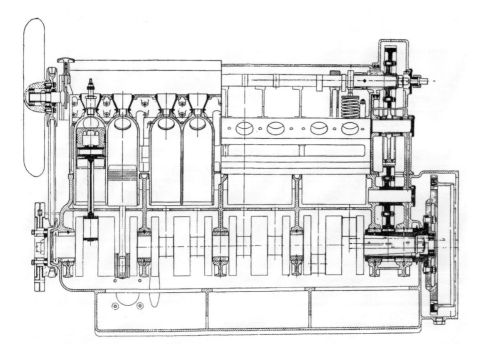

LEFT: Longitudinal section of the Bugatti Type 57 engine. The crankshaft ran in six plain main bearings. The rear two bearings straddle the power take-off to the gear tower. **ABOVE:** Transverse section of the Bugatti Type 57 engine.

The exhaust side of the 1937 Type 57 engine showing the rather unusual rearward 'bias' in the exhaust manifold, maybe not so critical on a touring car.

The right (inlet) side of the 1937 Type 57 dohc engine, showing the neat ducted wiring to the plugs.

same 3,257 cc (198.7 cu in) engine but with the help of a Roots supercharger delivered 160bhp (118 kW). Production totalled 96.

TYPE 57C TANK: A second 'Tank' version of a Bugatti based on the Type 57C. It was in this car that Jean Bugatti crashed and was killed.

TYPE 57S/SC: The 'S' stands for lowered, and the 'C' for supercharged. Originally production was 43 of the 57Ss and 2 of the 57SCs. But in fact most 57S were later converted to 57SC specification by retrofitting a supercharger. Power was up from 170bhp to 200bhp (148 kW), and 120mph was achievable. Four 57SCs were built as Atlantics, one of the most highly prized of all classic cars.

TYPE 57S/SC ATALANTE: Similar to the Atlantic. Production totalled 17.

TYPE 57S45: A one-off special using a 4,743 cc (289 cu in) engine.

TYPE 57G TANK: The 57S based 57G tank won Le Mans and the 1936 French Grand Prix. Only 3 units were produced.

TYPE 101: A most unusual series of cars, being essentially pre-war Type 57s cloaked in 1950s' bodywork and sold as the Type 101, or Bugatti Coach. Seven or eight cars (plus a prototype) were made from left-over pre-war parts, and six were sold in 1951-52. Amazingly one was not completed until 1965. The 101 had a 3,257 cc (199 cu in), 135 bhp (100 kW) engine with two valves per cylinder and a bore of 72 mm (2.8 in) and stroke of 100 mm (3.9 in).

TYPE 101C: The supercharged version of the 101 with 190bhp (141 kW).

THE TYPE 41 SERIES

The Type 41, also known as the Bugatti Royale, was hardly a series, with just seven similar cars made. It was intended by Bugatti to be the ultimate luxury car, and the chassis alone cost $30,000 (equivalent to around $1.8 million today). The engine was a massive 12,763 cc (778 cu in) unit with 125 mm

The 1955 Bugatti Type 251 with its amazing transverse rear mounted pre-war engine.

(4.9 in) bore and 130 mm (5.1 in) stroke, giving a near-square bore:stroke ratio of 96%, and 3 valves per cylinder controlled by a sohc driven from a centrally located gear train. It could deliver 275-300 bhp (204-224 kW), had nine crankshaft bearings and a dry sump. In the end only three of the seven were sold to 'real' customers.

THE PROTOTYPES

In addition to the production cars, there was a small number of prototype or 'one off' straight eights. These included the 1,493 cc (91.1 cu in) Type 36, the 3,801 cc (231.9 cu in) Type 45, the 2,986 cc (182.2 cu in) Type 47 and 4,432 cc (270.4 cu in) Type 64 with 'gull wing' bodywork, of which it appears no example was completed. Finally, there was the extraordinary Type 251, a Grand Prix contender with a unique rear-mounted transverse straight eight engine of pre-war design. This was also Bugatti's first and only 'over square' engine, and the first with a De Dion rear axle. Another interesting feature was that the drive to the gearbox was taken from the centre of the crankshaft by a set of spur gears. There was a second set of spur gears joining the gearbox to the final drive.

The table provides an overview summary of the different series.

A 1937 Bugatti 57SC. The 'S' stands for lowered, and the 'C' for supercharged, making this one of the greatest of all Bugattis.

The inlet side of the 1937 Bugatti 57SC engine with the supercharger clearly in view. **INSET:** The exhaust (left) side of the sensational 57SC's engine, but still with the rather odd 'rear bias' on the exhaust system.

BUGATTI EIGHT MODELS

Model		Type 30	Type 35	Type 35A	Type 35C	Type 38	Type 39	Type 39A
Year introduced		1922	1924	1926	1926	1926	1926	1926
Displacement	cc	1,991	1,991	1,991	1,991	1,991	1,493	1,493
	cu in	121	121	121	121	121	91	91
Power output	bhp	50+	90	70	120-130	60	80-90	110-120
	kW	37+	67	52	89-97	45	59-67	82-89
	@ rpm	3,800	3,800	3,800	3,800			
Specific output	bhp/litre	25.1+	45.2	35.2	60.3-65.3	30.1	53.5-60.3	73.7-80.4
	bhp/cu in	0.41+	0.74	0.58	0.99-1.07	0.50	1.00-1.13	1.38-1.50
	kW/litre	18.6+	33.7	26.1	44.7-48.7	22.6	39.5-44.9	54.9-59.6
	kW/cu in	0.31+	0.55	0.43	0.74-0.80	0.37	0.74-0.84	1.03-1.11
Bore	mm	60	60	60	60	60	60	60
	inches	2.40	2.40	2.40	2.40	2.40	2.40	2.40
Stroke	mm	88	88	88	88	88	66	66
	inches	3.50	3.50	3.50	3.50	3.50	2.60	2.60
Bore:stroke ratio		68%	68%	68%	68%	68%	91%	91%
Valve gear		sohc 24 v	sohc 24v	sohc 24v	sohc 24v	sohc 24v	sohc 24v	sohc 24v
Carburettor		2xZenith or Solex	2x Solex	2xZenith or Solex	s/c 1xZenith	2xZenith or Solex	1xZenith	s/c 1xZenith

Model		Type 35B	Type 38A	Type 43/43A	Type 44	Type 46	Type 41	Type 46S	Type 49
Year introduced		1927	1927	1927	1927	1929	1930	1930	1930
Displacement	cc	2,262	1,991	2,262	2,991	5,359	12,763	5,359	3,257
	cu in	138	121	138	182	327	778	327	199
Power output	bhp	120-130	100	120	80	140	275-300	160	85
	kW	89-97	67	89	59	104	204-224	118	63
	@ rpm								
Specific output	bhp/litre	53.1-58.6	50.2	53.1	26.7	26.1	21.6-23.5	29.9	26.1
	bhp/cu in	0.87-0.94	0.83	0.87	0.44	0.43	0.35-0.39	0.49	0.43
	kW/litre	39.4-42.9	33.7	39.3	19.7	19.4	16.0-17.6	22.0	19.3
	kW/cu in	0.64-0.70	0.55	0.64	0.32	0.32	0.26-0.29	0.36	0.32
Bore	mm	60	60	60	69	81	125	81	72
	inches	2.40	2.40	2.40	2.70	3.20	4.90	3.20	2.80
Stroke	mm	100	88	100	100	130	130	130	100
	inches	3.90	3.50	3.90	3.90	5.10	5.10	5.10	3.90
Bore:stroke ratio		60%	68%	60%	69%	62%	96%	62%	72%
Valve gear		sohc 24v	sohc 24v	sohc 24v	sohc 24v	sohc 24v	sohc 24v	sohc 24v	sohc 24v
Carburettor		s/c 1xZenith	s/c 1xZenith	s/c 1xZenith or Solex	1xSchebler	1xSmith Barriquand	1xZenith	s/c 1xSmith Barriquand	1xSchebler

Model		Type 50	Type 50T	Type 51	Type 51 (2)	Type 51A	Type 53	Type 54	Type 55
Year introduced		1930	1930	1931	1931	1931	1932	1932	1932
Displacement	cc	4,972	4,972	1,991	2,262	1,493	4,972	4,972	2,262
	cu in	303	303	121	138	91	303	303	138
Power output	bhp	225	200	160	180	130	300	300	130
	kW	167	148	119	133	97	223	223	96
	@ rpm								
Specific output	bhp/litre	45.3	40.2	80.4	79.6	87.1	60.3	60.3	57.5
	bhp/cu in	0.74	0.66	1.32	1.30	1.43	0.99	0.99	0.94
	kW/litre	33.6	29.8	59.8	58.8	65.0	44.9	44.9	42.4
	kW/cu in	0.55	0.49	0.98	0.96	1.07	0.74	0.74	0.70
Bore	mm	86	86	60	64	60	86	86	60
	inches	3.40	3.40	2.40	2.50	2.40	3.40	3.40	2.40
Stroke	mm	107	107	88	88	66	107	107	100
	inches	4.20	4.20	2.60	2.60	2.60	4.20	4.20	3.90
Bore:stroke ratio		80%	80%	68%	73%	91%	80%	80%	60%
Valve gear		dohc 24v	dohc 24v	dohc 24v	dohc 24v	dohc 24v	dohc 24v	dohc 24v	dohc 24v
Carburettor		2xZenith or Schebler	2xZenith or Schebler	s/c 1xZenith	s/c 1xZenith	s/c 1xZenith	s/c 2xZenith	s/c 2xZenith	s/c 1xZenith

Model		Type 59	Type 57	Type 57S	Type 50B	Type 57C	Type 57SC	Type 101	Type 101C
Year introduced		1933	1934	1936	1937	1937	1937	1950	1950
Displacement	cc	3,257	3,257	3,257	4,972	3,257	3,257	3,257	3,257
	cu in	199	198.7	198.7	303	198.7	198.7	198.7	198.7
Power output	bhp	250	135	170	470	160	200	135	190
	kW	185	100	126	348	118	148	100	141
	@ rpm								
Specific output	bhp/litre	76.8	41.4	52.2	94.5	49.1	61.4	41.4	58.3
	bhp/cu in	1.26	0.68	0.86	1.55	0.81	1.01	0.68	0.96
	kW/litre	56.8	30.7	38.7	70.0	36.2	45.4	30.7	43.3
	kW/cu in	0.93	0.50	0.63	1.15	0.59	0.74	0.50	0.71
Bore	mm	72	72	72	86	72	72	72	72
	inches	2.80	2.80	2.80	3.40	2.80	2.80	2.80	2.80
Stroke	mm	100	100	100	107	100	100	100	100
	inches	3.90	3.90	3.90	4.20	3.90	3.90	3.90	3.90
Bore:stroke ratio		72%	72%	72%	80%	72%	72%	72%	72%
Valve gear		dohc 24v	dohc 24v	dohc 24v	dohc 16v	dohc	dohc	dohc	dohc
Carburettor		s/c 2xZenith	1xStromberg	1xBugatti or Stromberg	s/c 1xZenith or Schebler	s/c 1xStromberg	s/c 1xStromberg or Bugatti	1xWeber	s/c 1xWeber

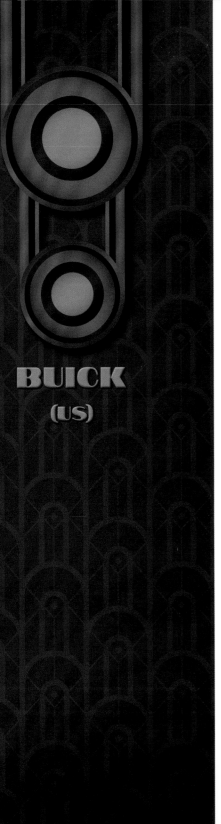

The first Buicks, just two automobiles, were made in 1899 and 1900 at the Buick Auto-Vim and Power Company. These two vehicles were made by chief engineer, Walter Marr, but he failed to convince owner David Buick that there was a future in motor cars. Marr left the company and was replaced by Eugene Richard who applied for a patent on Marr's ohv engine design under the name of Buick; in future Buick would use only ohv engines. Car production proper began in 1904. By 1908 around 8,000-9,000 vehicles a year were being built, taking the number-one spot ahead of Oldsmobile, Ford and Maxwell. The success of Buick, with profits allowing co-owner William C Durant to acquire other businesses, led to the creation of General Motors in 1908.

Buick occupies an important position in the history of the straight eight. In 1931 the straight six in all Buick cars was replaced with a straight eight, and the company produced only straight eights until 1953. Unlike Packard, and many other major manufacturers, overhead valves were used from the outset and there was never a flathead model. In 1936 the variety of engines was rationalised to two, a 233 cu in version for the lower range cars and a larger 320.2 cu in for the higher range models. The last year of a Buick straight eight was 1953, by which time it was only installed in the 'entry' model, the Special, and after that all Buicks used the V8 'Nailhead' engine.

Buick straight eight cars progressed through the following series:

SERIES 40: The 'entry level' Series 40 started life in 1930 as a 4,220 cc (257.5 cu in) six-cylinder model producing 80.5 bhp (60 kW) at 2800 rpm. The six-cylinder version was discontinued in 1934 and was re-launched in 1935 with a 3818 cc (233.0 cu in) straight eight engine.

40 SPECIAL: In 1936 the Series 40 was renamed as the Special, still the entry model, but with a new 4.1-litre (248 cu in) engine in place of the 3,818 cc (233 cu in) unit. In 1951 the engine was changed to a larger 4.3-litre (263.3 cu in) Fireball straight eight, which continued in this model until 1953.

SERIES 50: When the 40 was temporarily discontinued in 1934 the Series 50 became, for a short while, the entry model for Buick. The Series 50 originally, in 1930, had a six-cylinder engine, but a straight eight 3,616 cc (220.7 cu in) engine delivering 77bhp (57 kW) was an option from 1931. In 1932 the displacement was increased slightly to 3,776 cc (230.4 cu in) raising power to 82.5 bhp (61kW), and in 1933 power was further raised to 86 bhp (64 kW), and finally to 88 bhp (65 kW) in 1934. In 1935 a new engine of 3,818 cc (233.0 cu in) was installed which delivered 93 bhp (69 kW).

50 SUPER: As with the Series 40, the Series 50 acquired the name Super in 1936, and the 4,065 cc (248.0 cu in) Fireball engine. With a compression ratio of 6.3:1, it delivered 107 bhp (79 kW). In 1941 compression was raised to 7.0:1 and 'compound carburettion' was introduced, improving power output to 125 bhp (93 kW). But in 1942 the compound carburettion was dropped, and the compression ratio lowered to 6.3:1 reducing power output to 110 bhp (82 kW).

SERIES 60: The 60 was intended to be a sportier version of the 50, with the same Fireball engine in a lighter body. The Series 60 started in 1931 with the 4,829 cc (294.7 cu in) engine delivering 90 bhp (67 kW). In 1933 power was raised to 97 bhp (72 kW), then in 1934 a new 4,561 cc (278.3 cu in) 100 bhp (74 kW) engine was introduced.

60 CENTURY: In line with the 1936 'naming', the Series 60 became the Century. It acquired the 5,247 cc (320.2 cu) in 120 bhp (89 kW) Fireball engine, but the model was discontinued in 1942. The name was re-instated in 1954 with the Nailhead V8.

SERIES 80: The Series 80 appeared in 1931, featuring the 5,649 cc (344.7 cu in) engine delivering 104 bhp (78 kW) at 2,800 rpm. In 1932 a higher power 113 bhp (84 kW) unit was used.

80 ROADMASTER (AND LIMITED AFTER 1940): In 1936 the Series 80 was renamed the Roadmaster, initially with a 5,247 cc (320.2 cu in) 120 bhp (89 kW) Fireball engine. For 1938 the compression ratio was raised to 6.5:1, producing 141 bhp (104 kW), up 21 bhp on the previous version. A further increase to 7.0:1 later produced 165 bhp (122 kW), before the compound carburettor was dropped, and the compression ratio reduced back to 6.6:1, giving 144 bhp (107 kW). After 1940 the Series 80 changed its name from Roadmaster to Limited, the name previously used for the Series 90.

SERIES 90: The Series 90 was the top of the Buick range, and had the highest level of trim. It appeared in 1931 with the 5,650 cc (344.8 cu in) engine delivering 104 bhp (78 kW) at 2,800 rpm. In 1932 power increased to 113 bhp (84 kW), and further rose to 116 bhp in 1934.

90 LIMITED: With the introduction of names in 1936, the Series 90 became the 90 Limited. From 1936 to 1939 it used the 5,243.9 cc (320 cu in) engine delivering 120 bhp (89 kW). In 1940 the Limited name was switched to the Series 80 models. To confuse matters, in 1940 some names were moved around. The name Roadmaster was used for a new Series 70, whilst the 1940 Series 80 was renamed Limited.

70 ROADMASTER: The 1940 70 Roadmaster used the same 5,243 cc (320 cu in) 120 bhp (89 kW) engine as in the 90 Limited, a model which was dropped in 1940.

The Buick 60 Series was intended to be a sportier version of the 50 Series, with, by 1934, a 4.6-litre ohv 100 bhp engine. **INSET:** The left (inlet/exhaust) side of the 1934 Buick 66C 4.6-litre ohv engine. **OPPOSITE:** The right-hand side of the engine, with just the spark plugs. The plate on the valve cover displays the firing order 1-6-2-5-8-7-4.

A 1941 Buick Roadmaster. From 1940, the Roadmaster used the same 5.2-litre engine as the 90 Limited, a model which was dropped in 1940.

The 'Fireball Dynaflash Eight' engine in the Roadmaster, proudly boasting 'valve in head'.

A large 1939 Buick Super 90, which was the top of the Buick range. **INSET:** 15.9 The inlet/exhaust (left) side of the Super 90's engine. **OPPOSITE:** The right-hand side of the Super 90's 5.2-litre ohv engine. Buick only ever used ohv with their 'eights'.

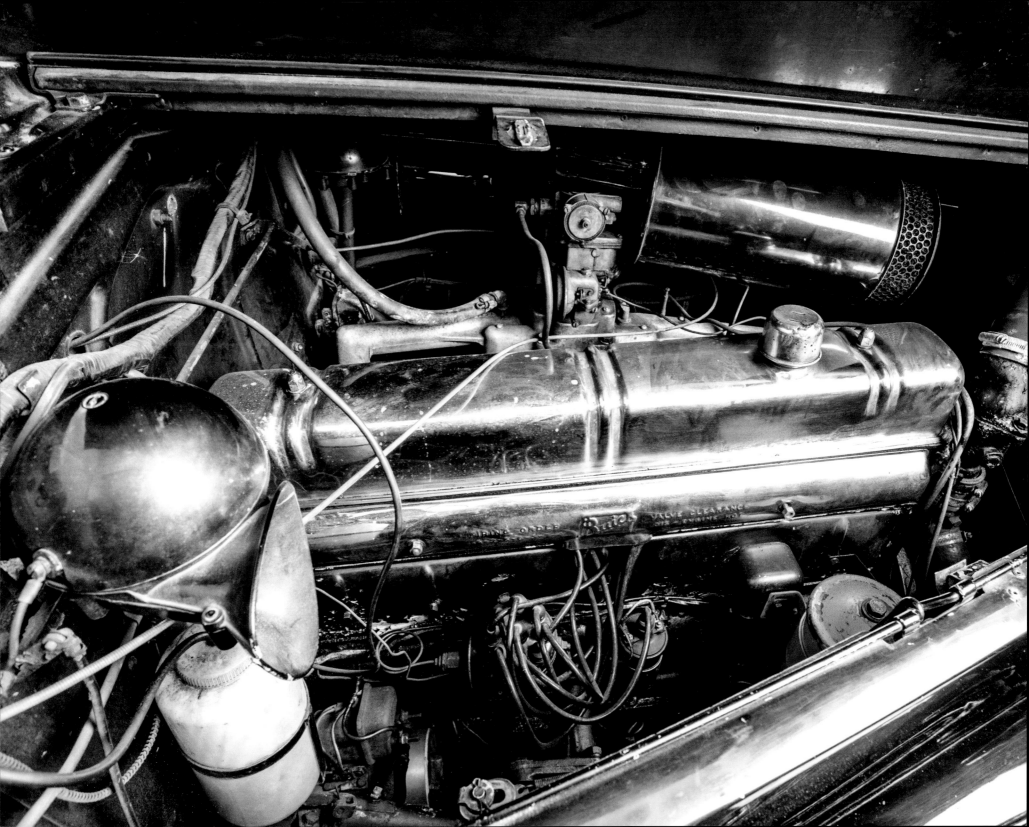

BUICK EIGHT MODELS

Model		Series 50	Series 60	Series 80	Series 90	Series 50 ii	Series 80 ii	Series 90 ii	Series 50 iii
Year introduced		1931	1931	1931	1931	1932	1932	1931	1933
Displacement	cc	3,616	4,829	5,649	5,649	3,776	5,649	5,649	3,776
	cu in	220.7	294.7	344.7	344.7	230.4	344.7	344.7	230.4
Power output	bhp (max)	77	90	104	104	82.5	113	113	86
	kW	57	67	78	78	61	84	84	64
	@ rpm	3,200	3,000	2,800	2,800	3,200	2,800	2,800	3,200
Specific output	bhp/litre	21.3	18.6	18.4	18.4	21.8	20.0	20.0	22.8
	bhp/cu in	0.35	0.31	0.30	0.30	0.36	0.33	0.33	0.37
	kW/litre	15.8	13.9	13.8	13.8	16.2	14.9	14.9	16.9
	kW/cu in	0.26	0.23	0.23	0.23	0.26	0.24	0.24	0.28
Compression ratio		4.75:1	4.63:1	4.5:1	4.5:1	5.09:1	4.5:1	4.5:1	5.09:1
Bore	mm	73.0	77.8	84.1	84.1	74.6	84.1	84.1	74.6
	inches	2.87	3.06	3.31	3.31	2.94	3.31	3.31	2.94
Stroke	mm	108.0	127.0	127.0	127.0	108.0	127.0	127.0	108.0
	inches	4.25	5.00	5.00	5.00	4.25	5.00	5.00	4.25
Bore:stroke ratio		68%	61%	66%	66%	69%	66%	66%	69%
Valve gear		ohv 16v	ohv 16v	ohv 16v	ohv 16v	ohv 16v	ohv 16v	ohv 16v	ohv 16v
Carburettor		1xMarvel	1xMarvel	1xMarvel	1xMarvel	1xMarvel	1xMarvel	1xMarvel	1xMarvel
Main bearings		5	5	5	5	5	5	5	5

Model		Series 90 iii	Series 40	Series 50 iv	40 Special	50 Super	60 Century	80 Roadmaster
Year introduced		1934	1935	1935	1936	1936	1936	1936
Displacement	cc	5,649	3,818	3,818	4,065	4,065	5,247	5,247
	cu in	344.7	233.0	233.0	248.0	248.0	320.2	320.2
Power output	bhp (max)	116	93	93	107	107	120	120
	kW	86	69	69	80	79	89	89
	@ rpm	2,800	3,200	3,200	3,400	3,600	3,200	3,600
Specific output	bhp/litre	20.5	24.4	24.4	26.3	26.3	22.9	22.9
	bhp/cu in	0.34	0.40	0.40	0.43	0.43	0.37	0.37
	kW/litre	15.2	18.1	18.1	19.7	19.4	17.0	17.0
	kW/cu in	0.25	0.30	0.30	0.32	0.32	0.28	0.28
Compression ratio		4.5:1	5.09:1	5.09:1	6.15:1	6.3:1	6.3:1	6.35:1
Bore	mm	84.1	78.6	75.4	78.6	78.6	87.3	87.3
	inches	3.31	3.09	2.97	3.09	3.09	3.44	3.44
Stroke	mm	127.0	98.4	108.0	104.8	104.8	109.5	109.5
	inches	5.00	3.87	4.25	4.12	4.12	4.31	4.31
Bore:stroke ratio		66%	80%	70%	75%	75%	80%	80%
Valve gear		ohv 16v	ohv 16v	ohv 16v	ohv 16v	ohv 16v	ohv 16v	ohv 16v
Carburettor		1xMarvel	1xStromberg	1xMarvel	1xMarvel	1xStromberg	1xStromberg	1xMarvel
Main bearings		5	5	5	5	5	5	5

Model		90 Limited	80 Roadmaster ii	80 Roadmaster iii	80 Roadmaster iv	70 Roadmaster	50 Super ii	50 Super iii
Year introduced		1936	1938	1939	1939	1940	1941	1942
Displacement	cc	5,247	5,247	5,247	5,247	5,247	4,065	4,065
	cu in	320.0	320.2	320.2	320.2	320.0	248.0	248.0
Power output	bhp (max)	120	141	165	144	120	125	110
	kW	89	104	122	107	89	93	82
	@ rpm	3,200	3,600	3,600	3,600	3,600	3,600	3,600
Specific output	bhp/litre	22.9	26.9	31.4	27.4	22.9	26.3	26.3
	bhp/cu in	0.38	0.44	0.52	0.45	0.38	0.43	0.43
	kW/litre	17.0	19.8	23.3	20.4	17.0	19.4	19.4
	kW/cu in	0.28	0.32	0.38	0.33	0.28	0.32	0.32
Compression ratio		6.3:1	6.5:1	7.0:1	6.6:1	6.9:1	7.0:1	6.3:1
Bore	mm	84.1	87.3	87.3	87.3	87.3	78.6	78.6
	inches	3.31	3.44	3.44	3.44	3.44	3.09	3.09
Stroke	mm	127.0	109.5	109.5	109.5	109.5	104.8	104.8
	inches	5.00	4.31	4.31	4.31	4.31	4.12	4.12
Bore:stroke ratio		66%	80%	80%	80%	80%	75%	75%
Valve gear		ohv 16v	ohv 16v	ohv 16v	ohv 16v	ohv 16v	ohv 16v	ohv 16v
Carburettor		1xMarvel	1xMarvel	1xMarvel	1xMarvel	1xStromberg	1xStromberg (compound)	1xStromberg
Main bearings		5	5	5	5	5	5	5

By any standards the Burney Streamline was a most unusual vehicle. The car was the brainchild of Sir Dennistoun Burney, an aeronautical engineer/designer best known for his work on the airship R100. Burney set up Streamline Cars Ltd in 1927 to produce large streamlined cars essentially to showcase some of his more advanced ideas. The car was never intended for volume production, and only 12 were made. Later Crossley Motors took over some of the ideas for its Crossley-Burney cars, a much 'diluted' version of Burney's original concept, but these were not a commercial success. Just 25 of these were produced of which two survive. None of the original straight eight Streamlines is still around.

Aside from advanced features such as independent suspension all round, hydraulic brakes, and controls operated by flexible cables inside copper tubing (just as in contemporary aircraft design), and the highly unconventional styling, the car was unusual in having an engine at the rear cantilevered outwards from the bodywork on a long overhang.

The first nine cars were powered by a Beverley-Barnes overhead cam straight eight engine, the same 4,825 cc (294.4 cu in) 90 bhp engine used in the Beverley-Barnes 30/90. But in the Burney it proved to be unreliable, possibly due to overheating in its rear location in the car. Two more Streamlines used straight eight Lycoming engines, and one a six-cylinder Armstrong Siddeley unit. In the Beverley-Barnes 30/90, the original engine was good for 70 mph. With the better streamlining of the Burney the top speed was probably higher, but little information about performance survives.

It is interesting that the factory in Maidenhead, Berkshire where the Burneys were built was later used by Marendaz who experimented with small capacity straight eights, but also with no commercial success.

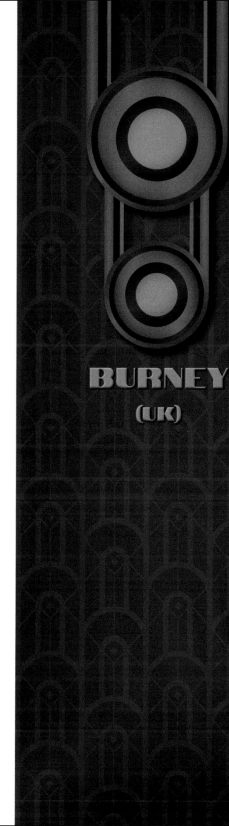

BURNEY

(UK)

1927 Burney Streamline: a rare photograph of an early Streamline. No original Streamlines survive, the only survivor being one of the later Crossley Streamlines which did not feature a straight eight engine.

THE PRINCE AND A NEW-TYPE STREAMLINE MOTOR-CAR : THE " BURNEY " LENT TO
H.R.H. BY MRS. STEPHEN COURTAULD PENDING DELIVERY OF HIS OWN.

to render her uncapsizable. Her maximum speed is about 40 miles an hour, and she is intended
for cruising as well as for racing. She was designed by Captain John Palethorpe, and she has a
Sharland engine.— His Royal Highness's new car is one of those built to the specification of
Sir Dennistoun Burney, the designer of the airship " R101." The engine is at the back.

ABOVE: This Burney was lent to the Prince of Wales by Mrs. Courtauld while he awaited delivery of his own car. It is not known whether the Prince actually acquired one.

TOP RIGHT: A contemporary 'cut away' view of the original 1927 Burney Streamline.

RIGHT: A contemporary photograph of a 1927 Burney Streamline showing the Beverley-Barnes engine first fitted to the car.

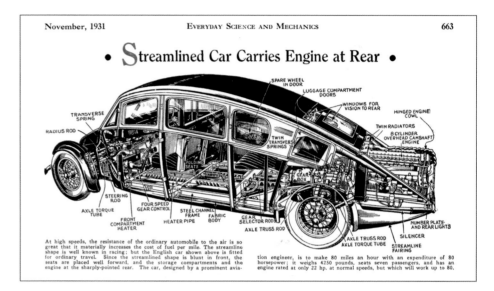

November, 1931   EVERYDAY SCIENCE AND MECHANICS   663

• Streamlined Car Carries Engine at Rear •

At high speeds, the resistance of the ordinary automobile to the air is so great that it materially increases the cost of fuel per mile. The streamline shape is well known in racing; but the English car shown above is fitted for ordinary travel. Since the streamlined shape is blunt in front, the seats are placed well forward, and the storage compartments and the engine at the sharply-pointed rear. The car, designed by a prominent avia- tion engineer, is to make 80 miles an hour with an expenditure of 80 horsepower; it weighs 4250 pounds, seats seven passengers, and has an engine rated at only 22 hp. at normal speeds, but which will work up to 80.

The Chandler Motor Car Company was founded in 1913 in Cleveland, Ohio by Frederick Chandler. The company's aim was to make good quality automobiles for the middle-class car buyer in the United States. By 1920 it offered a range of six cars which grew to 10 by 1922. Chandler's peak year was 1927 when 20,000 cars were sold. But like many other manufacturers it expanded too quickly and tried to compete in too many parts of the market, and by the end of 1928 the business was deeply in debt. In 1929 the assets were acquired by the Hupp Motor Car Company and the Chandler name was dropped.

The top-of-the-range Chandler was the Royal Straight Eight 85, which was a relatively straight-forward flathead 'eight', although the engine had a neat appearance. The other 'eight' was the Royal Straight Eight 75, which features in the photographs.

A contemporary photograph of the left side of the engine of the 1929 Chandler Royal Eight 75.

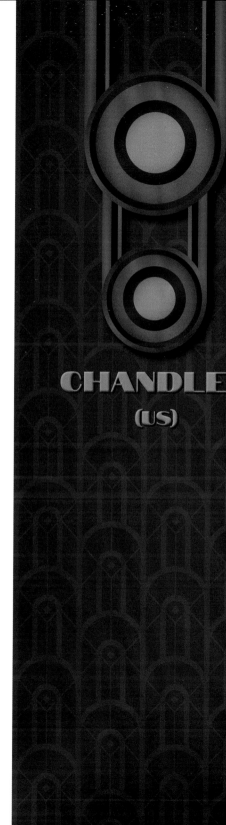

CHANDLE

(US)

First American Car to Offer Westinghouse Vacuum Brakes!

Chandler *today* anticipates the mode and the needs of *tomorrow!*

New Royal Eights and new Sixes that today give you tomorrow's smart body styles—tomorrow's speed-suggestive lines—tomorrow's ground-hugging lowness—and new vacuum brakes designed for the 1928 Chandler by the Westinghouse Air Brake Company!

Westinghouse Vacuum Brakes are beyond question the greatest safeguard ever introduced in an automobile. A 5-year-old schoolgirl can stop these new cars with absolute ease and safety. A gentle touch on the pedal applies all four brakes instantly and evenly, with positive control.

And these new cars give you real high-compression power—tremendous in volume and range—always vibrationless and quiet.

Chandler has today what all fine cars must have eventually—*centralized automatic chassis lubrication*. Chandler pioneered this great advance—and is still the lowest-priced car that offers it.

CHANDLER-CLEVELAND MOTORS CORPORATION, CLEVELAND

CHANDLER

SIXES & ROYAL EIGHTS · $995 to $2195, f. o. b. factory · SEE—DRIVE—COMPARE

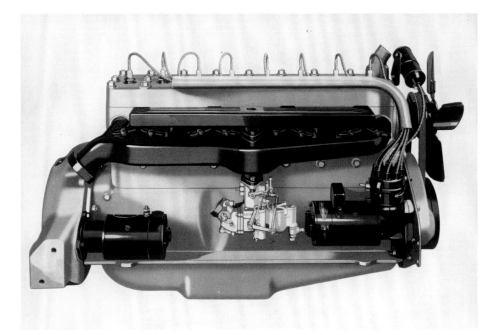

ABOVE: A contemporary photograph of the right side of the Royal Eight 75's engine with the single carburettor and inlet and exhaust manifolds.

LEFT: A contemporary advertisement for the Chandler Royal Eight extolling the car's 'ground hugging lowness' and its vacuum brakes.

Chenard, Walcker et Cie was founded in 1899, and the company initially manufactured motor tricycles, and later quadricycles. Its first real car was the Chenard et Walcker Type A in 1900. By 1910 1,500 cars a year were being built, making them the ninth largest car maker in France. Before the First World War, 'fours' and 'sixes' in three sizes: 2.0-litre (120 cu in), 2.6-litre (160 cu in) and 3.0-litre (180 cu in) were offered. After the war only the 'six' was built until, in 1920, a brand new 2,648 cc (161.6 cu in) four was added.

Around this time, the company was perhaps best known for winning the first Le Mans 24 Hour race in 1922 with a three-litre, six-cylinder model. For the 1924 Le Mans it developed a straight eight model, which was effectively a larger version of the 22CV 'six'. This had two 2-litre blocks end to end with a single cylinder head, giving a

capacity of 3,945 cc (240.7 cu in). The bore was 69.5 mm (2.74 in) and the stroke was 130 mm (5.12 in), giving a low bore:stroke ratio of 53%. The engine featured double overhead camshafts, and two valves per cylinder. The car was certainly rapid, holding off the winning Bentleys in both the 1924 and 1925 Le Mans until engine failure occurred. In the 1924 race the Chenard et Walcker had been in the lead for the first 20 hours.

After the 4-litre, the company did not develop any more straight eights, although much later, in 1938, it did produce a 20 hp Ford V8-powered vehicle with independent front suspension which, nominally, lasted until the post-war period. But this vehicle was basically a 'parts bin' car and lacked the unique character of the earlier models.

A 1924 Chenard et Walcker 22CV. A low-quality contemporary photograph of the 1924 22CV, possibly one of the Le Mans vehicles.

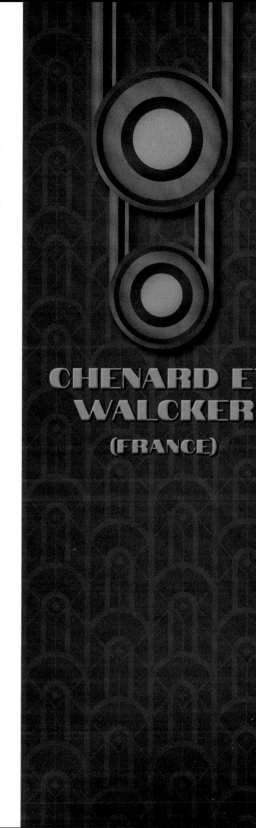

CHENARD ET
WALCKER
(FRANCE)

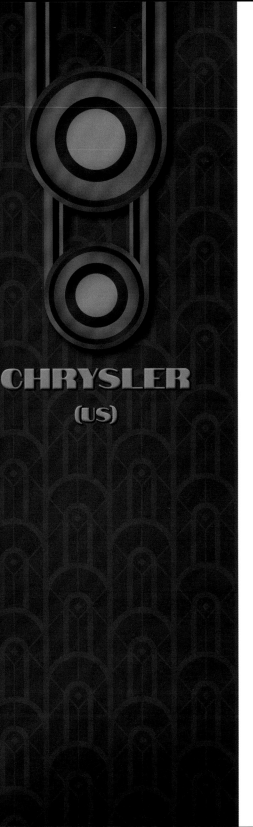

Although Chrysler was probably the world's most prolific producer of straight eight models, with at least 58 different engine series between 1931 and 1950, all these engines were remarkably similar apart from displacement and power output; one of the few differences was the number of crankshaft bearings used, whilst the carburettion also varied. They were all side valve, iron block, 16 valve units which all looked similar apart from a few cosmetic changes. The six photographs of engines show examples from 1931, 1933, 1934, 1936, 1937 and 1938, and there is little differentiation over time. The table shows the variants by year and application by vehicle.

THE VARIANTS OF THE CHRYSLER STRAIGHT EIGHT 1930-1950

Year	cc	cu in	BHP	Variants
1930	3403	207.7	70	DeSoto S-CF
	3617	220.7	75	Dodge S-DC
	3403	207.7	70	DeSoto S-CF
	3617	220.7	75	Dodge S-DC
			77	DeSoto S-CF Second Series
1931	3938	240.3	84	Dodge S-DG
			82	Chrysler S-CD-8
	4273	260.8	90	Chrysler S-CD-8
	4623	282.1	95	Chrysler S-DeLuxe 8
	6306	384.8	125	Chrysler S-Imperial
	3617	220.7	75	Dodge S-DC

YEAR	cc	cu in	Bhp	Variants
1931			77	DeSoto S-CF Second Series
	3938	240.3	84	Dodge S-DG
1932	4623	282.1	90	Dodge S-DK
			95	Chrysler S-CD
	4893	298.6	100	Chrysler S-CP-8
	6306	384.8	125	Chrysler S-CG, CH,CL
	4487	273.8	90/98	Chrysler S-CT
1933	4623	282.1	92	Dodge S-DO
	4895	298.7	108/100	Chrysler S-CQ
	6306	384.8	135/125	Chrysler S-CL
	4895	298.7	122	Chrysler S-CU

YEAR	cc	cu in	Bhp	Variants
1934	5301	323.5	130	Chrysler S-CV,CX
	6306	384.8	150	Chrysler S-CW
	4487	273.8	110	Chrysler O-CZ
			105	Chrysler S-CZ
		323.5	138	Chrysler O-C-2,C-3
1935	5301	323.5	130	Chrysler S-C-2, C-3
		323.5	120	Chrysler O-C-1
		323.5	115	Chrysler S-C-1
	6306	384.8	150	Chrysler S-CW
	4487	273.8	110	Chrysler O-C-8
1936			105	Chrysler S-C-8
	5301	323.5	130	Chrysler S-C-10, C-11
			115	Chrysler S-C-9
	4487	273.8	115	Chrysler O-C-14
1937			110	Chrysler S-C-14
	5301	323.5	138	Chrysler O-C-17, C-15
			130	Chrysler S-C-17, C-15
	4895	298.7	122	Chrysler O-C-19
1938			110	Chrysler S-C-19

YEAR	cc	cu in	Bhp	Variants
1938	5301	323.5	138	Chrysler O-C-20
			130	Chrysler S-C-20
			138	Chrysler O-C-24
1939	5301	323.5	132	Chrysler S-C-24
			130	Chrysler S-C-23
			143	Chrysler O-Traveler, NY, Saratoga, C/Imperial
1940	5301	323.5	135	Chrysler O-Traveler, NY, Saratoga
			132	Chrysler S-Crown Imperial
			143	Chrysler S-Crown Imperial
1941	5301	323.5	140	Chrysler O-Saratoga, NY
			137	Chrysler S-Saratoga, NY
1942	5301	323.5	140	Chrysler S-others
1946	5301	323.5	135	Chrysler S-others
1947	5301	323.5	135	Chrysler S-others
1948	5301	323.5	135	Chrysler S-others
1949	5301	323.5	135	Chrysler S-others
1950	5301	323.5	135	Chrysler S-others

A 1935 Chrysler Airflow, showing how by 1935 the 'extreme' styling of the original Airflow had been toned down, and a more conventional bonnet (hood) incorporated into the design. **OPPOSITE**: The 1935 Chrysler Airflow used a very conventional 5.3-litre 'flathead' engine.

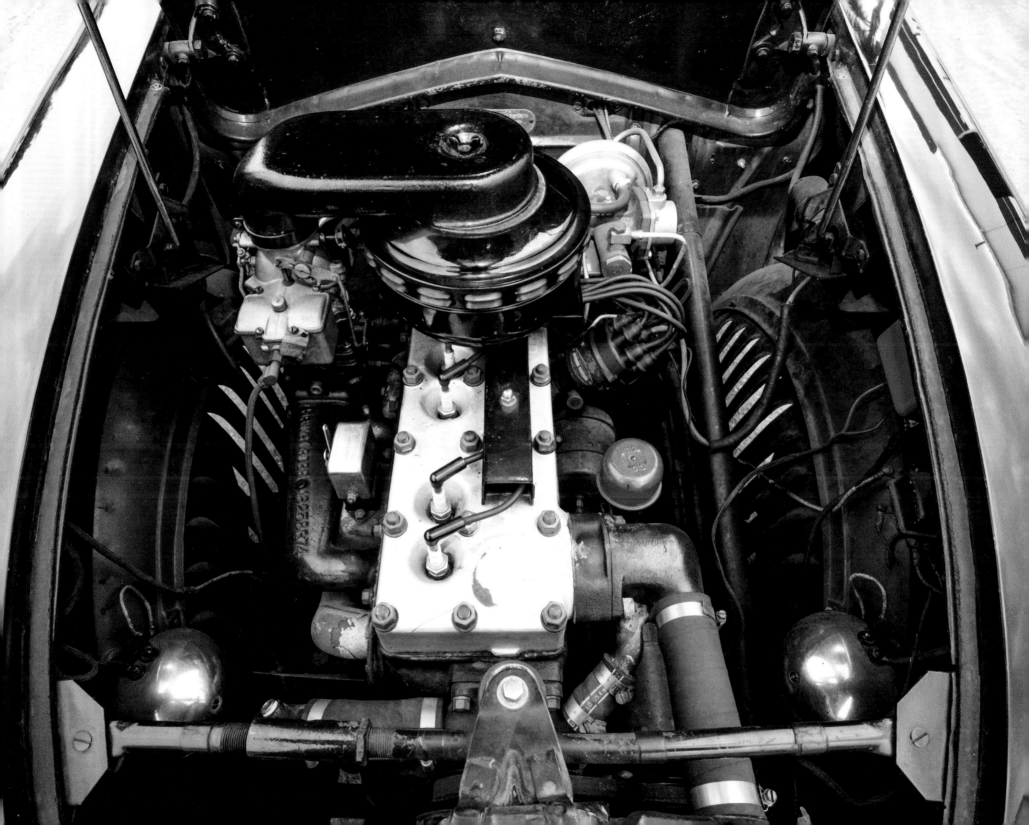

The 6.3-litre side valve engine of the 1932 Chrysler Imperial CL. The Imperial CL was a conventional-looking upmarket vehicle which preceded the bizarre Airflow design.

Chrysler persevered with a straight eight until the 1950s with the Chrysler s-Crown Imperial. The table shows six examples illustrating the relatively limited range changes.

Model Variant		CG	CG Red Head	CW	Airflow 8	Touring Limousine	Crown
Year introduced		1931	1931	1934	1936	1937	1940
Displacement	cc	6,306	6,306	5,301	5,301	4,487	5,301
	cu in	384.8	384.8	323.5	323.5	273.8	323.5
Power output	bhp (max)	125	135	115	123	115	137
	kW	93	100	86	92	86	102.4
	@ rpm	3,200	3,200	3,400	3,400	3,400	3,400
Specific output	bhp/litre	19.8	21.4	21.7	23.2	25.6	25.8
	bhp/cu in	0.32	0.35	0.36	0.38	0.42	0.42
	kW/litre	14.7	15.9	16.2	17.4	19.2	19.3
	kW/cu in	0.24	0.26	0.27	0.28	0.31	0.32
Compression ratio		5.2:1	6.2:1	6.2:1	6.2:1	6.2:1	6.2:1
Bore	mm	88.9	88.9	82.6	82.6	82.6	82.6
	inches	3.50	3.50	3.25	3.25	3.25	3.25
Stroke	mm	127	127	123.8	123.8	104.8	123.8
	inches	5.00	5.00	4.87	4.87	4.12	4.87
Bore:stroke ratio		70%	70%	67%	67%	79%	67%
Valve gear		2 valves/cyl	2 valves/cyl	2 valves/cyl	2 valves/cyl	2 valves/cyl	2 valves/cyl
Carburettor		1xChrysler	1xChrysler	1xChrysler	1xStromberg	1xStromberg	1xStromberg
Main bearings		9	9	5	5	6	5

THESE TWO PAGES: A 1946 Chrysler Town & Country. In the mid-1940s, the 'town and country' look was popular, whilst Chrysler had returned to a more conventional look after the Airflow. In spite of the name 'Spitfire' the engine in the 1946 Chrysler Town & Country was just a conventional side valve engine.

By 1941, Chrysler was building conventional looking cars, such as this New Yorker. The 5.3-litre Spitfire flathead straight eight was the mainstay from 1938 to 1950.

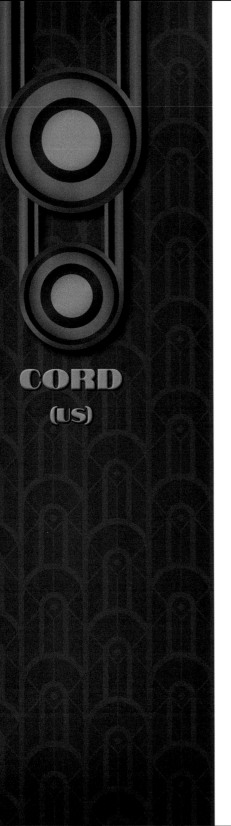

The Cord Corporation was founded and run by E. L. Cord as a parent company for his many transport interests, which included Auburn. Cord's designs were noted for being technologically advanced, and for sporting some highly streamlined and innovative coachwork. He introduced front wheel drive on powerful up-market cars, and with the 810 and 812 models incorporated concealed headlights, a feature which would not become common until the 1960s. He also introduced a form of electro-mechanical pre-selector gearbox.

Although Cord would become better known for his iconic 810 and 812 models, with their sensational Gordon Buehrig bodywork, his first model, the L-29, was equally groundbreaking, if not so sensational to look at. It had front wheel drive using constant velocity joints, and inboard brakes. The absence of a driveshaft to the rear axle allowed the bodywork to sit low down, permitting some rakish styling.

The L-29 was powered by the same five bearing Lycoming 4,894 cc (298 cu in) flathead inline eight used by Auburn, but mounted 'back to front' with the flywheel on an extended crankshaft at the front of the engine. With a compression ratio of 5.25:1 this delivered

125 bhp (93kW) at 3,400 rpm which, given the gearing in both the transmission and front axle, was barely adequate. At around 4,700 lbs (2,100 kg) the under-powered car struggled to reach 80 mph (130 kph). This was way behind the likes of competitors such as Stutz, Marmon, Lincoln and Packard which were of a similar price, around $3,000. But it was clothed in attractive bodywork and the handling was reportedly 'superb', even though it required four turns of the steering wheel to go from lock to lock; so it lacked a little in the sporting stakes. Later the engine was changed to a 5,276 cc (322 cu in) Lycoming 'FF' unit to improve performance.

Unfortunately, like so many luxury cars, it could not weather the depression and production ceased in 1932 after 4,400 had been sold.

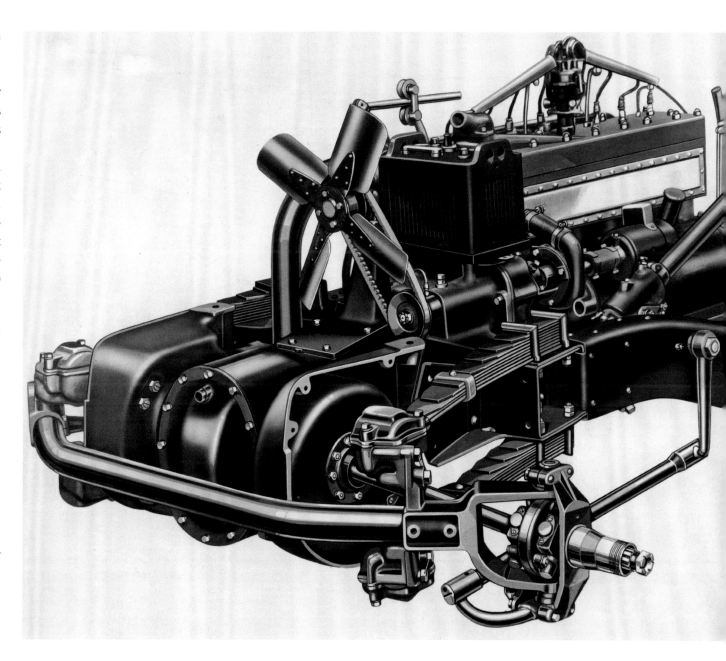

RIGHT: A contemporary photograph of a 1929 Cord showing the differential and inboard brake drums supported and located by four quarter elliptic leaf springs.

OPPOSITE: A fine contemporary photograph showing the transmission layout and the gear change rod on the Lycoming engine.

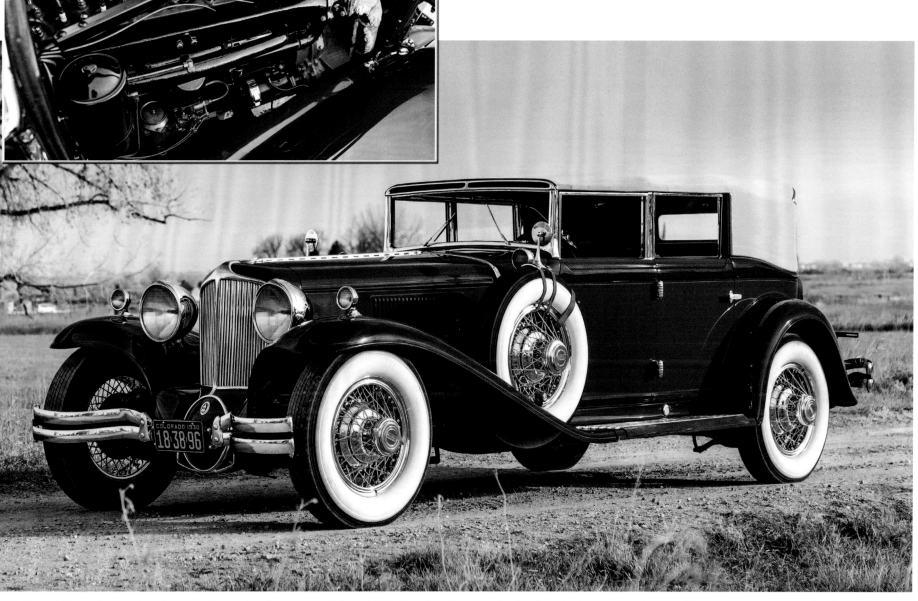

A 1930 Cord L29. Prior to the Gordon Buehrig-designed 810 and 812 Cord's offerings looked entirely conventional, although the car was far from ordinary with its front wheel drive. **INSET:** The Lycoming engine showing the complex gear change rod running between two pulleys to the front of the engine. **OPPOSITE:** The right side of the highly conventional eight-cylinder Lycoming engine powering the 1930 Cord L29.

LEFT: The 1931 Cord La Grande Speedster was a rakish two-seater. **ABOVE:** The rakish appearance of the La Grande Speedster concealed the same 4.2-litre Lycoming engine.

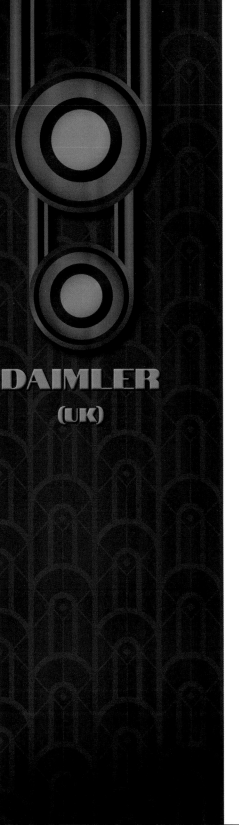

DAIMLER
(UK)

During the mid- to late-1920s Daimler's top-of-the-range models had been organised around the complex V12 'double six' engine, in various sizes from 7.1 litres for the Double-Six 50 down to 3.7 litres for the Double-Six 30. These V12 sleeve valve engines were highly complex and required great care if they were to work reliably. The very large area of lubricated surface of the sleeves could, if the oil were not regularly changed and the engine frequently turned over, seize up. By the early 1930s Daimler was looking for ways to simplify the engines for their top models, and started exploring the straight eight format, with simple poppet valves, as a solution. As it turned out, the straight eight would be the mainstay of their top models for over 20 years, and their last straight eight, the DE36, occasionally sported some of the most spectacular coachwork seen on a British car. The evolution of their straight eights is as follows;

1934: The first Daimler straight eight was the Twenty-Five V26 in both saloon and limousine variants. This featured a 3,746cc (228.6 cu in) ohv engine with an alloy block, bore of 72mm (2.8 in) and stroke of 115mm (4.5in), and a nine-bearings crank with a vibration damper. The compression ratio was 5.5:1, and the engine was fed by a twin choke Stromberg downdraft carburettor. Power output was 89 bhp (66kW) at 3,600 rpm.

1935: The next model was the Thirty-Two V4.5, which was essentially a bored out Twenty-Five V26. The engine displacement was raised to 4,624cc (282.2 cu in) by increasing the bore to 80mm (3.15in) from the previous 72mm (2.8 in). It retained the nine-bearing crankshaft

and twin choke Stromberg carburettor. The compression ratio was increased from 5.5:1 to 6.0:1, giving 90 bhp (67 kW) at 3,600 rpm. The Thirty-Two was capable of around 72 mph, depending on coachwork.

1936: The Daimler Light Straight Eight E3.5 model had an entirely new engine. The car was intended to be livelier, and was aimed at the owner driver. The engine was a 3,421cc (208.8 cu in) unit with a bore of 72mm (2.83 in) and a stroke of 105mm (4.13in). Again, the unit had a nine-bearing engine with a vibration damper, and was fed by a twin choke Stromberg carburettor. The compression ratio was 5.5:1, and power output was 90 bhp (67 kW) at 4,000 rpm allowing a top speed of around 85-90 mph.

1938: In August 1938 the Light Straight Eight engine was bored out to 77.5mm giving a displacement of

The 3.4-litre engine in a 1938 Light Eight undergoing renovation.

3,960cc (241.7 cu in). Power output increased to 95 bhp (71kW) at 3,600 rpm

1946-1953: The last Daimler straight eight was the DE36, with a 5,460cc (333.2 cu in) engine with a bore of 85.1mm (3.35in) and a stroke of 120.0mm (4.73in). These were the same cylinder dimensions as in the smaller six-cylinder DE27. This larger unit produced 150 bhp (112kW) at 3,600 rpm, and 252 ft lb (342 Nm) of torque at 1,200 rpm. The engine was fed by two SU carburettors. Depending on coachwork, the DE36 was good for 0-50 mph (80 kph) in around 14.5 seconds, going up to a top speed of around 85 mph. The DE36 attracted some of the most beautiful and flamboyant coachwork of the 1950s, including the infamous 'Docker Daimlers', one of which, the 'Golden Daimler', had 7,000 gold stars along the sides below the waistline. In total 205 DE36s were manufactured.

DAIMLER EIGHT MODELS

Model		25	32	Light 8	Light 8	DE36
Year introduced		1934	1935	1936	1938	1946
Displacement	cc	3,746	4,624	3,421	3,960	5,460
	cu in	228.6	282.2	208.8	241.7	332.2
Power output	bhp	89	90	90	95	150
	kW	66	67	67	71	112
	@ rpm	3,600	3,600	4,000	3,600	3,600
Specific output	bhp/litre	23.8	19.5	26.3	24.0	27.5
	bhp/cu in	0.39	0.32	0.43	0.39	0.45
	kW/litre	17.6	14.5	19.6	17.9	20.5
	kW/cu in	0.29	0.24	0.32	0.29	0.34
Compression ratio		5.5:1	6.0:1	5.5:1		6.3:1
Bore	mm	72	80	72	77.5	85.1
	inches	2.8	3.15	2.83	3.05	3.35
Stroke	mm	115	115	105	105	120
	inches	4.5	4.5	4.13	4.13	4.73
Bore:stroke ratio		63%	70%	69%	74%	71%
Valve gear		ohv	ohv	ohv	ohv	ohv
Carburettor		1xStromberg	1xStromberg	1xStromberg	1xStromberg	2xSU
No of main bearings		9	9	9	9	9
Lubrication		wet sump	wet sump	wet sump	wet sump	wet sump

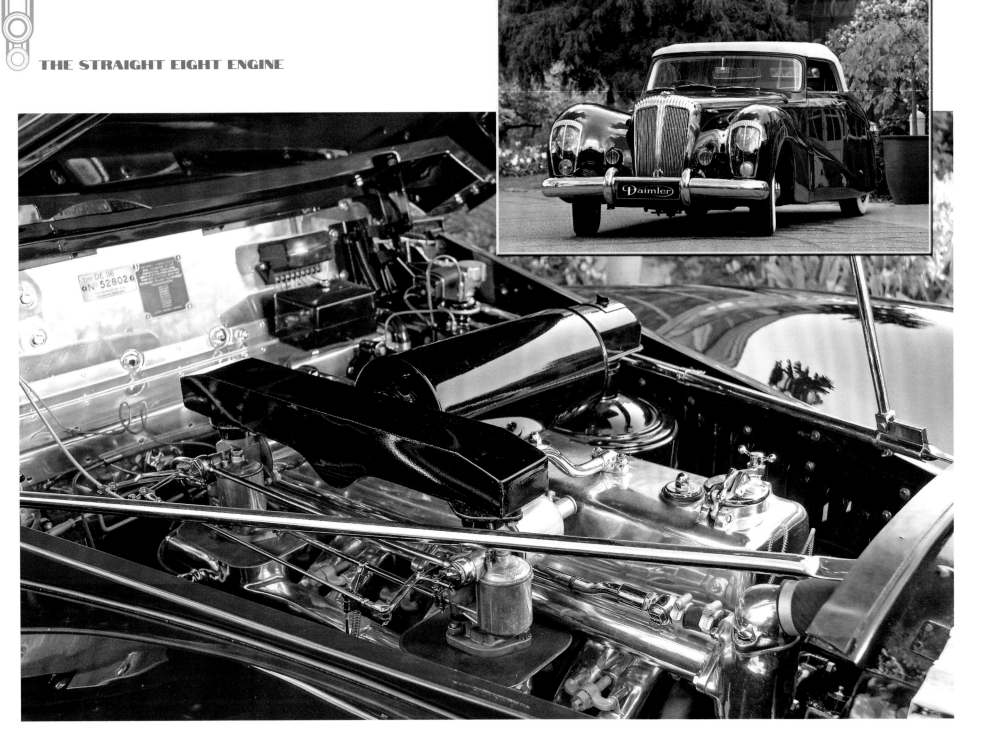

THIS PAGE: The 3.4-litre 1939 Daimler Light Eight was aimed at the owner/driver.
OPPOSITE: The immaculate engine compartment of the 1948 DE36 showing the twin SU carburettors, and the beautifully polished 5,460cc straight eight block. The 1948 Daimler DE36 was one of the largest cars ever made, at around 20 feet long and seven feet wide.

In two-door drophead form, the 1948 Daimler DE36 shows its vast bulk to great effect. **OPPOSITE:** Twin SUs feed the 5.5-litre 'eight' in the vast DE36.

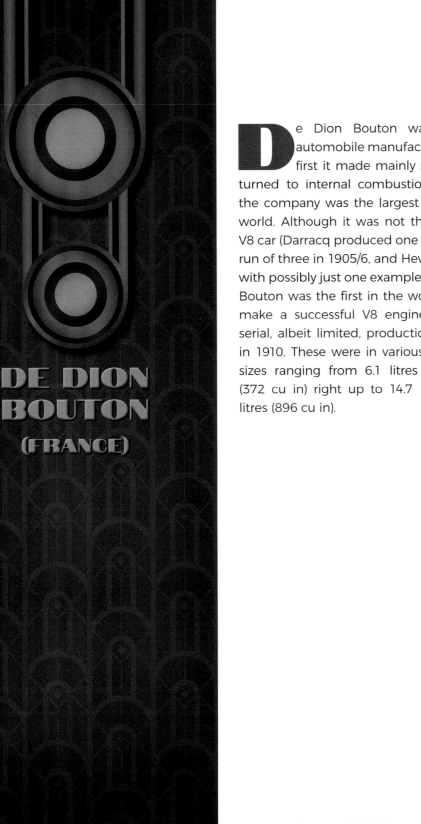

DE DION BOUTON

(FRANCE)

De Dion Bouton was one of the earliest automobile manufacturers, starting in 1883. At first it made mainly steam vehicles, but soon turned to internal combustion engines and by 1900 the company was the largest car manufacturer in the world. Although it was not the first to manufacture a V8 car (Darracq produced one in 1905, Rolls-Royce a run of three in 1905/6, and Hewitt in the US with possibly just one example) De Dion Bouton was the first in the world to make a successful V8 engine in serial, albeit limited, production in 1910. These were in various sizes ranging from 6.1 litres (372 cu in) right up to 14.7 litres (896 cu in).

After the First World War the company was virtually dormant until 1923, and although having a new range of models the factory closed for most of 1927. When it re-opened, two models were offered; the Type LA was a 1,982 cc (120.9 cu in) 'four' whilst the Type LB was a 2,496 cc (152.3 cu in) straight 'eight'. The straight eight was extremely expensive and sales were dismal, in spite of (or maybe because of!) moving up market with an increase in capacity to 3-litres (180 cu in) in 1930.

This brief excursion into the straight eight sector came to an end in 1932 when De Dion Bouton completely ceased automobile manufacture.

Although De Soto was part of the Chrysler empire, it deserves a separate mention here as the Chrysler Group first entered the straight eight market through this brand. In 1929 De Soto was represented by the six-cylinder K Series, and this continued into 1930 as a 'first series 1930 model'. De Soto was Chrysler's mid-range brand, but by 1930 the straight eight was becoming the engine of choice for medium-priced cars. De Soto's entry into the straight eight sector began with the 1930 CF model. Apparently, this came as quite a surprise to the car buying public, especially De Soto customers, at the time.

The CF's engine was a relatively basic side valve straight eight with an iron block. The bore and stroke of 73 mm x 102 mm (2.9 in x 4.0 in) gave a displacement of 3,404 cc (208 cu in), the smallest straight eight the Chrysler Group would produce. With a single Carter carburettor, it produced a modest 70 bhp (51.5 kW) at 3,400 rpm and generated 132 ft lb of torque at 1,200 rpm. The low speed torque, which would be an ongoing feature of Chrysler engines, made the CF highly attractive to buyers, as did the price. At $895 - $1,075

($14,600 - $16,300 at 2020 prices) it undercut rivals like Graham, whose cheapest eight was $1,445 ($23,570 at 2020 prices), but was much on a par with Hudson, whose straight eights ranged from $885 to $1,295.

De Soto disappeared as a brand in 1961, largely as a result of a shift in Chrysler's strategy. Since the 1920s De Soto had been the mainstay of Chrysler's mid-range, with Chrysler itself as the premium brand. But the Chrysler Group, as a result of changing consumer tastes, moved Chrysler down into the mid-range, retaining the name Imperial for the high-end models. This effectively killed off De Soto's reason for existing, so the brand name was dropped and De Soto models became the Chrysler Newport range.

The 1930 Desoto CF Series was powered by a 3,404cc (208 cu in) straight eight, the smallest straight eight Chrysler would ever use.

DE SOTO
(US)

DELAGE
(FRANCE)

Delage was founded in 1905 by Louis Delage and produced its first model in 1906, a voiturette powered by a single cylinder De Dion Bouton engine. By 1909 the company was making exclusively four-cylinder models, and was involved in racing as well as selling road cars. During the First World War car production all but stopped in favour of munitions manufacture. After the war Delage moved away from small cars and entered its first 'golden era' of fast, expensive and exclusive road cars. The second, even more golden era, started in 1930 with the launch of the D6 (six-cylinder), followed in 1933 by the D8 (eight cylinder) series. Delage only made the rolling chassis for these models, the cars themselves being clothed by some top coachwork companies in France and beyond.

During the production run of the D8, the size of the engine changed a number of times, sometimes the result of tax changes. The chronology was as follows:

D8 (1929): The original D8 engine was the first straight eight in the French auto industry. The 4,061 cc (247.8 cu in) engine had a single, centrally positioned, overhead camshaft and produced 80 bhp (60 kW) at 3,500 rpm. Bore and stroke were 77 mm (33.03 in) and 109 mm (4.29 in) respectively. There was a more powerful D8-S version producing 120 bhp (89 kW) as an option. Performance depended on the bodywork, but the standard version was good for 75 mph (120 kph) whilst the D8-S could achieve around 82 mph (130 kph).

D8-15 (1933-34): in 1933 the engine size was reduced to 2,668 cc (163 cu in) to place the vehicle in the 15CV tax bracket. As with the original car, the D8-15

was available in both 'normale' and 'S' versions. But the reduction in engine size moved the D8-Somewhat downmarket, and it was withdrawn in 1934.

D8-85 (1934-35): 1934 saw the launch of a 3,570 cc (218 cu in) version with an output of 85 bhp (63 kW) at 4,000 rpm.

D8-105 (1934-35): the engine in the D8-105 was similar to that in the D8-85 but the unit was tuned to produce 105 bhp (78 kW). This was fitted in a shorter chassis. In April 1935 the company experienced financial problems and the D8-85 and D8-105 were withdrawn from production.

D8-100 (1936-40): The Delage Company was slowly being absorbed into the Delahaye business, and the future was seen as continuing to build Delage engines but place them in Delahaye chassis, Delahaye not having a straight eight engine of its own. The new engine displaced 4,302 cc (262.5 cu in) giving a rise in tax bracket to 25CV. Output was listed as 90 bhp (67 kW), but this increased to 105 bhp (78 kW) by 1937. A pre-selector Cotal gearbox was now an option. 97 mph was possible, with 0-60mph in around 17-18 seconds.

D8-120 (1937-40): In 1937 a 4,743 cc (289.4 cu in) D8-120 was on offer, which was a D8-100 bored out by 4 mm from 81 mm to 85 mm (3.35 in), the stroke remaining at 107 mm (4.21 in). Power was up at 120 bhp (89kW) at 4,000 rpm, and torque was 180 ft lbs (244 Nm) at 2,000 rpm. In 1939 the larger engine also found its way into the D8-100, but passenger car production came to a halt in 1940. Total production of the D8-120 was 66.

Delage also produced a sophisticated straight eight for Grand Prix racing in 1926. The 1.5-litre engine had twin overhead cams, and initially two small Roots superchargers each feeding a block of four-cylinders. Later this was changed to one large supercharger driven off the nose of the crankshaft. This engine produced a record breaking 114 bhp per litre and proved invincible in 1927.

DELAGE EIGHT MODELS

Model		D8	D8-S	D8-15	D8-85	D8-105	D8-100	D8-100	D8-120
Year introduced		1929	1929	1933	1934	1934	1936	1937	1937
Displacement	cc	4,061	4,061	2,668	3,570	3,570	4,302	4,302	4,743
	cu in	247.8	247.8	163	218	218	262.5	262.5	289.4
Power output	bhp (max)	80	120	80	85	105	90	105	120
	kW	60	89	60	63	78	67	78	89
	@ rpm	3,500	3,500	4,400	4,000	4,000	3,500	3,500	4,000
Specific output	bhp/litre	19.7	29.5	30.0	23.8	29.4	20.9	24.4	25.3
	bhp/cu in	0.32	0.48	0.49	0.39	0.48	0.34	0.40	0.41
	kW/litre	14.8	21.9	22.5	17.6	21.8	15.6	18.1	18.8
	kW/cu in	0.24	0.36	0.37	0.29	0.36	0.26	0.30	0.31
Bore	mm	77	77	75	79.3	79.3	81	81	85
	inches	3.03	3.03	2.95	3.10	3.10	3.17	3.17	34.00
Stroke	mm	109	109	75.5	90.5	90.5	107	107	107
	inches	4.29	4.29	2.97	3.60	3.60	4.26	4.26	4.20
Bore:stroke ratio		71%	71%	99%	88%	88%	76%	76%	79%
Valve gear		ohv 16v	ohv 16v	sohc 16v	sohc 16v	sohc 16v	sohc 16v	sohc 16v	sohc 16v

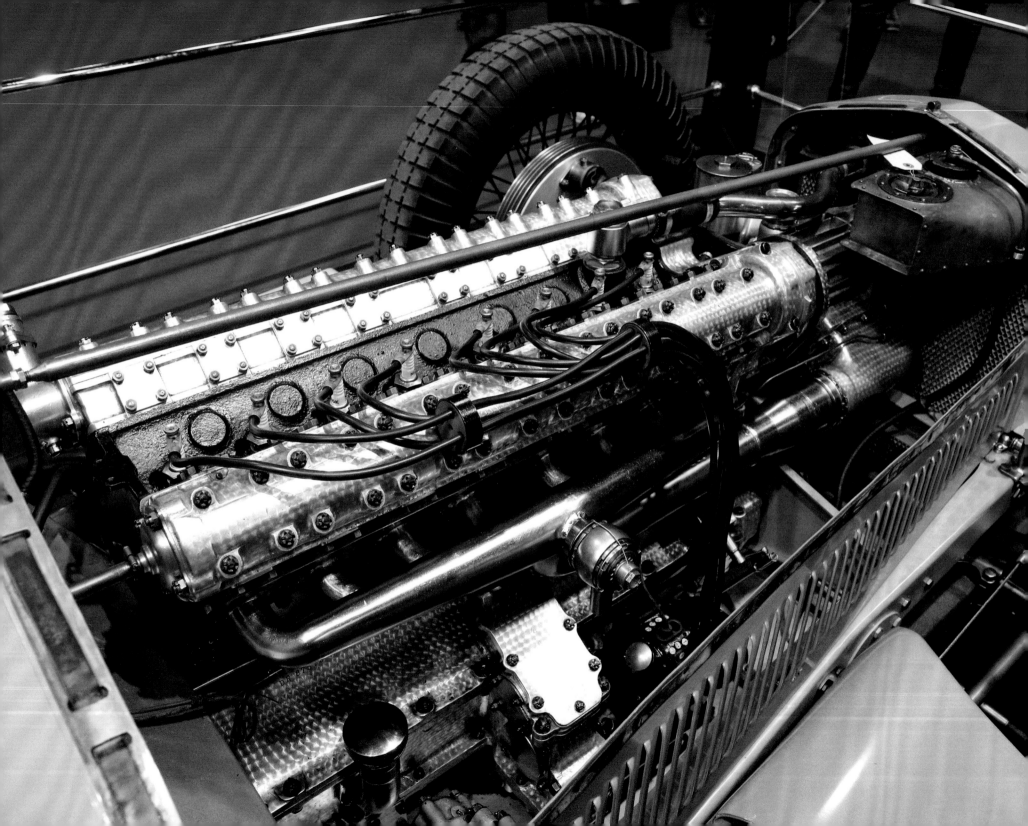

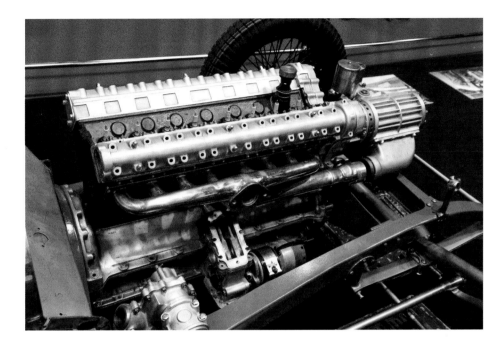

THESE TWO PAGES: Delage 15S 8 GP, taken at the 2017 Retromobile, Paris.

A very elegant 1937 Delage D8 120. By 1937, Delage was becoming absorbed into Delahaye, and would soon disappear as a distinct brand. **TOP:** The neat 4.3-litre sohc engine (left) and Delage D8 120's impressive exhaust system (right), reminiscent of the Duesenberg SJ.

The exhaust (right) side of a 1931 Delage D8-C powered by a 4.1-litre engine. The capacity would later be reduced to 2.7 litres to place the car in the 15CV tax bracket.

The 1933 Delage D8-S, the very elegant 'close coupled' performance model, good for 82 mph. **INSET:** The brass plate on the engine of the 1933 D8-S denotes the firing order as being 1-3-7-4-8-6-2-5 and states that the oil should be changed at 2,000 kms and the valve clearances should be checked every 5,000 km. **OPPOSITE:** The impressive row of four carburettors of the high performance D8-S version.

A stately 1936 Delage D8 100. **INSET:** The inlet/exhaust side of the D8 100's engine, and single downdraft carburettor. **OPPOSITE:** The left-hand side of D8 100's 4.3-litre (263.5 cu in) single overhead cam engine with neat ducted wiring.

The Diana Motor Company, based in St. Louis, produced vehicles between 1925 and 1928 and was a subsidiary of the Moon Motor Car Company. It assembled cars from third-party components and sourced its engines from Continental. The 1925 Straight Eight's five bearing side valve Continental engine had a bore of 76.2 mm (3.0 in) and a stroke of 108 mm (4.25 in) giving a displacement of 3,940 cc (240.4 cu in). The compression ratio was a low 4.6:1 and power output was a modest 72 bhp (54 kW) at 2,950 rpm. But torque was a reasonable 153 ft lbs (207 Nm) at an impressively low 1200 rpm, offering great flexibility. Just 12 Diana Straight Eights are known to survive. Unusually, the Continental engine used in the car was a Continental design but unique to the Diana.

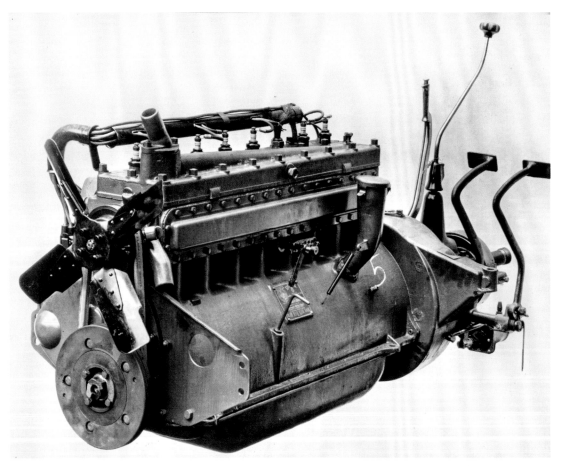

Front three quarters view of the 1926 Diana's engine showing the Lanchester damper and the rather bulbous crankcase.

ABOVE: A contemporary photograph of the right-hand side of the Diana's engine, with the firing order 1-6-2-5-8-3-7-4 embossed on the exhaust manifold. **RIGHT:** 1926 Diana: front of the engine showing the Lanchester damper and the heavy pressed steel engine brackets.

DIATTO
(ITALY)

Diatto and Maserati were closely linked. Diatto was originally a railway engineering and iron founding business which began making cars around 1905/6. It was ambitious and launched a range of six cars, 8 hp and 10 hp 'twins', and 12 hp, 20 hp, 35 hp and 50 hp 'fours'. Unfortunately, there was a major recession in Italy around this time, and the company had to cut back to just one model, the 15.9 hp 'four'.

The Diatto was not the great sporting success the company hoped for, with just an eighth place in the 1914 Targa Florio and a third place in 1919. Post-war models were a 10 hp and a 20 hp, both with four-cylinder engines, of 1.0 and 2.7 litres respectively. For the 1923 season, Diatto announced a more exciting new model, the 15 hp four, using the 20 hp chassis, but with a 15.9 hp, sohc, 2-litre (122 cu in) engine of great potential, developing 52 bhp (39 kW) in standard guise. It appealed to the sporting market, and tuned racing versions were soon developed.

Among the most effective tuners of this engine were the Maserati brothers. Alfieri Maserati had already driven a tuned overhead cam 3-litre Diatto to a number of class wins; in 1924, he entered a modified 2-litre Diatto with twin overhead camshafts for the Spanish San Sebastian Grand Prix, and made his way to third place before the engine gave out. But its performance had been convincing enough for Diatto to commission the Maserati brothers to design a proper racing car in the shape of the straight eight 2-litre (122 cu in) Type 30 GP model. The engine had a bore of 65.5 mm (2.58 in) and a stroke of 74 mm (2.91 in), giving a bore:stroke ratio of a high 89%. The cylinder block and head were aluminium, whilst the pistons were initially made of electron although these were soon switched to aluminium as well. At first the engine used two or four Zenith carburettors, but later a Roots supercharger and two pressurised Memini carburettors were use. On a mix of petrol and benzol the engine delivered around 150 bhp (112 kW). The car made only one appearance, at the 1926 Italian Grand Prix, where sheared blower bolts forced its retirement. By this time Diatto was in deep financial trouble, and the company gave the car to the Maseratis for further development work and withdrew. In effect, this vehicle became the first Maserati in all but name. Details are given in the section on Maserati.

The photograph shown in the 'Maserati' section dates from 1925 and shows Alfieri Maserati at the wheel of what is almost certainly the Diatto Type 30, although it is possible it is a Maserati Tipo 26, which essentially was the Diatto Type 30.

In one respect, Dodge as a brand is a great survivor. In 1914 a large number of new makes, 146 in total, went into production in the United States, although this included many small enterprises, as was typical of the day. Of those only one, Dodge, survives to this day. Prior to producing their own cars, the Dodge brothers supplied engines and various assemblies to Ford for several years. The first Dodge car appeared in November 1914, a four-cylinder vehicle selling for $785. The early cars were a great success and a range of four- and six-cylinder models was developed throughout the 1920s.

DODGE EIGHT MODELS

Model		DC	DG	DK	DO	CUSTOM 8
Year introduced		1930	1931	1932	1933	1938
Displacement	cc	3,617	3,938	4,622	4,622	4,894
	cu in	221	240	282	282	299
Power output	bhp (max)	75	84	90	100	110
	kW	56	63	67	75	82
Specific output	bhp/litre	20.7	21.3	19.5	21.6	22.5
	bhp/cu in	0.34	0.35	0.32	0.35	0.37
	kW/litre	15.5	16.0	14.5	16.2	16.8
	kW/cu in	0.25	0.26	0.24	0.27	0.27
Bore	mm	73	76.2	82.6	82.6	82.6
	inches	2.88	3.00	3.25	3.25	3.25
Stroke	mm	108	108	108	108	114.3
	inches	4.25	4.25	4.25	4.25	4.50
Bore:stroke ratio		68%	71%	76%	76%	72%
Valve gear		s/v	s/v	s/v	s/v	s/v

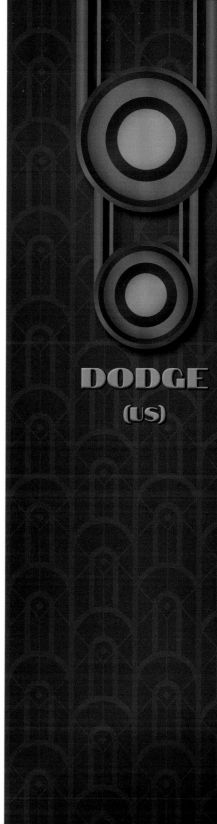

DODGE
(US)

In line with so many other car manufacturers Dodge decided to introduce a straight eight model in 1930, despite the Great Depression. Fortunately, the 'eight' would not be a 'kiss of death' for Dodge, although the model was not long-lived. The car initially had a 3,617 cc (220.7 cu in) engine with a single downdraft carburettor. For an 'eight' the car was quite short for its time, with a wheelbase of just 2.9 metres (114 inches). Between 1930 and 1938 the eight went through a number of transitions shown in the table.

Alongside the eight, the 'six' was continued on an even shorter wheelbase of 2.8 metres (109 inches).

For 1931, a free wheel was made available on both the 'eight' and the 'six', and this would become a standard feature in 1932. 1931 also saw the appearance of the famous Rocky Mountain ram on the radiator. In 1932 an automatic clutch became an option, whilst improved Chrysler-designed 'Floating Power' engine mounts became standard. In 1933 the body styling was modernised

with a slanting 'V' shaped grille, and the gears became all helical, or constant mesh, reducing engine and gearbox noise considerably.

1934 saw a shift to the less expensive six-cylinder models, and the 'eight' was dropped. It had been short-lived but, unlike many other manufacturers, the adventure into the world of the straight eight had not damaged the business.

A 1931 Dodge Eight Roadster. The Eight was an unusually short car for a straight eight, and only lasted until 1934. The Dodge Eight used a simple straight-forward 3.6-litre (220.7 cu in) 'flathead' engine, with somewhat untidy wiring (above). The Roadster had a single downdraught carburettor above the inlet and exhaust manifolds. The firing order is shown as 1-6-2-5-8-3-7-4 on the inlet manifold (opposite).

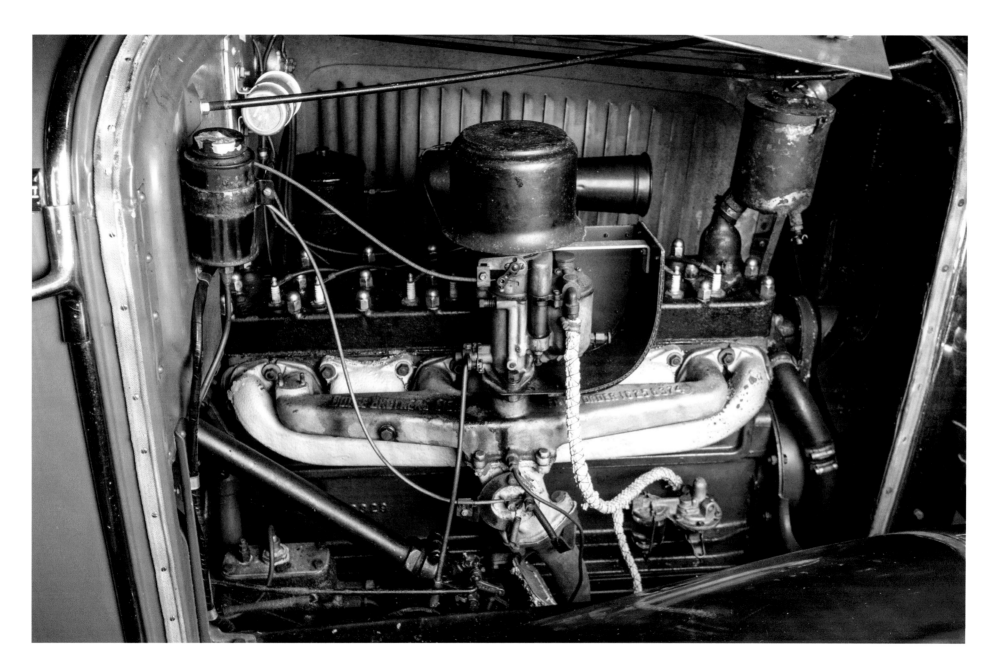

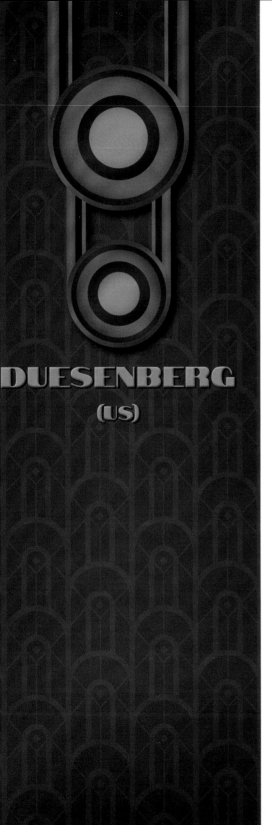

DUESENBERG
(US)

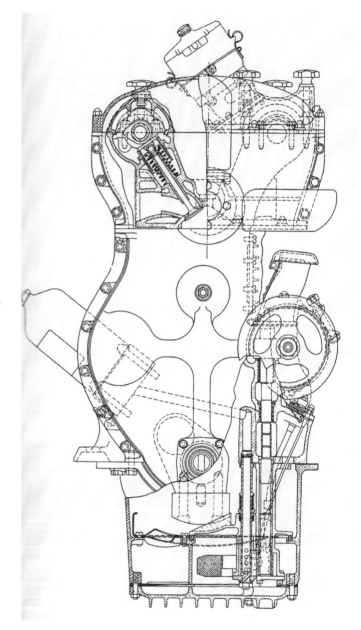

Duesenberg built some of the most spectacular straight eight-engined cars, and today they are amongst the most valuable vehicles of all.

Duesenberg was founded in 1913 in Saint Paul, Minnesota, by August and Fred Duesenberg. At first their business was building engines and racing cars, the engines initially being straight fours. When war came, they moved to New Jersey to build aircraft and marine engines for the military, including 25.7-litre V12s and 55.6-litre V16s. After the war the Duesenberg brothers used the expertise they had developed to build automobile engines, at first for racers, and later for cars for road use.

Their first racing straight eight appeared in 1919, a 4,260 cc (260 cu in) ohv unit. The subsequent evolution of these racing engines is summarised on page 177.

The first road car was the Duesenberg Straight Eight (otherwise known as the Model A) introduced in 1920. But it would not reach production until the end of 1921, as Fred Duesenberg was not happy with aspects of the valve gear. The engine in the 'A' had a cast-iron block, a detachable iron cylinder head, and an aluminium crankcase and sump. The crank ran in just three bearings, unusual for such an 'up market' vehicle. The prototype revealed in 1920 had horizontal valves, but the re-designed engine at launch used a shaft-driven single overhead camshaft, operating via rockers with two valves per cylinder mounted in the hemispherical combustion chamber.

The engine had a bore of 73 mm (2.87 in) and a stroke

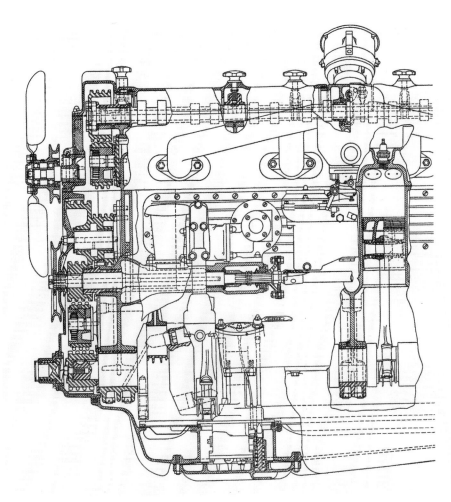

ABOVE: Longitudinal section of a Duesenberg Model J engine.

OPPOSITE: Cross section of the Duesenberg Model J engine with details of the exhaust valve gear and sump. Tappet clearance was adjusted by changing the valve stem caps.

of 127 mm (5.0 in) giving a displacement of 4,261 cc (260.0 cu in). Fed by a single Stromberg carburettor (later to be changed for a Wheeler-Schebler unit) the engine with a compression ratio of 5.0:1 delivered 88 bhp (66 kW) at 3,000 rpm. The carburettor was mounted on the right-hand side of the engine, from where fuel mixture passed through the block via a duct, to the inlet manifold on the left side. The Model A (depending on bodywork) could typically attain 82 mph (132 kph). 650 Type As were built between 1921 and 1927, along with a small number, believed to be around 13, of a more highly tuned version, with power up from 88 bhp (66 kW) to 100 bhp (75 kW), allowing a top speed of 100 mph (161 kph).

Towards the end of 'A' production, Duesenberg was purchased by E. L. Cord, the owner of the Auburn brand. Cord's motivation was to use the engineering expertise of the Duesenberg brothers to build a car to rival the best from the UK and Europe, and in particular Rolls-Royce, Isotta Fraschini and Hispano Suiza. For reasons that are not clear, Cord did not want August Duesenberg involved in the design of the new engines and models. However August would remain closely involved but in the background, within a separate business away from the main Duesenberg site.

The new model, the 'J', was introduced in 1928 following the end of Type A production. It could have been a disastrous time to launch such an up-market car as the stock market crash would happen the following year, followed by the Great Depression. However, the sensational J turned out to be a great success. Technologically it was a leap forward from the Type A, featuring dual overhead camshafts and four valves per cylinder. The engine was based on the company's successful racing engines of the 1920s, and whilst the design was pure Duesenberg the actual units were built by Lycoming, another business within E. L. Cord's empire. The engine was significantly larger than that in the outgoing Type A. With a bore of 95.3 mm (3.75 in) and a stroke of 120.5 mm (4.74 in), the displacement was 6,876 cc (419.6 cu in). Fed by a single Wheeler-Schebler carburettor, and with a compression ratio of 5.2:1, the engine could deliver 265 bhp (198 kW) allowing a top speed of around 115 mph (185 kph). Acceleration was impressive for the time, 0-50 mph (80 kph) taking just 8.6 seconds, and 0-100 mph (160 kph) 21 seconds. The J was a very expensive car, the typical complete vehicle with bodywork costing around $13,000 - $19,000, equivalent today to $192,000 - $281,000. It is believed that 443 Model Js were produced, of which 79% still survive.

In 1932, alongside the 'ordinary' J, a supercharged 'SJ' appeared. The SJ had the same size engine as the J, but the addition of a Duesenberg-designed supercharger boosted power from 265 bhp (196 kW) to 320 bhp (237 kW) at 4200 rpm. The supercharger was located alongside the engine, necessitating a redesign of the exhaust system to make room for the supercharger drive shaft that resulted in the distinctive four exposed exhaust pipes emerging from the side of the bonnet. This design was patented by E. L. Cord and used in his Auburn and Cord vehicles as well. A one-off Duesenberg Special, based on the SJ, but highly tuned, broke the 24-hour speed record at 135.57 mph (218,2 kph), a record which would stand until 1961. Just 36 SJs were built.

Even more extreme than the SJ was the vehicle generally (but not officially) known as the SSJ. With dual carburettors, and a 'rams horn' inlet manifold, power rose to a mighty 400 bhp (298 kW). Only two examples were built, these being owned by Gary Cooper and Clark Gable.

Another version of the J, unofficially called the 'JN', appeared in 1935, and ten were built.

Duesenberg disappeared as a company in 1937 following the collapse of E. L. Cord's business empire. Today Duesenberg straight eights are amongst the most desirable and valuable classic cars.

DUESENBERG EIGHT MODELS

Model		Model A	J	SJ	SSJ
Year introduced		1920	1928	1932	1935
Displacement	cc	4,261	6,876	6,876	6,876
	cu in	260	419.6	419.6	419.6
Power output	bhp (max)	88	265	320	400
	kW	66	198	239	298
	@ rpm	3,000	4,200	4,750	4,750
Specific output	bhp/litre	20.7	38.5	46.5	58.2
	bhp/cu in	0.34	0.63	0.76	0.95
	kW/litre	15.5	28.8	34.8	43.3
	kW/cu in	0.25	0.47	0.57	0.71
Compression ratio		5.0:1	5.2:1	5.2:1	5.7:1
Bore	mm	73	95.3	95.3	95.3
	inches	2.87	3.75	3.75	3.75
Stroke	mm	127	120.5	120.5	120.5
	inches	5.00	4.74	4.74	4.74
Bore:stroke ratio		57%	79%	79%	79%
Valve gear		sohc	dohc 32v	dohc 32v	dohc 32v
Carburettor		1xStromberg	1xSchebler	s/c 2xSchebler	s/c 2xSchebler
Main bearings		3	5	5	5

OVERVIEW OF DUESENBERG RACING ENGINES

Year	Bore mm	Bore in	Stroke mm	Stroke in	Displ cc	Displ cu in	Camshaft	Valves/cyl	Plugs/cyl	Bearings
1919	73	2.88	127	5	4260	260	ohv	2	1	3
1919	76	3	133	5.25	4850	296	sohc	3	2	3
1920	63	2.5	117	4.63	2980	182	sohc	3	1	3
1922	63	2.5	117	4.63	2980	182	dohc	4	1	3
1923	60	2.38	87	3.42	1990	121	dohc	4	1	3 or 5
1924	60	2.38	87	3.42	1990	121	dohc	2	1	3
1926	58	2.29	70	2.75	1480	90	dohc	2	1	5
1926	58	2.29	70	2.75	1480	90	*		1	5
1927	55	2.19	76	3	1485	90	dohc	2	1	5

*rotary inlet valves

Duesenberg SSJ shown at the Gooding Auction, Pebble Beach, 2018.

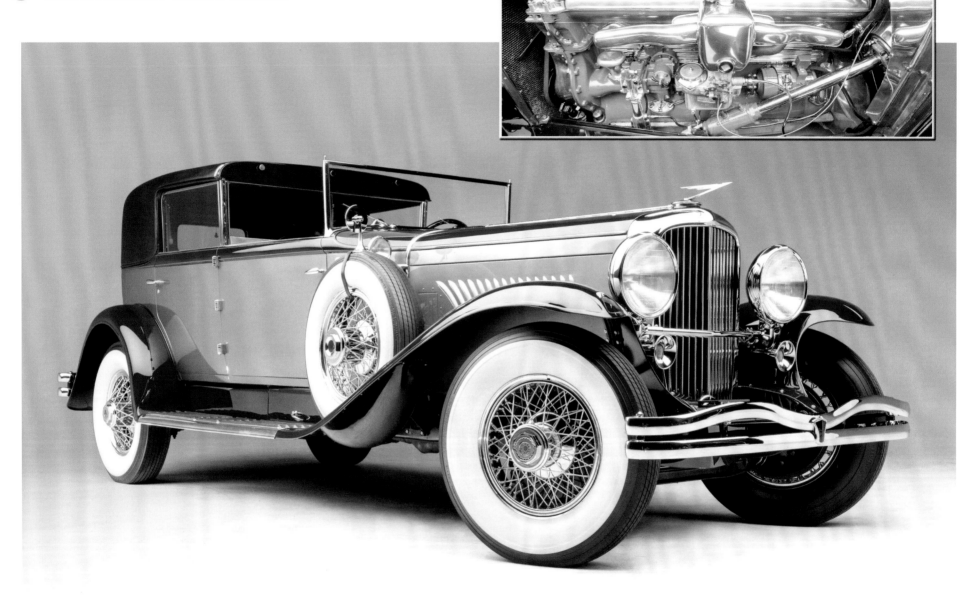

The sensational Duesenberg Model J, introduced in 1928, would become a great success for the company. This is a 1930 example of the model.
INSET: The immaculate inlet side of the Model J's engine with its single Schebler carburettor. **OPPOSITE:** The impressive dual overhead cam, four-valve, 6.9-litre engine powering the Model J.

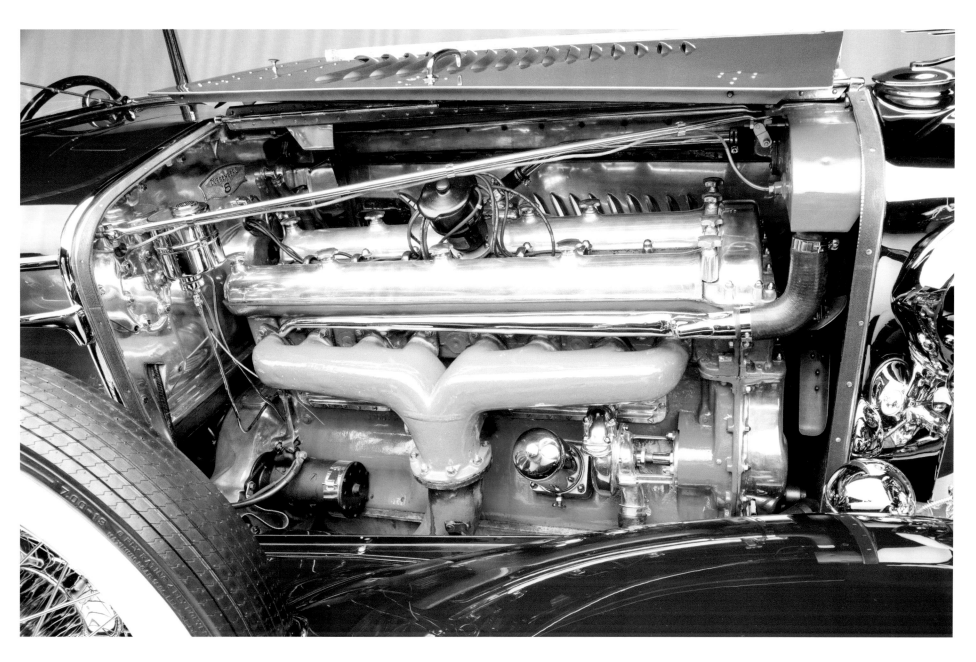

A slightly later 1932 Duesenberg J. On the 1932 model, the four separate chromed exhausts are similar to those on the super-charged SJ (see opposite).

DUPONT

(US)

Between 1919 and 1931 Dupont built a small number of upmarket cars, including one straight eight model. Du Pont Motors was founded by E. Paul du Pont to make marine engines during the First World War. After the war, in 1919, Paul du Pont started the DuPont Car Company.

The first car was the Model A, followed in 1920 by the Model B, of which 120 were made. The Model C used a six-cylinder Continental engine, whereas for the Model D the company switched to a six-cylinder Wisconsin unit. The next two models were not a success; the Model E was an experiment with supercharging, but the car did not meet expectations, whilst the Model F had a production run of three.

The Model G was more successful, enjoying a production run of 200 between 1928 and 1931. This vehicle used a straight eight 5,274 cc (321.8 cu in) side valve Continental engine with a bore of 85.7 mm (3.37 in) and stroke of 114.3 mm (4.5 in) fed by twin carburettors and delivering 125 bhp (92 kW) at 3,600 rpm. The company attempted to launch a Model H on a Stearns-Knight chassis, but the Great Depression effectively killed it off after only three had been built,

Despite their high quality and popularity with actors and actresses, in 1931 the company was bankrupt, and was absorbed into the Indian Motorcycle Company, also owned by du Pont. In total 537 cars were made.

1929 Dupont Model G: contemporary photograph of the eight-cylinder Continental engine with the cover removed from the flathead.

A 1930 Dupont Model G, one of the just 200 straight eight Model Gs made between 1928 and 1931.

LEFT: A contemporary photograph of the right side of the Model G's engine, with the firing order 1-6-2-5-8-3-7-4 embossed on the cover plate.

BELOW: The left-hand side of the side valve 5,273 cc (321.8 cu in) Continental engine in the 1929 Model G. The impressive cover concealing the spark plugs and leads 'alludes to' an overhead cam but actually just hides a conventional flathead block.

The Elkhart Carriage and Motor Car Company, owned by William and George Pratt, started to manufacture cars in 1915. Their first vehicles were branded as Elkharts, and between 1905 and 1911 they produced three models, the 30/35 from 1905 until 1909, the 4.2-litre Sterling from 1909 to 1911, and the Komet in 1911 which continued to 1915. In that year the vehicles were re-branded as Elcars as a series of four and six-cylinder cars powered by Lycoming and Continental engines, and then in 1925 the first straight eight was launched.

The 8-80 model had a 4,273 cc (260.9 cu in) Continental side valve unit with a five-bearing crankshaft and a single Swan carburettor. In Roadster form it cost $2,315. In 1926 the 8-81 brought a larger 4,894 cc (298.7 cu in) Continental engine delivering 115 bhp (86 kW). The 1927

8-82 used a smaller 'eight', also from Continental. With a bore of 69.9 mm (2.75 in) and a stroke of 120.7 mm (4.75 in) the displacement was 3,705 cc (226.1 cu in). This still had the five-bearing crankshaft and the single Swan carburettor. In Roadster form it cost $1,870, less than the previous model.

In 1929 the model became the 120 and reverted to the 4,894 cc (298.7 cu in) Continental engine which produced 115 bhp (86 kW) at 3,000 rpm. The carburettor changed from Swan to Schebler and in Roadster form the price was increased to $2,465. In 1930 the company experimented with fitting the complex 'Lever' engine designed by Alvah Leigh Powell, but only four Elcar-Levers were built.

By 1930 the business was in trouble. A venture to supply 'El-Fay' taxis to Larry Fay for use in New York City was hit by the Great Depression, and Larry Fay was shot dead by a disgruntled employee. A final attempt to keep the business going by selling the 1930 Elcar as the 1931 Mercer came to nothing, and the business closed.

1928 Elcar 8-91 Continental side valve engine.

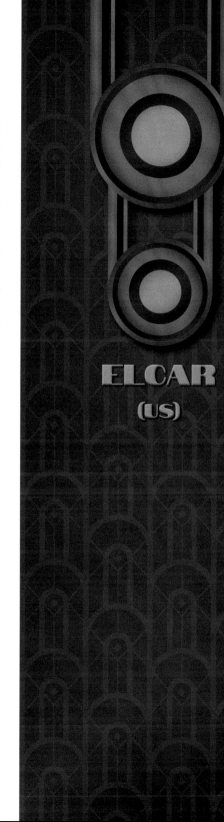

ELCAR

(US)

ABOVE: An elegant open two seat 1928 Elcar 8-91 with the 3,705 cc (226.1 cu in) Continental side valve engine.

OPPOSITE: A contemporary cross-sectional drawing of Alvah Leigh Powell's complex 'Lever Engine' which was installed in just four Elcars in 1930, by which time the business was in serious trouble.

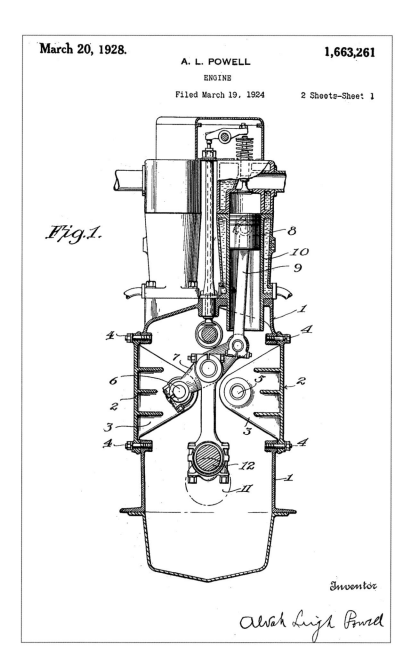

March 20, 1928.

A. L. POWELL

1,663,261

ENGINE

Filed March 19, 1924

2 Sheets—Sheet 1

Fig.1.

Inventor

Alvah Leigh Powell

Model		8-80	8-81	8-82	120
Year introduced		1925	1926	1927	1929
Displacement	cc	4,273	4,894	3,705	4,894
	cu in	260.9	298.7	226.1	298.7
Power output	bhp (max)	100	115	87	115
	kW	75	86	65	86
	@ rpm	3,000	3,000	3,000	3,000
Specific output	bhp/litre	23.4	23.5	23.5	23.5
	bhp/cu in	0.38	0.39	0.38	0.39
	kW/litre	17.6	17.6	17.5	17.6
	kW/cu in	0.29	0.29	0.29	0.29
Compression ratio					
Bore	mm	77.2	82.6	69.9	82.6
	inches	3.00	3.25	2.75	3.25
Stroke	mm	114.3	114.3	120.7	114.3
	inches	4.50	4.50	4.75	4.50
Bore:stroke ratio		68%	72%	58%	72%
Valve gear		s/v 16v	s/v 16v	s/v 16v	s/v 16v
Carburettor		1xSwan	1xSwan	1xSwan	1xSchebler
Main bearings		5	5	5	5

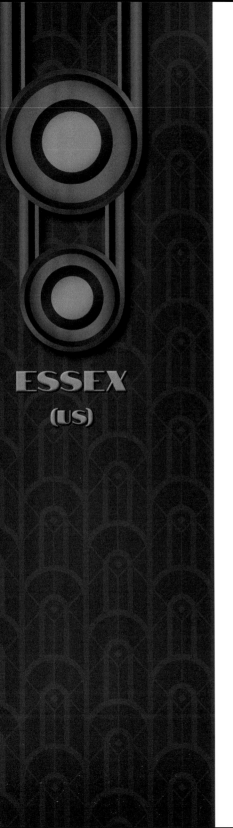

The histories of Essex, Hudson and Terraplane (and even Railton) are inextricably entwined together... and not easy to unravel.

Hudson had started manufacturing the Essex in 1919 as a lower priced vehicle, initially as a separate entity. But in 1922 Hudson absorbed Essex into the parent company, and this move substantially helped Hudson recover from difficult times in the early 1920s. But the effects of the Great Depression combined with declining Essex sales necessitated a rethink by Hudson, and it introduced a car with lower production costs at a lower price. This was the Essex Terraplane which was launched in 1932 and helped Hudson survive the tough economic conditions of the early 1930s. In 1932 only the Model K with a 3.2-litre (244 cu in) six-cylinder side valve engine was available. For 1933 the Model K was continued but

A 1933 Essex Terraplane chassis, showing the inlet/exhaust side of the simple side valve Terraplane engine with its single downdraft carburettor.

alongside a Model KU on a longer wheelbase and a Model KT with a 4,010 cc (244 cu in) side valve straight eight with a bore of 75 mm (2.95 in) and a stroke of 114 mm (4.49 in). The engine produced 94 bhp at 3,200 rpm and was fed by a single downdraft Carter carburettor. The engine was basically the same as that in the Hudson, but with a slightly smaller bore. The Model KT cost $615 and over 38,000 were produced.

The 1933 Essex Terraplane Eight, with the lighter bodywork, had one of the highest power-to-weight ratios of any car at the time, and was as a result a popular choice of gangsters! For 1934 the word Essex was dropped from the name and then, in 1938, knowing they were going to abandon the name Terraplane completely, phased in its demise by changing the name to Hudson Terraplane. This was virtually identical to the contemporary Hudson Model 112.

A contemporary photograph of a 1933 Essex Terraplane 8 convertible with the distinctive '8' on the wheel hubs.

FERRARI
(AUTO AVIO 815)
(ITALY)

This car appears here as a 'Ferrari' because, to all intents and purposes, it was a Ferrari, although it could not be called that at the time. It was named the Auto Avio Costruzioni 815, of which two were built.

The problem with the name arose because Enzo Ferrari left Alfa Romeo in 1938 after running its racing team under the name Scuderia Ferrari and part of the separation agreement was that Ferrari would not resurrect the Scuderia Ferrari name for four years, so he founded Auto Avio Costruzioni (AAC) in Modena to manufacture aircraft components. Then in 1939 he was commissioned by the splendidly named Marchese Lotario Rangoni Macchiavelidi di Modena to build two sports racing cars for himself and Alberto Ascari to drive in the Brescia Grand Prix in 1940.

The 815 was designed by Enrico Nardi and two ex-Alfa engineers, with the name 815 derived from its having eight cylinders and being 1.5 litres (1,496 cc or 91 cu in) in displacement. The engine was based on two four-cylinder blocks from the 1,100 cc Fiat Balilla 508C placed end to end and joined by a single custom-built alloy crankcase. The bore and stroke were reduced, and a five-bearing crankshaft was used. The Fiat valve gear was retained, but driven by a sohc. The connecting rods and cylinder heads, one for each block of four, were also retained. Four Weber carburettors were used and a power output of 75 bhp (56kW) was achieved at 5,500 rpm.

In the Brescia Grand Prix, both cars suffered mechanical failures and were withdrawn.

This was in effect the first 'Ferrari', albeit by a different name. The first car using Ferrari's name was the 125 S, but the Auto Avio 815 would remain Enzo Ferrari's only straight eight.

The Auto Avio 815 was a Ferrari in all but name.

The Auto Avio 815 featured the first 'Ferrari' engine and would remain Ferrari's only straight eight. The four carburettors on this small 1.5-litre (91 cu in) engine would have taken very careful balancing.

Although Fiat never made a straight eight road car, the company did produce a sensational racing engine in the shape of the 3-litre twin cam 402 in 1921. This engine had no fewer than ten main bearings, all roller bearings, and shaft/bevel gear-driven twin overhead camshafts. The big end bearings were also split cage roller bearings. Whereas previous Fiat racing engines had used twin plugs and four valves per cylinder, the company reverted to single plugs and two valves in a hemispherical combustion chamber for the 402. At its time the output of 40 bhp/litre was only exceeded by the new three litre Miller engine. The Fiat T.801, powered by the 402 engine, set a new lap record at Monza. Unfortunately, the displacement formula expired before it could enjoy racing success.

But a four-cylinder version of the 402 did have considerable success, coming 1st, 2nd, 3rd and 4th in the Voiturette Grand Prix at Monza in 1922. For the 2-litre GP formula, which came into being also in 1922, Fiat developed a six-cylinder version.

Fiat returned with another straight eight in 1923 with the 405 engine, this being basically a development of the previous year's 'six' with two extra cylinders. This straight eight was supercharged, initially with a Wittig blower. But it proved unreliable and was replaced by a Roots type. The 405 engine was successful, taking the first two places in the Grand Prix of Europe at Monza.

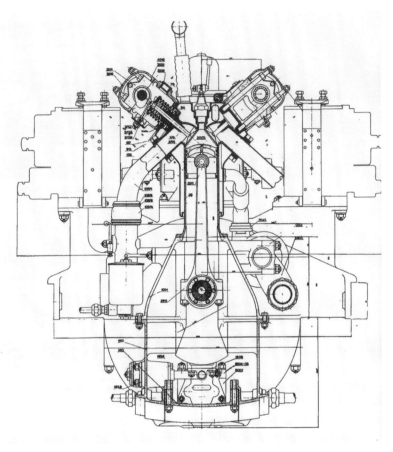

ABOVE: The cross section shows the dohc with two valves per cylinder. The combustion chambers closely approached hemi-spherical form.

OPPOSITE: The 3-litre 402 had ten main bearings, and the con rod bearings and crankshaft bearings were all rollers. At the flywheel end of the engine a spur gear and bevel shaft camshaft drive can be seen in the diagram.

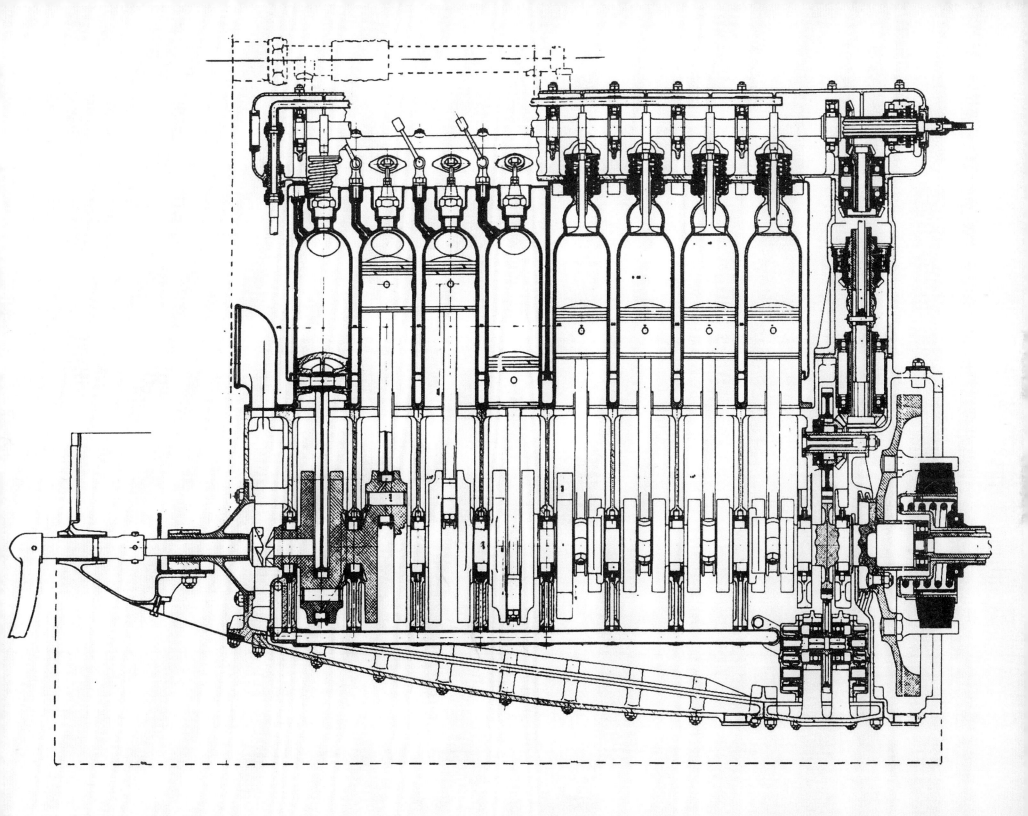

The Belgian company FN, whose full name was Fabrique Nationale d'Armes de Guerre (or National Manufacturer of Weapons of War), is a classic example of an automobile business which stretched itself too far at the wrong time, even within its own area of expertise. By the start of the 1930s, just a few years before its demise, it had no fewer than sixteen different models within its established repertoire. Launching a straight eight, out of its comfort zone, at the same time did nothing to prevent the inevitable end even though the range was later cut back to just two models.

FN launched its first car, the twin cylinder 'Spider', in 1900. The first four-cylinder model followed in 1904, and one year later saw the luxurious FN Type 30-40,

a car used by both the Belgian Royal Family and the Shah of Persia.

Until 1931 the company focused on up-market four- and six-cylinder models. Then the first and only eight was launched, the FN 16CV. This had a 3,257 cc (198.8 cu in) straight side valve engine of 72 mm (2.83 in) bore and 100 mm (3.94 in) stroke, fed by one Amal carburettor. It was capable of 62 mph (100 kph).

Car production came to an end in the mid-1930s, but even so it remains the longest running automobile manufacturer in Belgian history.

Although the 16CV was only made in small numbers, it does have the distinction of appearing on a Belgian postage stamp!

Although only made in small numbers, the Belgian FN 16CV has the rare distinction of appearing on a postage stamp.

Frontenac was another important player in the North American racing engine industry, but unlike Miller and Offenhauser, Frontenac also made road cars, although only a small number with an 'eight' engine.

Most of Frontenac's racing experience was with four-cylinder engines, and one of its areas of expertise was a twin cam four valve 'Peugeot-type' head conversion for the Model T Ford engine, producing a spectacularly entertaining unit.

For the 1921 season, inspired by Ballot, Frontenac designed a three-litre sleeve valve straight eight essentially based on two of its previous 'fours' joined together. Like the 'fours' the 'eight' was unusual in that the crankshaft bearings, five in total, were incorporated within the block, so the block supported the crank. The crankcase was therefore relegated to the humble role of oil holder.

The straight eight Frontenac engine powered the winner of the 1921 Indianapolis 500.

Some straight eight road-going Frontenacs were made. The photograph of the engine shows the company name and firing order on a plate on the block. Unfortunately, information on the straight eight road cars is hard to find.

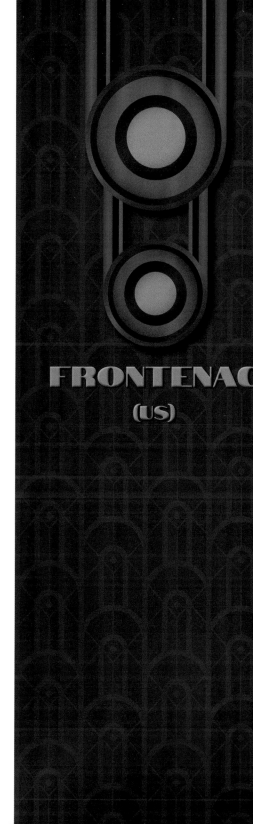

FRONTENAC

(US)

LEFT: A contemporary photograph from 1925 of one of the rare road-going Frontenac 'eights'.
RIGHT: The uncluttered left-hand side of the 1925 Frontenac engine with the unusual firing order 1-6-3-7-4-6-2-8 displayed on a plate.

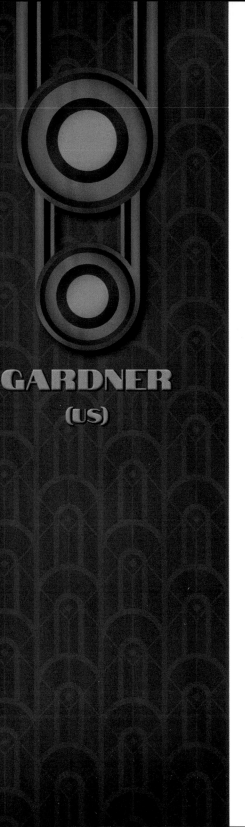

GARDNER

(US)

Gardner, based in St. Louis, Missouri, had a comparatively short life from 1920 to 1931. The company originated in the first two decades of the 20th century when Russell E. Gardner, already a successful businessman, started assembling Chevrolets in St. Louis, and also had control over all Chevrolet business west of the Mississippi. After Gardner sold his business to General Motors, and his three sons had returned from the war, the family decided to start manufacturing motor cars of their own design, and the Gardner Motor Company was founded. Having been familiar with car assembly with Chevrolets, it seemed natural that they would manufacture cars from bought-in components. Throughout the life of the company, engines were sourced from Lycoming.

A four-cylinder model was introduced in 1919. Sales were good, reaching 3,800 cars in 1921 and 9,000 in 1922. In 1924 they expanded the product range and by 1925 the range included 'fours', 'sixes' and 'eights'. The four-cylinder models were dropped at the end of 1925 leaving the company to focus on its 'sixes' and 'eights'. From 1927 to 1929 the range was rationalised even more, and only straight eight engines were used. Then in 1930 they dropped the 'eights' and reverted to six-cylinder models only. In 1931 Russell Gardner announced that the company was no longer profitable on account fierce competition from the larger manufacturers who, he claimed, controlled so much of the supply chain of parts, and the business closed.

Throughout the eleven years of production Lycoming engines of various sizes were offered. The largest engine was a 4,894 cc (298.7 cu in) five bearing version with a bore of 83 mm (3.25 in) and a stroke of 114 mm (4.5 in), which delivered 75 bhp (56 kW) in single Schebler carburettor form, or 86 bhp (64 kW) with twin carburettors.

Most body styles also offered a smaller engine option. These varied over time and included a 3,699 cc (225.7 cu in) 70 bhp (52 kW) unit, a 4,040 cc (246.5 cu in) 86 bhp (64 kW) version and a 4,528 cc (276.3 cu in) power plant, all straight eights.

RIGHT: The engine of a 1929 Gardner Series 120, an elegant sporting two-seater produced during the period 1927-29 when the company only produced 'eights'.

OVERLEAF: The 1929 Gardner Series 120 used a simple 'off-the-shelf' 4.9-litre side valve Lycoming engine.

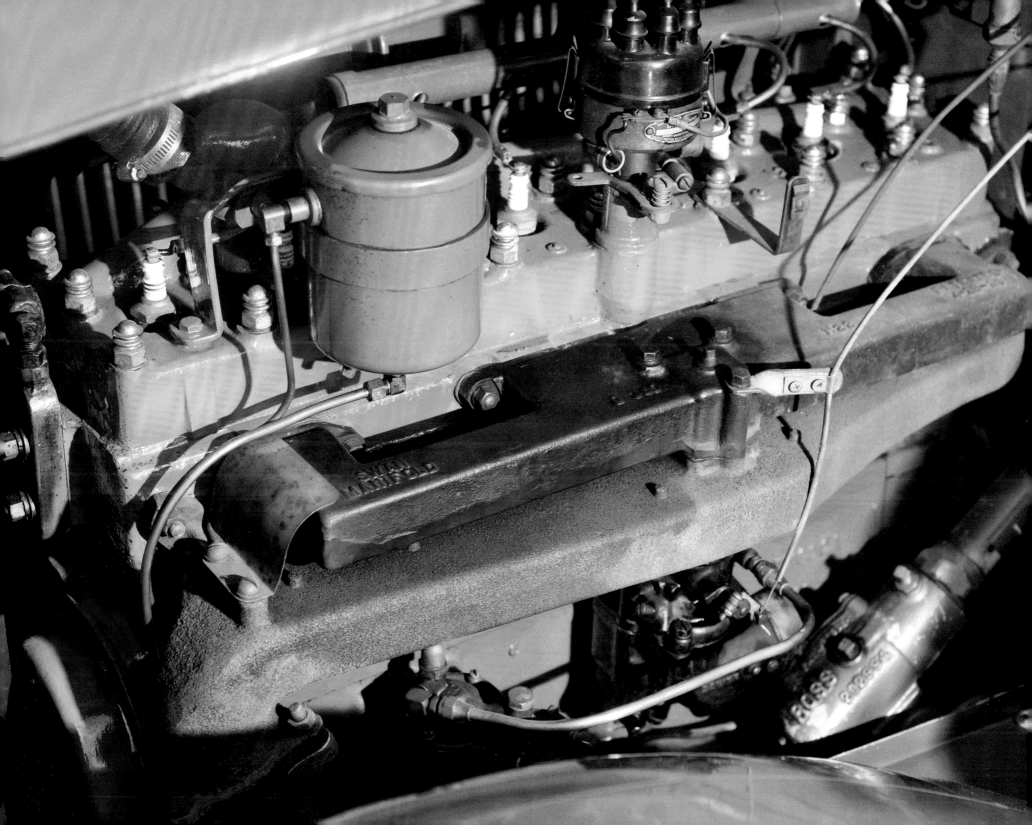

GARDNER EIGHT MODELS

Model		Eight	8-A	Eight	Eight ii	Eight
Year introduced		1925	1926	1927	1927	1928
Displacement	cc	3,699	4,528	4,894	4,894	4,040
	cu in	225.7	276.3	298.7	298.7	246.5
Power output	bhp (max)	70	69	75	86	86
	kW	53	52	56	65	64
	@ rpm	3,200	3,200	3,200	3,200	3,200
Specific output	bhp/litre	18.9	15.2	15.3	17.6	21.3
	bhp/cu in	0.31	0.25	0.25	0.29	0.35
	kW/litre	14.3	11.5	11.4	13.3	15.8
	kW/cu in	0.23	0.19	0.19	0.22	0.26
Bore	mm	70	79	83	83	73
	inches	2.75	3.13	3.25	3.25	2.87
Stroke	mm	121	114	114	114	121
	inches	4.75	4.50	4.50	4.50	4.75
Bore:stroke ratio		58%	69%	73%	73%	60%
Valve gear		s/v 16v	s/v 16v	s/v 16v	s/v 16v	s/v 16v
Carburettor		1xSchebler	1xSchebler	1xSchebler	2xSchebler	1xSchebler
Main bearings		5	5	5	5	5

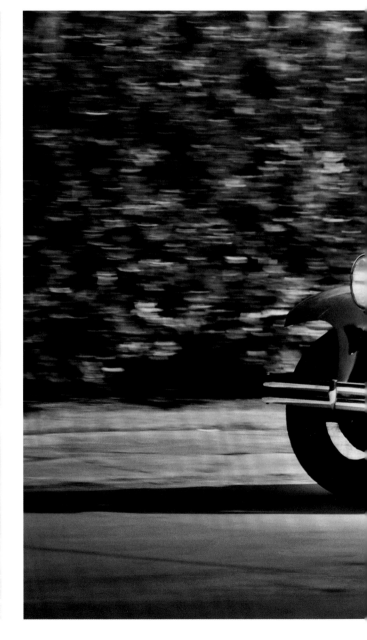

A conservatively styled 1930 straight eight Gardner 4-door Sedan.

The 1930 4-door Sedan used the same Lycoming flathead engine with a single Schebler carburettor.

GRÄF & STIFT
(AUSTRIA)

The Austrian company Gräf & Stift is generally better known for manufacturing lorries, buses and trolley buses, but before the Second World War it also produced high-end luxury cars. Gräf & Stift cars also have an unusual claim to 'fame'; the Archduke Franz Ferdinand of Austria was riding in a Graf & Sift Double Phaeton limousine owned by Count Franz von Harrach when he was assassinated in Sarajevo, the event which precipitated the First World War.

Gräf & Stift made its first car between 1895 and 1898, a voiturette with a single cylinder De Dion Bouton engine driving the front wheels. It was possibly the first front wheel drive car. From 1920, when it resumed motor car production after the war, until 1930 it manufactured luxury four- and six-cylinder cars. Then in 1930 the first straight eight model, the Tipo Sp 8, was produced.

The Tipo Sp 8 had a 5,992 cc (365.7 cu in) sohc engine, with a bore of 85 mm (3.35 in) and a stroke of 132 mm (5.2 in). Its crankshaft was well supported by nine main bearings. Power output was 125 bhp (93 kW). In 1937 the Sp 8 was replaced by the Sp 9.

The Sp 8 and Sp 9 were large and expensive vehicles, and in order to increase sales and support profits the company launched a range of smaller models, the G 35, G 36 and G 8, powered by a 4.6-litre straight eight engine. But these new models did not perform well enough to maintain future car production, and the last Gräf & Stift cars were made in 1938 allowing the business henceforth to focus on lorries and buses.

1931 Gräf & Stift SP 8: the straight eight was very large, very expensive and very rare. This is a contemporary photograph in relatively low quality.

The Graham-Paige business began in 1927 when the Graham brothers, Joseph, Robert and Ray, having previously manufactured trucks with Dodge engines under the Graham Brothers brand, decided to manufacture motor cars instead. They acquired the Paige Detroit Motor Company which made Jewett and Paige cars, and branded their new offerings as Graham-Paige.

Their first models were powered by a range of six- and eight-cylinder engines. The first 'eight' was the 835 with a flathead straight engine of 5,277 cc (322 cu in) developing 120 bhp. These engines were slightly unusual in that whilst they were manufactured by Continental, they were Graham-Paige designs. The 835 was joined by two variants, the 827 and 837; mechanically these were the same, but they came on 127 in and 137 in wheelbase chassis respectively, hence the model names. The Graham-Paige 837 has a claim to fame. One of this model became an early 'Popemobile'!

In 1932 a new model was launched with a Continental 'Blue Streak' engine. Although the name referred strictly to just the engine, the name was quickly adopted for the car itself. The 1932 model had a more regular side valve Continental engine with a bore of 79.4 mm (3.13 in) and a stroke of 101 mm (3.98 in) giving a displacement of 4,021 cc (245.4 cu in). It used a five-bearing crankshaft. The engine delivered 90 bhp (67 kW) allowing a respectable top speed of 80 mph. In 1934 a supercharged version was also offered.

In 1936 the range of 'eights' was dropped, and Graham-Paige continued manufacturing 'sixes' through various joint ventures, some disastrous, such as the notorious 'shark nose' models. The company dropped 'Motors' from its name in 1952 and branched out into real estate. The cars are variously referred to as Graham-Paiges or simply Grahams.

The company used eight variants of its in-house designed engine, and these are detailed in the table.

An elegant 1929 Graham-Paige straight eight sedan.

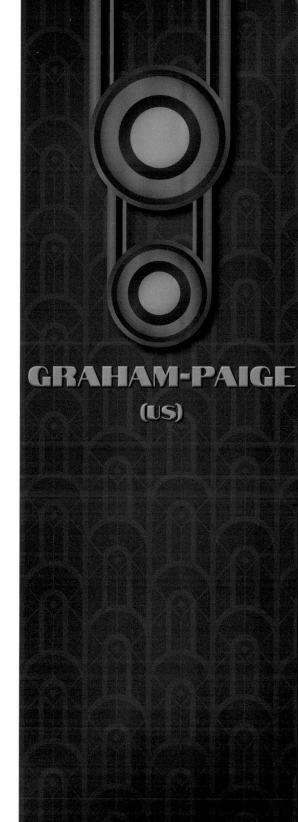

GRAHAM-PAIGE
(US)

A 1929 Graham-Paige Dual Cowl Phaeton. Although the engine was a Graham-Paige design, production of the 5.3-litre side valve was 'farmed out' to Continental, in the same way Duesenberg used Lycoming's production facilities.

GRAHAM-PAIGE EIGHT MODELS

Variant		1	2	3	4	5	6	7	8
Displacement	cc	5,277	5,277	4,893	4,021	4,021	4,021	4,021	4,349
	cu in	322	322	298.6	245.4	245.4	245.4	245.4	265.4
Power output	bhp (max)	120	120	100	85	90	95	95	135
	kW	89	89	75	63	67	71	71	101
@ rpm		3,200	3,200	3,400	3,400	3,400	3,400	3,400	4,000
Specific output	bhp/litre	22.7	22.7	20.4	21.1	22.4	23.6	23.6	31.0
	bhp/cu in	0.37	0.37	0.33	0.35	0.37	0.39	0.39	0.51
	kW/litre	16.9	16.9	15.3	15.7	16.7	17.7	17.7	23.2
	kW/cu in	0.28	0.28	0.25	0.26	0.27	0.29	0.29	0.38
Bore	mm	86	86	83	80	80	80	80	83
	inches	3.38	3.38	3.25	3.13	3.13	3.13	3.13	3.25
Stroke	mm	114	114	114	102	102	102	102	102
	inches	4.50	4.50	4.50	4.00	4.00	4.00	4.00	4.00
Bore:stroke ratio		75%	75%	72%	78%	78%	78%	78%	81%
Compression ratio		5.5:1	5.5:1	5.25:1	5.5:1	6.5:1	6.5:1	6.5:1	6.7:1
Valve gear		s/v	s/v	s/v	s/v	s/v	s/v	s/v	s/v
Main bearings		5	5	5	5	5	5	5	5
Carburation		Johnson	Detroit	Detroit	Detroit	Detroit	Detroit	Stromberg	Stromberg
Aspiration		normal	normal	normal	normal	normal	normal	normal	supercharged
Years used		1928, 1929	1930, 1931	1930-1932	1931	1932	1933	1934, 1935	1934, 1935

HAMPTON
(UK)

The Hampton Empire Sportsman straight eight of 1932 is one of the most obscure cars in this book and is perhaps the most inappropriately launched straight eight of all!

The cars were made by the Hampton Engineering Company which was founded in 1912 in Kings Norton near Birmingham, England. The founder William Paddon lived in Hampton-in-Arden and started the business as a car retailer, but also to manufacture light cars and motorcycles. In 1912, the Crowdy Car Company of Birmingham failed and the business was absorbed into Paddon's company. Paddon fitted a larger 1,726 cc (105 cu in) engine into the Crowdy 12/14 to create the Hampton 12/16. Before the First World War two new models were added, but when production stopped in 1914 the company went into receivership.

In 1919, the business was resurrected to make the Hampton 11.9 with either a 1,496 cc (91 cu in) or 1,795 cc (109 cu in) Dorman engine. But it failed again and was taken over by its major shareholder and continued under the same name. In 1925 it went into receivership yet again, but bounced back as Hampton Cars (London) Ltd. The company decided to move up-market with a six-cylinder model with a Meadows engine, but failed yet again in 1930.

The company bounced back once more as the Safety Suspension Car Company and, given its track record, made what must be one of the most stupid decisions in motoring history and produced an up-market straight eight, the Empire Sportsman. In fact, what the company did was order 50 2,496 cc (152 cu in) straight eight engines and 100 chassis from Röhr in Germany, with a plan to equip the second 50 chassis with Continental engines. The first 50 cars were simply 1931 Röhr 8 Type RA 10/55 bolted together in England. Of course, this business failed before even two cars had been bolted together! It is ironic that the Röhr business itself had been declared bankrupt in 1930 before bouncing back!

Technical details of the 'Hampton' can be found in the section on Rohr, as the cars were mechanically identical.

The Hartz was a remarkable one-off special. In 1932 Harry Hartz ordered a scaled-up version of the original eight-cylinder Miller 91 engine. The 2,998 cc (183 cu in) engine was installed in the Hartz Special and was entered in the 1932 Indy 500 within just two months of its first sketches on the drawing board. Half this engine, in four-cylinder form, became the Offy 91 cu in 'Midget'.

The Hartz Special won the Indianapolis 500 three times. In this contemporary photograph Harry Hartz proudly shows off the ten-foot high trophy!

The 1932 Hartz Eight-Cylinder Special used a scaled up (2,998 cc 183 cu in) version of the Miller 91 engine.

HARTZ

(US)

HILLMAN
(UK)

If Wolseley were an unexpected player in the British luxury straight eight car market, then Hillman is probably even more surprising to most people. Hillman had an image of addressing the lower end of solid middle-class motoring, the sort of car the senior bank clerk might buy, where his boss drove a Wolseley or Humber. Any foray into luxury cars is unexpected, but indeed it happened, and at the worst possible time for the business.

Having started as a bicycle manufacturer, Hillman branched out into automobiles in 1907. Success came with the small 9hp model in 1913, which evolved and sold successfully into the 1920s. In 1926 Hillman launched the 14hp, but the focus remained on modest-sized cars at modest prices. In 1928 Hillman became part of the Rootes Group, and one of its main brands along with Humber, Sunbeam and Singer. A six-cylinder, 2.1-litre model was added in 1931, later enlarged to 2.6 litres and called the Wizard. This sold alongside the smaller four-cylinder Minx which survived until World War Two.

It was in 1928, whilst becoming part of the Rootes Group, that the rather surprising decision was taken to launch a luxury model, the 2,620 cc (160 cu in) Straight Eight. With bore and stroke of 63 mm (2.5 in) and 105 mm (4.1 in), and overhead valves, it developed a modest 52.5 bhp (39 kW). This model marked Hillman's first use of ohv's, but the engine gained a reputation for big end problems. The engine was completely new in all aspects. Production delays put the launch back to 1929, just in time for the Great Depression. In hindsight the Straight Eight was a disastrous business decision, poorly executed. Commercially, it was a flop.

Of course, Hillman as a brand survived within the Rootes Group, but never again strayed outside its rather middle-class image. It did not have to as the Rootes Group had Humber to carry its 'up-market flag'.

The 1929 Hillman Straight Eight was an unusual model to appear from the Hillman company, a manufacturer better known for lower/mid-range vehicles. It was a commercial disaster and it's not known if any survive. This is a rare contemporary photograph.

Horch was one of the most successful manufacturers of 'quality' straight eight models, producing over 14,000 between 1926 and 1940, and if the later V8 cars are included, the total production of eight-cylinder models exceeded 25,000. Indeed, it was Horch's perceived success that prompted Mercedes-Benz to launch its first straight eight in 1928. Whereas the early Mercedes straight eights were side valves, Horch straight eights were from the outset much more advanced overhead cam units, the earlier ones being twin cams.

The company traces its roots back to 1899, when August Horch and Salli Herz set up August Horch and Cie Motorwagenwerke A.G. in Cologne, Germany. Various business problems, and the rights to use the name Horch, resulted in a second company, August Horch Automobilwerke GmbH, being formed in 1909 and the name Audi being registered by the business. The first four-cylinder car appeared in 1903, with a 'six' being launched in 1907. Then in 1926 Horch launched the Horch 8 303 model, the first German production model with eight cylinders.

Between 1926 and 1940 Horch produced 32 different straight eight models, utilising eight varieties of engine. The eight engine varieties are shown below:

The engine variety 4 was produced in two slightly different displacements, although the power output was quoted as the same.

Over time the basic engine grew from just over three litres to just under five litres, and power output doubled.

The only major difference over the 13 years was changing from dual overhead cams to single overhead cams in 1931.

In 1932 Horch, Audi, DKW and Wanderer merged to form the Auto Union, and it was under this new 'umbrella' brand that the later Horchs were marketed.

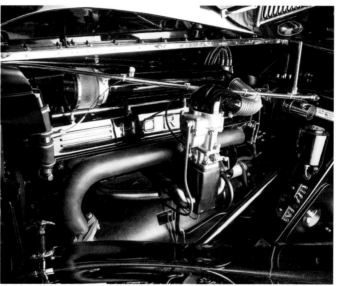

The 1938 Horch 853A had a 4.9-litre sohc engine with a single downdraft carburettor.

HORCH
(GERMANY)

HORCH EIGHT MODELS

Engine Variety	1	2	3	*4a	*4b	5	6	7	8
Years	1926-27	1927-28	1928-31	1931-32	1931-32	1931-33	1931-35	1931-37	1937-39
Capacity cc	3132	3378	3950	3009	3137	4014	4517	4944	4944
Capacity cu in	191.1	206.1	241	183.6	191.4	244.9	275.6	301.7	301.7
Bore mm	65	67.5	73	71	72.5	82	87	87	87
Bore in	2.56	2.66	2.87	2.8	2.85	3.23	3.43	3.43	3.43
Strole mm	118	118	118	95	95	95	95	104	104
Stroke in	4.65	4.65	4.65	3.74	3.74	3.74	3.74	4.09	4.09
bhp	60	65	80	65	65	80	90	100	120
kW	44	48	59	48	48	59	66	74	88
Valve	dohc	dohc	dohc	sohc	sohc	sohc	sohc	sohc	sohc
Models	303	305	350	430	430	410	420	480	851
	304	306	375			440	450	500	951
			400			470	470	500A	951A
			405				720	780	853
							750	780B	853A
							750B	500B	855
								850	
								850 Sport	

A supremely elegant 1938 Horch 853A two-door drophead model.

The very tidy right-hand side of the engine in a 1938 Horch 853A with a plate showing the firing order of 1-4-7-3-8-5-2-6.

ABOVE: A 1938 fixed head two-seater version of the Horch 853A, with its somewhat bulbous roofline.

OPPOSITE: The neat left side of the 1937 Horch 853A's engine with a plate detailing fuse sizes and electrical loads.

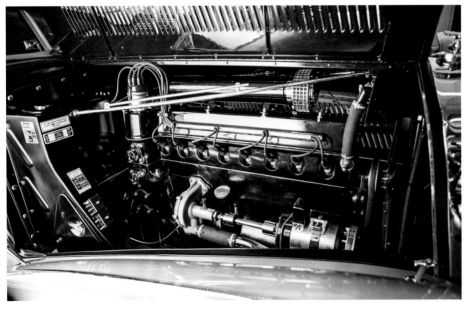

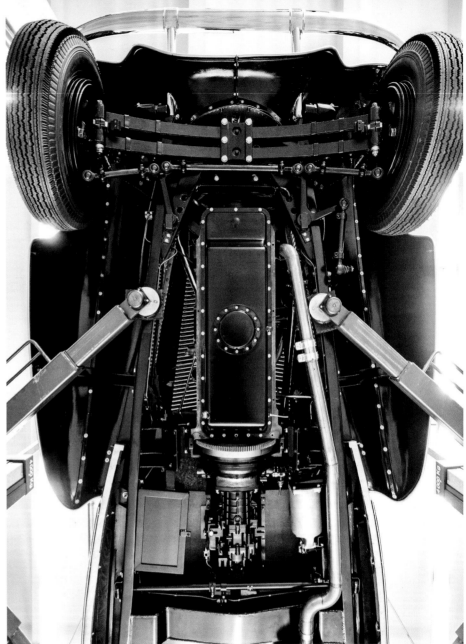

ABOVE: An unusual underside view of an 853 showing the neat sump design, the transverse front suspension and large front drum brakes.
TOP LEFT: The inlet/exhaust (left) side of engine with its single Solex carburettor. **LEFT:** The very tidy right side of the 853's engine.

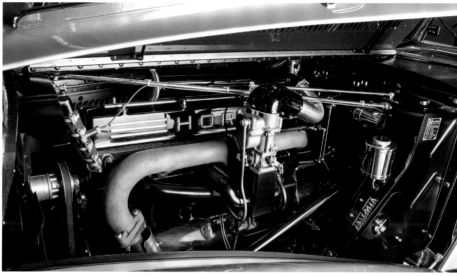

ABOVE: The right-hand side of the 1927 Spezialroadsters' 4.9-litre engine. The engine impressively fills the engine bay. The firing order plate can be seen on the cam cover, above the very neat wiring.

TOP RIGHT: The inlet/exhaust side of the Spezialroadster's in-line eight. RIGHT: An elegant 1937 Horch 853 Spezialroadster, the red bonnet, door caps and boot highlighting the sleek lines.

ABOVE: The 1934 Horch 780B had a 4,944 cc (301.7 cu in) engine delivering 100 bhp (74 kW). **INSET:** A classic teutonic design from the 1930s, a 1934 Horch 780B in a two-door four seat variant. The massive doors and folded drophead roof are characteristic of the era. **OPPOSITE:** The right side of the 1934 780B's 4,944 cc engine showing a clean, neat under-bonnet layout.

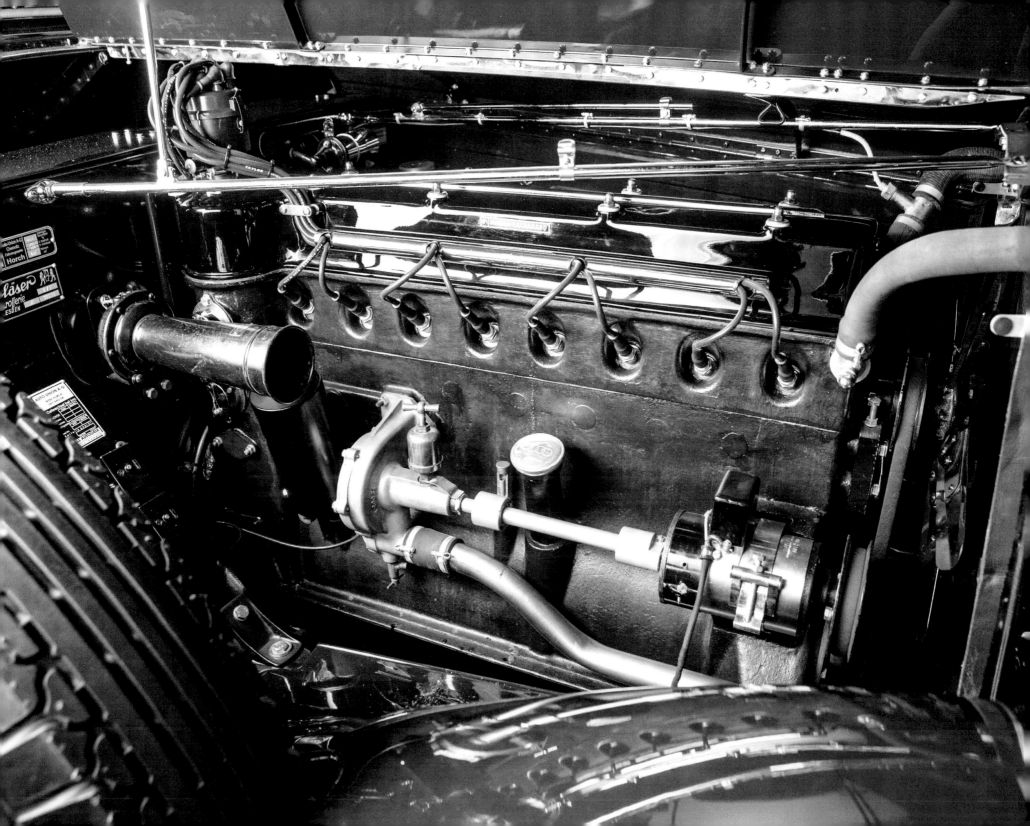

With its drophead roof up the 1937 Horch 853 Sport shows supreme elegance. **INSET:** The 'business side' of the 1937 Horch 853 Sport engine showing the single downdraft Solex carburettor. **OPPOSITE:** The 4,944 cc (301.7 cu in) engine on this 1937 Horch 853 Sport has been beautifully polished.

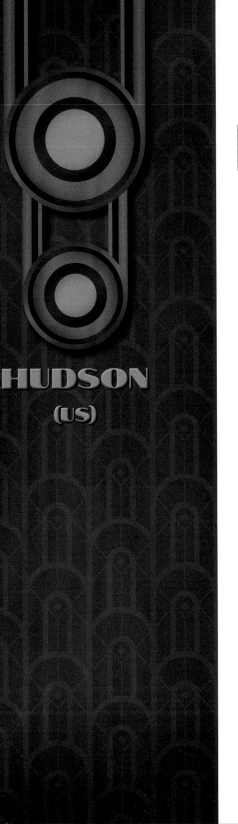

Hudson was one of the major players in the volume straight eight sector, producing straight eight models from 1930 to 1946, and also supplying engines for trans-Atlantic hybrids like Railton and Brough Superior in the UK. Hudson engines were always simple, straight-forward and reliable 'flathead' units, in many ways ideal for the hybrid market.

Hudson essentially used just one design of straight eight engine, the only variation being changes in the cylinder bore measurement. The first Hudson eight, called the Super Eight, had a 4,170 cc (254.5 cu in) engine with a bore of 76.2 mm (3.0 in), a stroke of 114.3 mm (4.5 in) and a five-bearing crankshaft. With twin Carter carburettors and a compression ratio of 6.5:1 it delivered 128 bhp (95 kW) at 4,250 rpm. Soon an alternative size of engine

became available with a reduced bore of 69.9 mm (2.75 in) but with the same stroke, giving a displacement of 3,509 cc (214.1 cu in). This smaller engine had a single carburettor whilst the larger unit had two.

This basic engine design remained unchanged through to the 1949 Hudson Commodore, a highly conservative design philosophy similar to that of Packard. Being more streamlined than the pre-war cars the 1949 Commodore was capable of 93 mph (150 kph).

Hudson engines also found their way in a number of 'specials', including the Kleinig Hudson 8 Special shown in the photographs. With four carburettors, and a separate exhaust from each of the eight cylinders arching over the engine, this was a sophisticated modification of the basic Hudson powerplant.

Straight-forward, with no frills, the Hudson Power Dome side valve straight eight engine was robust and reliable, and found its way into Railton and Brough Superior cars in the UK. **OPPOSITE:** The 1936 Hudson Stratton shows very conservative styling, apart maybe from the red 'rocket' mascot!

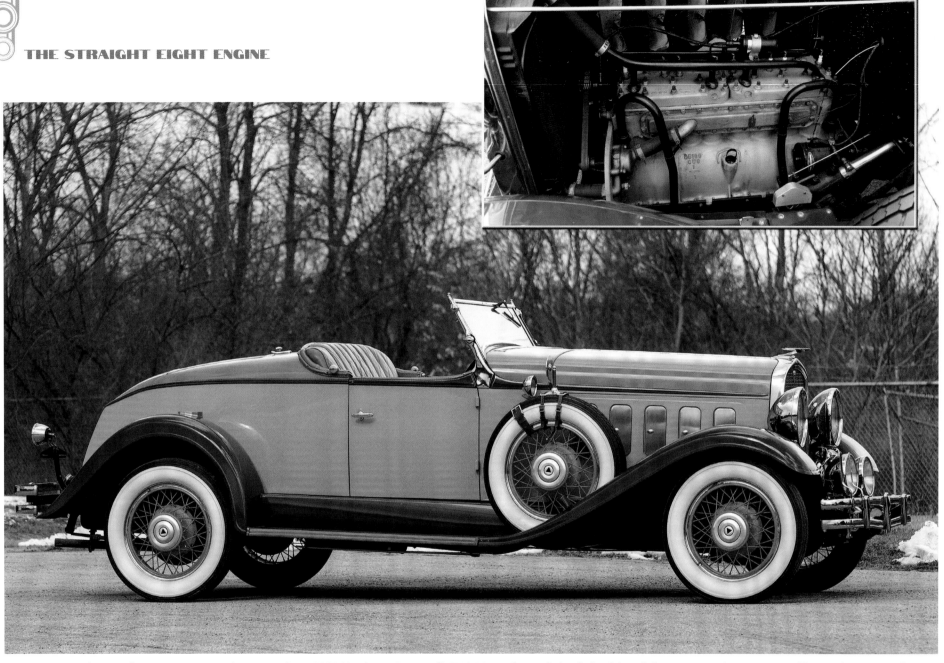

A more sporting style was seen on the two-door 1931 Hudson Boattail. **INSET:** A view of the left side of the 1931 Hudson Boattail's engine, showing the two-part flathead. **OPPOSITE:** The firing order of the 1931 Boattail is cast in the exhaust manifold, and whilst slightly unclear here, it's actually 1-6-2-5-8-3-7-4.

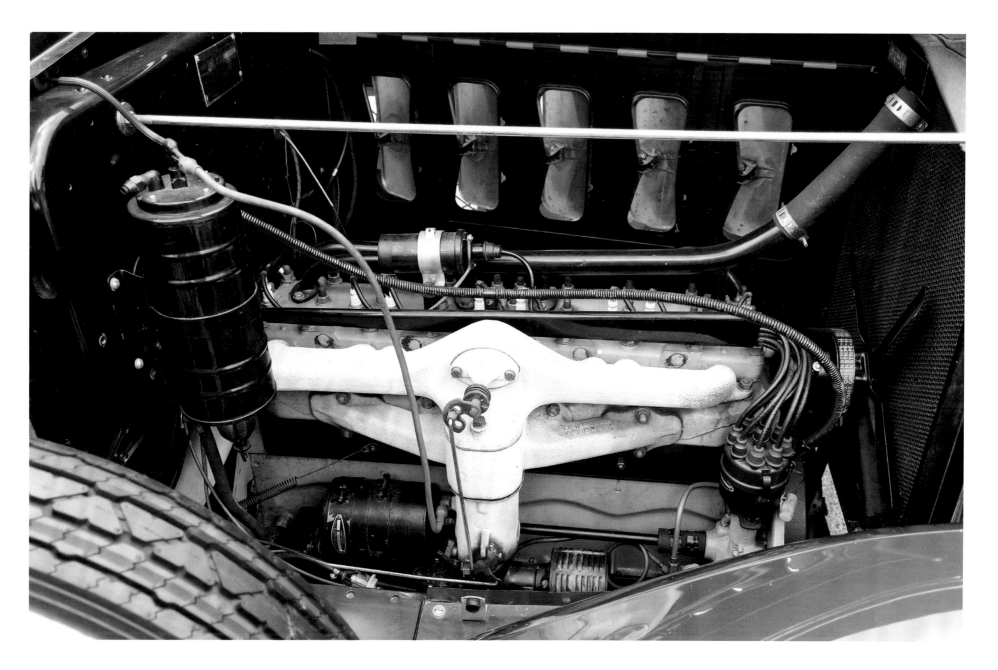

The two-door coupe was a popular style in the late 1930s. This 1936 Hudson Custom Eight Series 65 has a pre-selector gearbox. **OPPOSITE:** This 1936 Custom Eight Series 65 has a 4.2-litre (254 cu in) Hudson Power Dome engine.

OPPOSITE: The impressive modifications to the inlet and exhaust systems on the Kleinig Hudson 8 Special. **ABOVE:** The Kleinig Special in action. **RIGHT:** The Kleinig Special in the 'pits'.

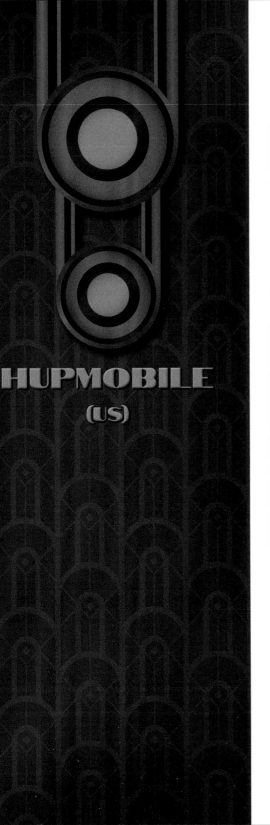

HUPMOBILE
(US)

Hupmobile is yet another example of a company that somehow took 'its eye off the ball', launched a straight eight at the wrong time and paid the price. Bobby Hupp co-founded the Hupp Motor Car Company with Charles Hastings who had been at Oldsmobile, and became one of the early investors in Hupp. At the 1909 Chicago Motor Show, Hupp secured advance cash deposits to enable him to start building the first model, the Hupp 20. The small car was a success, with 500 produced in the first year, and production rising to 5000 the following year. The later 1911 Hupp 32 was one of the first cars in the world to have all steel construction, although because of patent issues the company soon had to revert to conventional body construction.

Problems for Hupp began before the Great Depression. In 1925 the company decided to try to move 'up market' with the launch of a straight eight. The 621 had a 4,972 cc (303.4 cu in) engine with a bore of 81 mm

For the 1932 model year Hupmobile introduced a 4,109 cc (250.7 cu in) engine for its 222 Series.

(3.19 in) and a stroke of 120.6 mm (4.75 in) which produced 120 bhp (89 kW) at 3,500 rpm. It had five main bearings, a 5.8:1 compression ratio and a single Stromberg carburettor. The launch of the 621 'eight' was quickly followed by the end of 'four' production. Hupp had turned its back on the established loyal customers in an attempt to win new customers from more expensive brands.

Three more straight eight engines were used between 1926 and 1938. In 1926 a smaller 4,040 cc (246.5 cu in) version appeared with the bore reduced to 73 mm (2.87 in). The engine was revised in 1929 for the Century Eight 521 model, with the bore increased to 76.2 mm (3.0 in) but with the same stroke of 120.7 mm (4.75 in) used since 1925. Power was quoted at 70 bhp (52 kW) at 3,000 rpm.

In 1932 engine dimensions changed again for the Eight 222 Series, with the bore set at 74.6 mm (2.94 in) and the stroke at 117.5 mm (4.63 in) giving a displacement of 4,109 cc (250.7 cu in). Power rose to 93 bhp (69 kW) at 3,200 rpm on a 5.4:1 compression ratio.

The recipe changed yet again in 1938, with the engine reverting to the original dimensions of 1925, and compression being raised back to the 5.8:1 of the

HUPMOBILE EIGHT MODELS

Model		621	E2	Century Eight	Eight 222	8
Year introduced		1925	1926	1929	1932	1938
Displacement	cc	4,972	4,040	4,403	4,109	4,972
	cu in	303.4	246.5	268.6	250.7	303.4
Power output	bhp (max)	120	98	70	93	120
	kW	89	72	52	69	89
	@ rpm	3,500	3,500	3,000	3,200	3,500
Specific output	bhp/litre	24.1	24.3	15.9	22.6	24.1
	bhp/cu in	0.40	0.40	0.26	0.37	0.40
	kW/litre	17.9	17.8	11.8	16.8	17.9
	kW/cu in	0.29	0.29	0.19	0.28	0.29
Compression ratio		5.8:1	5.8:1	5.4:1	5.4:1	5.8:1
Bore	mm	81	73	76.2	74.6	81
	inches	3.19	2.88	3.00	2.94	3.19
Stroke	mm	120.6	120.6	120.7	117.5	120.6
	inches	4.75	4.75	4.75	4.63	4.75
Bore:stroke ratio		67%	61%	63%	63%	67%
Valve gear		s/v 16v	s/v 16v	s/v 16v	s/v 16v	s/v 16v
Carburettor		1xStromberg	1xStromberg	1xStromberg	1xStromberg	1xCarter
Main bearings		5	5	5	5	5

earlier model. The carburettor was changed to Carter from Stromberg, and this helped raise power to 120 bhp (89 kW) at 3500 rpm.

In an attempt to attack every sector of the 'eight' market, by using four variants of the engine in a wide variety of bodywork, the company was stretching itself too far, and at the same time had turned its back on its traditional, loyal clientele. Sales were in steep decline before the Great Depression struck, and Hupp's fate was sealed. Even turning to 'flashy' coachwork designed by Raymond Loewy, and also launching a cheaper version using modified Ford bodies, did not make a difference. In 1937 Hupp suspended production for nearly a year. A new line of six- and eight-cylinder models was fielded for 1938, but it was too little too late.

Desperate survival attempts included acquiring the dies for the Cord 810 with the aim of making a lower priced Cord 'lookalike' in the shape of the Hupp Skylark. Lacking adequate production capacity, having sold a lot of plant in 1936, Hupp teamed up with the ailing Graham-Paige concern, and production began in 1939. But it was too late, and Hupp closed its doors in the summer of 1939 after just 319 Skylarks had been produced.

One interesting legacy of Hupp is the Greyhound Line of coaches. In 1914 Eric Wickman had tried to set up a Hupmobile dealership but unable to sell his stock, he used the cars instead to transport miners, and this was the start of Greyhound!

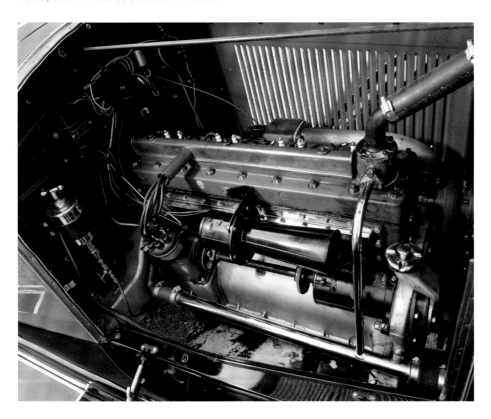

ABOVE: The 1925 Hupmobile 621 Eight was the company's first straight eight, introduced at the unfortunate time of the Depression. **LEFT:** Hupmobile's first straight eight engine was a 4.972 cc (303.4 cu in) side valve unit.

In many ways Isotta Fraschini, just like Duesenberg, epitomises one sector of the straight eight car market, which is the ultra top end of expensive motor cars. It had a one-model policy, and only built the running chassis, the customer being expected to commission a coachbuilder to complete the job, usually at vast expense. To put this in perspective, in 1931 a Tipo 8B chassis cost around $10,000, the US being its main target market, which equates to $166,000 at 2020 prices. The coachwork could easily have doubled the cost to over $300,000 in today's terms. In total around 1,380 were made before 1934, when the company was forbidden to make any more cars on the orders of the Italian Government, in order to focus on the war effort.

The first straight eight was the Tipo 8, made from 1919 until 1924. Before the First World War the company had made a variety of cars, but post-war it adopted a single-model policy. This would result in a succession of three straight eights, and then briefly a V8 in 1947/8. The Tipo A had a 5,902 cc (360.2 cu in) ohv engine producing 80bhp

The 7,370cc (449.7 cu in) ohv engine in the Tipo 8A is unusual in having no inlet manifold, internal ducting taking the mixture from four 'stub' pipes to the eight cylinders.

ISOTTA
FRASCHINI
(ITALY)

ISOTTA FRASCHINI EIGHT MODELS

Model		Tipo 8	Tipo 8 (later)	Tipo 8A	Tipo 8A (later)
Year introduced		1919	1920	1924	1925
Displacement	cc	5,902	5,902	7,370	7,370
	cu in	360.2	360.2	449.8	449.8
Power output	bhp (max)	80	90	115	160
	kW	60	67	86	119
	@ rpm	2,400	2,400	2,400	2,400
Specific output	bhp/litre	13.6	15.2	15.6	21.7
	bhp/cu in	0.22	0.25	0.26	0.36
	kW/litre	10.2	11.4	11.7	16.1
	kW/cu in	0.17	0.19	0.19	0.26
Bore	mm	85	85	95	95
	inches	3.35	3.35	3.74	3.74
Stroke	mm	130	130	130	130
	inches	5.12	5.12	5.12	5.12
Bore:stroke ratio		65%	65%	73%	73%
Valve gear		ohv	ohv	ohv	ohv

RIGHT: A 1929 Isotta Fraschini Tipo 8A two-door cabriolet with coachwork by Franay.

(60 kW) at 2,400 rpm. The power output was soon increased to 90 bhp (67 kW). The engine was novel in that there was no exterior inlet manifold, the twin carburettors being attached directly to the block which contained the necessary inlet ducting which gave a very clean appearance.

In 1924 the Tipo 8 was replaced by the larger Tipo 8A. By increasing the bore to 95 mm (3.74 in) but keeping the same stroke of 130 mm (5.12 in) the displacement rose to 7,370 cc (449.7 cu in). The enlarged engine produced 115-160 bhp (86-119 kW), making it the most powerful straight eight in the world at the time. In 1931 the Tipo 8A was replaced by the similarly engined Tipo 8B.

All production of automobiles ceased in 1934 so that the company could concentrate on military engines for both marine and air use. Ironically one of the British Royal Navy's fastest motor torpedo boats just before the Second World War was powered by a pair of Isotta Fraschini marine engines, quickly replaced by Packard units once war against Italy appeared inevitable.

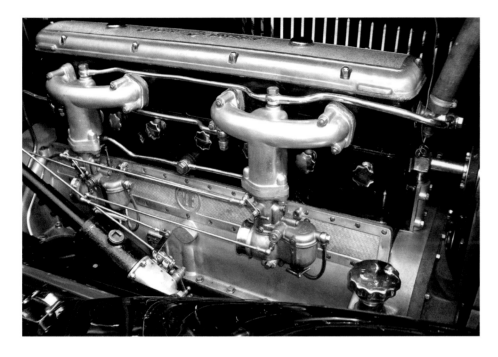

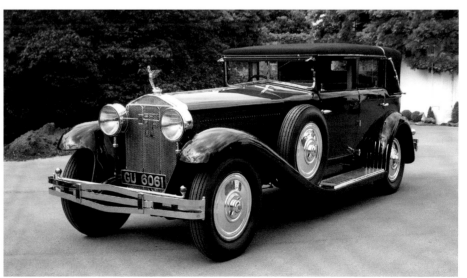

RIGHT: Carrozzeria Castagna of Milan supplied this 1929 Isotta Fraschini Tipo 8A with a very stately four-door sports landaulette body.
TOP LEFT: The inlet side of the four-door landaulette Tipo 8A's engine with the twin carburettors and discreet inlet ducting. **TOP RIGHT:** The left side of Tipo 8A's engine showing the two-part exhaust manifold with the final exhaust taken from the centre of the block.

OPPOSITE: A Lancefield-bodied 1931 Isotta Fraschini Tipo 8A. **INSET:** On the 1931 Tipo 8A, the neat and discreet exhaust manifold feeds the exhaust pipe at the rear of the engine, not the centre as in the 1929 models. The wiring to the plugs is extremely discreet. **ABOVE:** The two Zenith carburettors feed directly into internal ducting in the block with no external manifold at all.

The supremely neat exhaust (left) side of another 1931 Isotta Fraschini Tipo 8A's engine.

NO TWO ALIKE!

"Individuality" is as actual in these smart bodies of ultra-luxury as in the newest creations of a Paris couturière!

The Isotta Fraschini of your choice, although strictly custom-built, is ready for immediate delivery.

NEW YORK: 119 WEST 57

CHICAGO: 846 RUSH STREET

ISOTTA FRASCHINI

MADE IN MILAN, ITALY

Isotta Fraschini: a contemporary advertisement, aimed at the U.S. market, emphasising 'no two alike', mainly because most carried very expensive unique bespoke coachwork.

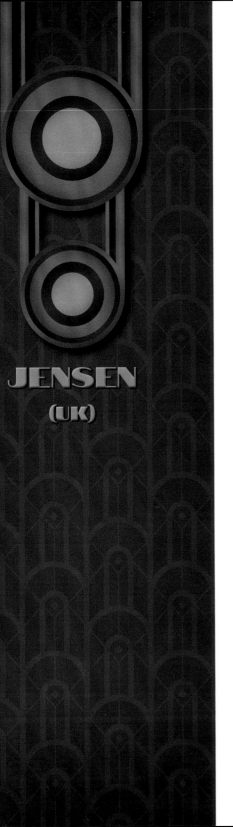

JENSEN
(UK)

The Jensen brothers gained much experience in the motor industry, particularly with W J Smith and Sons, before setting up their own business in 1934. Their first production model, the S-type with its 2.3-litre or 3.5-litre side valve Ford V8 engine, was a critical success although only 50 were produced.

In 1948 they expanded the range with a straight eight model that used a proprietary Henry Meadows engine of 3,860 cc (235.6 cu in) with bore and stroke of 85 mm x 85 mm (3.35 in x 3.5 in). A 'square' engine was unusual

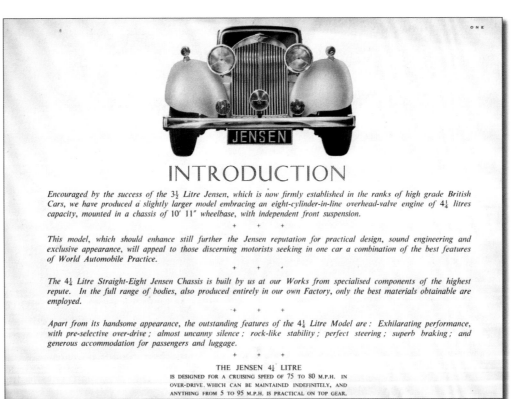

ONE

INTRODUCTION

Encouraged by the success of the 3½ Litre Jensen, which is now firmly established in the ranks of high grade British Cars, we have produced a slightly larger model embracing an eight-cylinder-in-line overhead-valve engine of 4¼ litres capacity, mounted in a chassis of 10' 11" wheelbase, with independent front suspension.

＋　　＋　　＋

This model, which should enhance still further the Jensen reputation for practical design, sound engineering and exclusive appearance, will appeal to those discerning motorists seeking in one car a combination of the best features of World Automobile Practice.

＋　　＋　　＋

The 4¼ Litre Straight-Eight Jensen Chassis is built by us at our Works from specialised components of the highest repute. In the full range of bodies, also produced entirely in our own Factory, only the best materials obtainable are employed.

＋　　＋　　＋

Apart from its handsome appearance, the outstanding features of the 4¼ Litre Model are : Exhilarating performance, with pre-selective over-drive ; almost uncanny silence ; rock-like stability ; perfect steering ; superb braking ; and generous accommodation for passengers and luggage.

＋　　＋　　＋

THE JENSEN 4¼ LITRE
IS DESIGNED FOR A CRUISING SPEED OF 75 TO 80 M.P.H. IN
OVER-DRIVE, WHICH CAN BE MAINTAINED INDEFINITELY, AND
ANYTHING FROM 5 TO 95 M.P.H. IS PRACTICAL ON TOP GEAR.

ABOVE: A rare magazine photograph of a Jensen straight eight.

LEFT: The introduction to a Jensen brochure for the very rare straight eight of 1948.

OPPOSITE: A 1948 Jensen advertisement for the straight eight model.

amongst straight eights, most of which had strokes much greater than the bore in order to reduce the overall length of the engine. The ohv unit had two valves per cylinder, a compression ratio of 6.25:1, and nine main bearings. With twin SU carburettors the engine produced 130 bhp at 4,300 rpm. The 'square' engine permitted higher revs than most straight eights, and maximum power being seen at the relatively fast 4,300 rpm.

The Meadows engine was, however, found to produce harsh vibrations so Jensen switched first to a straight eight engine from Nash, and then later to the better established 3,993 cc (243.7 cu in) straight six used in the Austin Sheerline.

Jensen advertising emphasised the flexibility of the engine, claiming 5mph to 90 mph can comfortably be done in top gear!

Only a handful was made.

The New JENSEN Straight-Eight 6-Seater Saloon

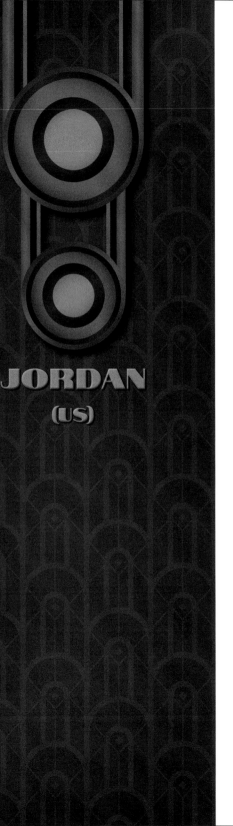

JORDAN

(US)

Jordan was another example of a 'parts bin' car, assembled from components supplied by other businesses. These included Continental engines, Timken axles, Bijur starter motors, Bosch ignitions, and bodies supplied complete from a number of different sources.

The company started making cars in 1916, and until 1925 they were all six-cylinder models Then in 1925 the first straight eight was launched. Called the Jordan A Great Line Eight, it was powered by a five bearing Continental engine of 4,402 cc (268.6 cu in) with 76.2 mm (3.0 in) bore and 120.7 mm (4.75 in) stroke. The following year saw the slightly smaller Jordan J Line Eight with a 4,040 cc (246.5 cu in) Continental unit. Both engines had five main bearings and a single Stromberg carburettor.

Jordan survived the 1929 stock market crash, but financial problems following the disastrous launch of a 'premium' model, allied with increasing competition, saw the business close a few years later.

Although a relatively minor manufacturer, Jordan was notable for two things; firstly, it was probably the first car company to give its models evocative names, which included Tomboy, Playboy and Friendly Three (the marketing slogan was 'seats two, three if they're really friendly!'). Secondly, in an era where most cars were black, Jordan offered a dazzling spectrum of colours including Apache Red, Egyptian Bronze and Chinese Blue. In that respect, but probably that respect only, it was years ahead of its time.

ABOVE: A 1929 Jordan 90 engine, a three-quarter view showing the Lanchester damper below the fan.

OPPOSITE: A 1929 Jordan 90 four-door sedan.

JORDAN EIGHT MODELS

Model		A Great Line Eight	J Line Eight
Year introduced		1925	1926
Displacement	cc	4,402	4,040
	cu in	268.6	246.5
Power output	bhp (max)	74	85
	kW	54	62
	@ rpm	3,500	3,500
Specific output	bhp/litre	16.8	21.0
	bhp/cu in	0.28	0.34
	kW/litre	12.3	15.3
	kW/cu in	0.20	0.25
Compression ratio		5.8:1	5.8:1
Bore	mm	76.2	73
	inches	3	2.87
Stroke	mm	120.7	120.7
	inches	4.75	4.75
Bore:stroke ratio		63%	60%
Valve gear		s/v 16v	s/v 16v
Carburettor		1xStromberg	1xStromberg
Main bearings		5	5

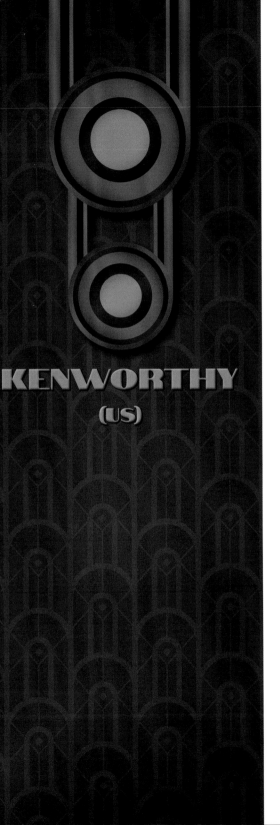

KENWORTHY
(US)

enworthy was based in Mishawaka, Indiana. Together with Duesenberg they were the first American manufacturers to offer a straight eight engine car. In 1921 it was also one of the first to offer four-wheel braking. The Kenworthy Line-O-Eight bore a close resemblance to the contemporary Rolls-Royce.

The Line-O-Eight used Kenworthy's own engine, a 4,633 cc (282.7 cu in) unit with bore and stroke of 76.2 mm (3.0 in) and 127 mm (5.0 in) giving a bore:stroke ratio of 60%. The engine had overhead inlet and side exhaust valves, one each per cylinder, a single Stromberg carburettor, and the crankshaft had just three bearings.

ABOVE: With the 1921 Kenworthy Line-O-Eight, the company deliberately imitated the radiator design of the contemporary Rolls-Royce to boost their image of quality. This is a rare contemporary photograph of a Line-O-Eight. This early 1921 example does not feature four-wheel braking.

LEFT: In the 1921 Kenworthy Line-O-Eight, the engine featured overhead inlet and side exhaust valves, and internal inlet ducting inside the block from the single carburettor.

The Kissel Motor Car Company was founded in 1906 by Louis Kissel and his two sons George and William. The family was originally from Prussia, Louis's father having emigrated to the United States in 1872. After various business ventures including manufacturing and distributing farming machinery, manufacturing outboard motor engines and house building, the Kissels started the car company and began production in 1907. The cars were marketed as KisselKar's, and from 1907 until 1931, when the business closed its doors, around 35,000 automobiles were made, although only 150 are believed to exist today. In addition to cars, the company was well known as a manufacturer of fire engines, hearses, taxis and lorries ranging in capacity from 0.75 tons to 5 tons.

Their first prototype car was a four-cylinder runabout, which entered production in 1906/7 using Beaver engines. The cars were noted for high quality, value and performance and the company even launched an ambitious 'double six' model in 1917 with a 6,379 cc (389.3 cu in) V12 ohv engine delivering a modest 82 bhp (61 kW). After the First World War the company struggled a little, but business picked up in the 'roaring twenties' with a range of high-quality sporty cars, including in

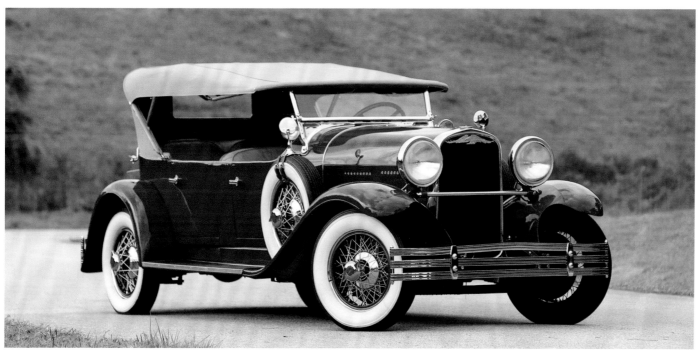

A 1929 classic-looking, four-door drophead Kissel 8-95.

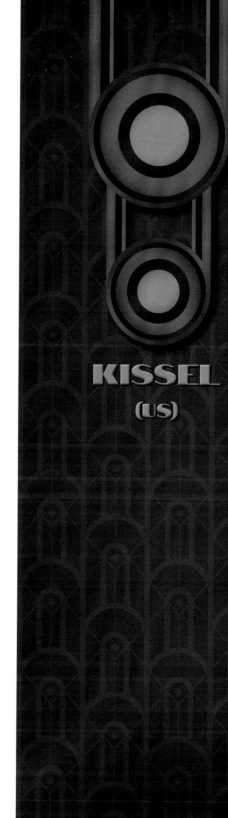

KISSEL
(US)

KISSEL EIGHT MODELS

Model		8-75	8-65	8-95	8-126
Year introduced		1924	1927	1927	1930
Displacement	cc	5,317	4,049	4,049	4,892
	cu in	324.5	247.1	247.1	298.6
Power output	bhp (max)	71	65	95	126
	kW	53	48	70	64
	@ rpm	3,000	3,000	3,200	3,200
Specific output	bhp/litre	13.4	16.1	23.5	25.8
	bhp/cu in	0.22	0.26	0.38	0.42
	kW/litre	10.0	11.9	17.3	13.1
	kW/cu in	0.16	0.19	0.28	0.21
Bore	mm	84	73	73	80
	inches	3.31	2.87	2.87	3.15
Stroke	mm	120	120	120	120
	inches	4.72	4.72	4.72	4.72
Bore:stroke ratio		70%	61%	61%	67%
Valve gear		s/v 16v	s/v 16v	s/v 16v	s/v 16v
Carburettor		1xSchebler	1xSchebler	1xSchebler	1xSchebler

particular the early six-cylinder Gold Bug which was popular with leading film stars of the time. In 1924 a straight eight version appeared, powered by a Lycoming engine.

The 8-75 model had a 5,317 cc (324.5 cu in) engine with a bore of 84 mm (3.31 in) and a stroke of 120 mm (4.72 in). The Lycoming unit was a straight-forward side valve with two valves per cylinder. Output was around 71 bhp (53 kW) at 3,000 rpm, and the 8-75 was good for 75 mph (121 kph).

A sportier version, the 8-65 (also using the same Golden Bug name as its six-cylinder cousin) was also produced with a 4,049 cc (247.1 cu in) Lycoming engine of similar stroke to the 8-75 but a smaller bore of 73 mm (2.87 in). With a smaller displacement this unit produced 65 bhp (48 kW) at 3,200 rpm, but was slightly faster than the 8-75 being good for 78 mph (126 kph).

A more powerful 8-95 appeared later, with the same capacity as the 8-65 but tuned to give 95 bhp (48 kW) at the slightly higher engine speed of 3,200 rpm. The 8-95 was also known as the White Eagle. Finally in 1930, the 8-126 Series appeared with power output increased to 126 bhp (64 kW) and displacement up by 843 cc (52 cu in) at 4,892 cc (298.6 cu in) by virtue of an increased bore. This would be the last model Kissel made before going into receivership in 1931. It is a shame that Kissel has descended into relative obscurity in the classic car world, and that the survival rate is an extremely low 0.4%.

Although basically quite a simple engine, the 5.3-litre (324.5 cu in) Lycoming engine in the 1929 Kissel 8-95 looks very smart indeed. **INSET:** The inlet/exhaust side of the same Lycoming engine.

The La Salle was manufactured and marketed by the Cadillac Division of General Motors. It was positioned as the second most prestigious model from GM, and priced significantly below Cadillac. Whereas Cadillac has never had a straight eight model, La Salle did, for three years at least.

Starting in 1934 La Salle was given a degree of freedom from Cadillac, and this resulted in the development of a straight eight model, the Series 50. The chassis was basically a Cadillac 355D, but equipped with a 3,940 cc (240.4 cu in) side valve engine sourced from Oldsmobile, but specially made for La Salle. With a bore of 76.2 mm

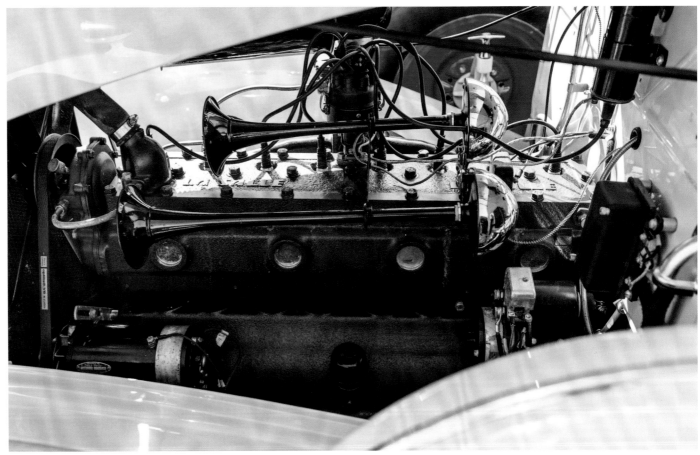

The left side of the 3,940 cc (240.4 cu in) engine in the Series 50 which was made by Oldsmobile specially for La Salle.

(3.0 in), a stroke of 108 mm (4.25 in), 16 valves and a compression ratio of 6.5:1 it delivered 95 bhp (71 kW) at 3,700 rpm, and was fed by a single Stromberg carburettor. The crankshaft was carried in five main bearings.

In 1936 the engine was enlarged to 5,527 cc (337.3 cu in) by increasing the bore and stroke to 87.7 mm x 114.3 mm (3.45 in x 4.5 in) resulting in enhanced power of 125 bhp (93 kW) at a slightly lower 3,400 rpm.

But sales of the Series 50 were not growing at the same rate as other brands within GM's portfolio, and in 1937 Cadillac decided to take tighter control of its La Salle subsidiary, and most significantly changed the engine in the Series 50 to a Cadillac V8. La Salle's brief journey into the world of the straight eight came to an abrupt end.

A 1935 La Salle Series 50, with elegant convertible coupe coachwork. The chassis was basically a Cadillac but equipped with a straight eight engine, an engine format never used by Cadillac itself.

LA SALLE EIGHT MODELS

Model		Series 50	Series 50 (2)
Year introduced		1934	1936
Displacement	cc	3,940	5,527
	cu in	240.4	337.3
Power output	bhp (max)	95	125
	kW	71	93
	@ rpm	3,700	3,400
Specific output	bhp/litre	24.1	22.6
	bhp/cu in	0.40	0.37
	kW/litre	18.0	16.8
	kW/cu in	0.30	0.28
Compression ratio		6.5:1	6.5:1
Bore	mm	76.2	87.7
	inches	3	3.45
Stroke	mm	108	114.3
	inches	4.25	4.5
Bore:stroke ratio		71%	77%
Valve gear		s/v 16v	s/v 16v
Carburettor		1xStromberg	1xStromberg
Main bearings		5	5

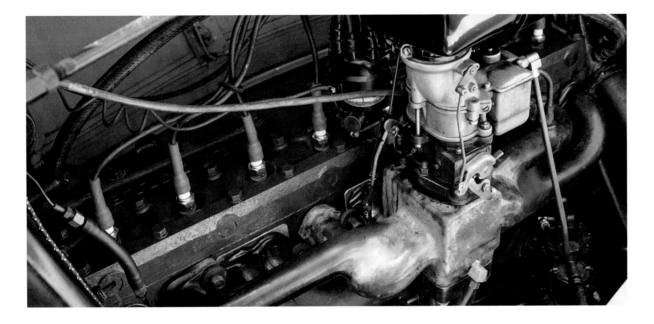

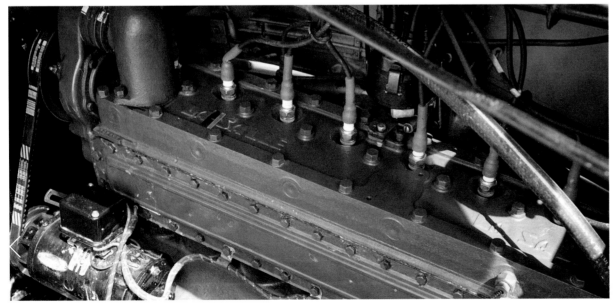

TOP: The inlet/exhaust side of the Series 50's engine with its single Stromberg downdraft carburettor. **BOTTOM:** Although made by Oldsmobile, the Series 50's engine proudly displays the La Salle name on the flathead.

OPPOSITE: A contemporary advertisement for the La Salle emphasising 'The New Extra Value' of the vehicle.

THE NEW
EXTRA VALUE

La Salle

Distinctive BEAUTY AND STYLE

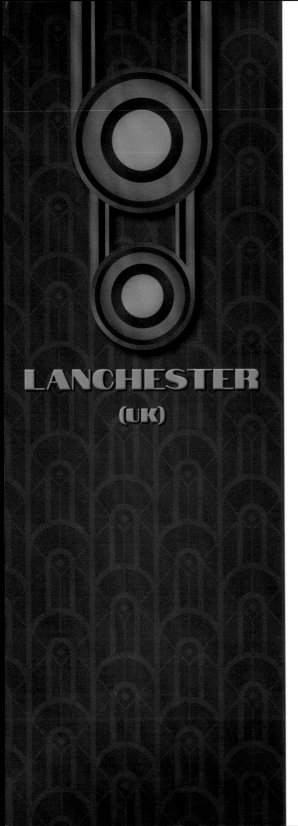

LANCHESTER (UK)

Lanchester was always a radical British car company, and it comes as no surprise that it had a straight eight on the books between the wars.

The Lanchester brothers started work on their first car as early as 1895, and started selling to the public in 1901. The cars were unconventional with steering by a side lever rather than a wheel. The brakes were revolutionary, being true disc brakes, albeit mechanically operated and on the front wheels only. Up to the First World War they produced a series of four and six-cylinder models, becoming increasingly conventional.

After the First World War the company adopted a single model policy, and the pre-war 40 was re-introduced with a 6.2-litre six-cylinder unit, now with a sohc rather than side valves, but still with epicyclic gears and a worm drive rear axle. The 40 was an extremely expensive car, more expensive even than the Rolls-Royce Silver Ghost. As the market was limited, Lanchester introduced a smaller model, the Twenty One, in 1924 that was a 3.1-litre six, now with a conventional gearbox. This model grew into the Twenty Three in 1926, and the aged Forty was finally replaced by the straight eight Thirty in 1928.

This straight eight marked the final entry into conventionality for Lanchester. The Thirty had a sohc engine of 4,436 cc (270 cu in), with a detachable head, which delivered 82bhp (61 kW) at 2,800 rpm. It had a bore of 78.7 mm (3.1 in) and a stroke of 114 mm (4.5 in) and 10 main bearings, and featured a dual choke carburettor, dual ignition and servo brakes. Depending upon bodywork, it was good for 75-90 mph. The car was extremely expensive, as all Lanchesters had been; in 1929 the chassis alone cost £1,325 (£79,240 in 2020 values), a Hooper bodied limousine £2,300 (£137,540 in 2020 values) and a Wendover coupe de ville was listed at £2,435 (£145,600 at present values). Mainly because of the high price, the Lanchester 30 remained a rare car, only 126 being made before the company encountered financial problems in 1930, the overdraft was called in, and the business was sold to BSA in early 1931. Thereafter Lanchester became a junior 'sibling' of Daimler, and only smaller models such as the four-cylinder Ten, and the six-cylinder Fourteen and Eighteen, were sold under the Lanchester brand. After the Second World War only the Ten and Fourteen struggled on until the Lanchester name disappeared completely in 1956.

The Lanchester straight eight did enjoy brief popularity in royal circles, the Duke of York (later to be King George VI) buying three for personal use by himself and his wife Lady Elizabeth Bowes-Lyon to drive their family around. For non-state occasions he always used Lanchester cars.

In 1939, as King, he purchased two more Lanchester straight eights, a limousine and a landaulette for state occasions. In reality, however, these two cars were not really Lanchesters at all, but 4.5-litre straight eight Daimlers, which were rebadged as Lanchesters because the King preferred the more modest image of this make over Daimlers. As with several other manufacturers, the foray into the straight eight territory came at a bad time for Lanchester, and the Thirty remains a rare animal.

OPPOSITE: The 4.5-litre Daimler engine in the 'Lanchester' 32. The 1939 Lanchester 32 was a 'fake' Lanchester, because in reality it was a Daimler badged as a Lanchester. This was because the Duke of York (later King George VI) preferred the more modest image of the Lanchester. Only 126 Lanchester 32s were made.

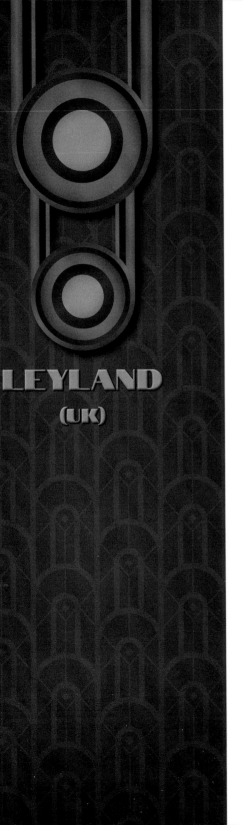

eyland was an interesting small player in the straight eight market. The Leyland Eight was designed by J.G. Parry-Thomas and Reid Railton with the specific and sole aim of exceeding the excellence of the Rolls-Royce Silver Ghost, and was the first straight eight produced in the UK. Parry-Thomas was chief engineer at Leyland and Railton was his assistant. It is possible they achieved their goal; reports at the time were highly complimentary about the Eight, comparing it favourably against contemporary Rolls-Royce and Napier vehicles. With a chassis-only cost in 1920 of £2500 (equivalent to around £119,000 today), and with bodywork easily doubling this cost, it should have been a superb offering! In total just 14-18 were

made, making it an extremely exclusive car. Only one is known to survive, this being the one at the British Motor Museum at Gaydon in Warwickshire, UK. This vehicle was actually assembled by Thomson and Taylor from spares in 1929 six years after production ceased.

The 1920 model had a 6,968cc (425.2 cu in) straight eight engine with a bore and stroke of 89 mm x 140 mm (3.5 in x 5.51 in). It was quite advanced in having a single overhead camshaft, hemispherical combustion chambers, a triple eccentric cam drive, Delco coil ignition (rather than a magneto, which was more usual at the time), a six-bearing crankshaft and dry sump lubrication. The little ends were lubricated via ducts in the connecting rods. With a 5:1 compression ratio and a single Zenith carburettor it delivered 115 bhp (86 kW). Interestingly the engine used leaf valve springs, rather than coil springs, and these provided a degree of desmodromic action. The cylinder block and the upper half of the dry sump crankcase were cast in one piece.

For 1921 the engine displacement was increased to 7,266cc (443.4 cu in) by increasing the stroke from 140 mm to 146mm. Power increased to 145 bhp (108 kW) by virtue of twin Zenith carburettors, one on each side of the engine. Under normal operation just one of these carburettors was used, the second Zenith being brought into action via a lever on the steering wheel when extra power was needed. Use of the second carburettor increased the bhp per litre by 20% from a modest 4% increase in engine displacement.

In 1922 Parry-Thomas left Leyland and set up premises at Brooklands, taking possibly three chassis and a large quantity of spares. At Brooklands he constructed the Leyland-Thomas Special, based on the Leyland Eight. After Parry-Thomas's death on Pendine Sands in that car the facility was taken over by Thomson and Taylor who then built the car now at Gaydon from the spares they inherited.

OPPOSITE: One of the rare Leyland Eights, of which just 14-18 made. This one is in the British Motor Heritage Centre at Gaydon. It is powered by a 7-litre ohc eight with hemispherical combustion chambers and two Zenith carburettors.

LEYLAND EIGHT MODELS

Model		1920 EIGHT	1921 EIGHT
Displacement	cc	6,968	7,266
	cu in	425.2	443.4
Power output	bhp	115	145
	kW	86	108
	@ rpm	2,500	3,000
Specific output	bhp/litre	16.5	19.9
	bhp/cu in	0.27	0.33
	kW/litre	12.3	14.9
	kW/cu in	0.2	0.24
Compression ratio		5:1	5:1
Bore	mm	89	89
	inches	3.5	3.5
Stroke	mm	140	146
	inches	5.51	5.75
Bore:stroke ratio		64%	61%
Valve gear		sohc	sohc
Carburettor		1x Zenith	2xZenith*
No of main bearings		6	6
Lubrication		dry sump	dry sump

second carburettor selectable as required

LOCOMOBILE
(US)

ocomobile began as a company building steam cars, hence the name Locomobile, a cross between locomotive and automobile. In 1904 it started producing internal combustion-engined cars, and specialised in expensive high-quality vehicles from the outset. The 1908 Locomobile forty Runabout sold for $4,750, equivalent to around $130,000 today, or thirty Model T Fords in its day.

In 1922 Locomobile was acquired by Durant Motors, but Durant continued to use the Locomobile name for its top of the range vehicles, including the successful six-cylinder Model 48 which pre-dated the takeover. In 1925 the first new Locomobile under Durant's ownership was launched, the 8-66 Junior Eight with a straight eight ohv, five bearing engine designed in-house but built under licence by Continental. The 3,260 cc (198.9 cu in) unit

had a bore of 68 mm (2.69 in), a stroke of 102 mm (4.0 in), and a single Stromberg carburettor, delivering 66 bhp (49 kW). This was followed by the 8-70, and in 1929 new 8-86 and 8-88 models appeared, also Continental powered. But the focus on straight eights in the difficult economic climate of the late 1920s could not sustain the business, and by 1933 the brand had disappeared.

ABOVE: The Continental engine in a 1927 Locomobile 8-70.
OPPOSITE: The 1927 Locomobile 8-70 was a very expensive car launched at a challenging time for the luxury car market.

LOCOMOBILE EIGHT MODELS

Model		8-66 Junior 8	8-70	8-86
Year introduced		1925	1928	1929
Displacement	cc	3,260	4,044	4,895
	cu in	198.9	246.7	298.6
Power output	bhp (max)	66	70	90
	kW	49	52	67
	@ rpm	3,000	3,000	3,200
Specific output	bhp/litre	20.2	17.3	18.4
	bhp/cu in	0.33	0.28	0.30
	kW/litre	15.0	12.9	13.7
	kW/cu in	0.25	0.21	0.22
Compression ratio		5.0:1	5.0:1	5.0:1
Bore	mm	68	73	82
	inches	2.69	2.88	3.25
Stroke	mm	102	121	114
	inches	4.00	4.75	4.50
Bore:stroke ratio		67%	60%	72%
Valve gear		ohv	ohv	ohv
Carburettor		Stromberg	Schebler	Schebler
Main bearings		5	5	5

MARENDAZ (UK)

arendaz cars were made between 1926 and 1936, and for the last four of these years were manufactured in the same factory in Maidenhead, Berkshire that had been used by Dennistoun Burney to make his Streamline.

Donald Marendaz had served an apprenticeship with Siddeley Deasey before The First World War. After the war he joined Alvis, but was sacked from there, and then started a company called Marseal manufacturing gearboxes for the Emscote car business. Emscote did not take all the gearboxes Marseal made, and the surplus gearboxes were mated with Coventry Climax engines and formed the basis of a new complete car, the Marseal. Before Marseal closed for business in 1925 it is believed around 1,200 cars may have been made.

After a brief break from motorcars, Marendaz started DMK Marendaz Ltd, initially in Brixton, London. The Marendaz cars were sporty, good-looking cars rather in the Bentley mould. Initially they had side valve four-cylinder Anzani engines of either 1,496 cc (91 cu in) or 1,094 cc (67 cu in). Then in 1929, the company rather surprisingly announced a straight eight model, the 14/55 Special, which used a special Anzani crank married to a Marendaz designed block, based on a pair of Anzani 'fours'. It had overhead input and side exhaust valves. At just 1,495 cc (91 cu in) it was one of the smallest straight eights to date, with each cylinder being just 187 cc (11 cu in). It is not recorded how many were made, but the number was certainly small. In addition, a supercharged version of the 14/55 was developed, although it is not certain any production examples were ever made.

From 1932, until the business closed in 1936, it produced only six-cylinder models. In total around 80-120 Marendaz cars were produced, but only a few were 'eights'.

Today Marmon is probably best known for its V16, a car the company had hoped would be the world's first production V16. The company had started to develop this car in 1927, but technical problems delayed the launch until 1931 by which time Cadillac had stolen the V16 'crown'. Marmon is less well-known for its excellent straight eights.

Marmon started producing cars in 1902 when Howard Marmon built for his own use an air-cooled V-twin. The next year, he built six V-fours which were sold mostly to friends, but by 1905 production was running at 25 cars, and that year a one-off V6 prototype was constructed. In 1909 the Model 32 appeared, and would be the company's mainstay until 1914. In 1915 the six-cylinder ohv Model 34 was launched, featuring aluminium block and crankcase, which helped establish Marmon's reputation for performance and quality. But it was expensive, selling for around 40% more than a similar specification Cadillac.

At the time Marmon's main business was manufacturing milling machinery, and as a sideline the motor car production was probably not receiving the attention it deserved, and sales were disappointing. As a consequence, the car business was spun off with a new management team who decided, much to the disgust of Howard Marmon, to develop a medium-priced straight eight to gain volume sales. Concerned that a 'cut price' Marmon would damage the car's image, Howard Marmon no longer took an active part in the car business.

The medium-priced car, known as the Little Marmon, appeared in 1927 and featured a 3,144 cc (190 cu in) L-head straight eight engine delivering 64 bhp (48 kW).

A 1930 Marmon Roosevelt Sedan.

By 1928 it was decided that the name Little Marmon was not very flattering, and it was renamed the 68 Series, with a slightly larger engine of 3,341 cc (201.9 cu in), but still a side valve unit. There was also a 78 Series with overhead valves and a slightly larger 3,540 cc (216 cu in) engine.

In 1929 the company launched the Roosevelt as a separate model. This was a lower-priced Marmon, the first straight eight in the United States to sell for under $1,000. In 1931, the separate Roosevelt brand identity was abandoned, and the Roosevelt became the Model 70 Marmon. More than 22,000 of this model were made.

In 1930 sales fell by over 60%, and the business never properly recovered. For 1931 and 1932 the company offered the 69 Series and the 79 Series. The 69 Series had a 3,440 cc (209.9 cu in) engine delivering 84 bhp (62 kW), whilst the 79 Series had a larger 4,954 cc (302.2 cu in) power unit delivering 110 bhp (81 kW). Also, from 1930, the company offered the Big Eight with a capacity of 5,166 cc (315.2 cu in), a bore of 83 mm (3.25 in) and a stroke of 121 mm (4.75 in), which delivered 124 bhp (92 kW) at 3,400 rpm.

Marmon finally launched its V16 in 1931/2 after a long delay in development, and whilst it should have been a success it was well over a year behind the offering from Cadillac, and never realised its true potential. It carried a high price tag of $5,100-$5,400 ($77,000-$82,000 at 2020 values).

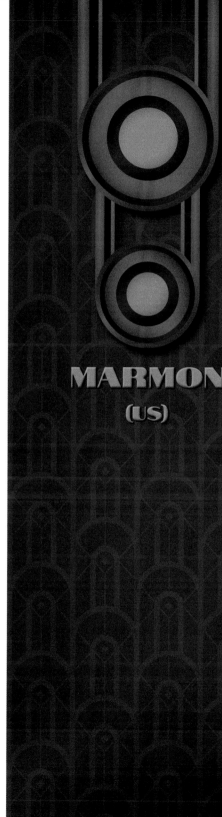

MARMON
(US)

MARMON EIGHT MODELS

Model		Little Marmon	68	78	Roosevelt	Big Eight	69	79
Year introduced		1927	1928	1928	1929	1930	1931	1931
Displacement	cc	3,144	3,341	3,540	3,309	5,166	3,440	4,954
	cu in	190	201.9	216.8	201.9	315.2	209.9	302.2
Power output	bhp (max)	64	72	86	77	124	84	110
	kW	48	54	64	57	92	62	81
	@ rpm	3,200	3,200	3,400	3,400	3,400	3,400	3,400
Specific output	bhp/litre	20.4	21.6	24.3	23.3	24.0	24.4	22.2
	bhp/cu in	0.34	0.36	0.40	0.38	0.39	0.40	0.36
	kW/litre	15.3	16.2	18.1	17.2	17.8	18.0	16.4
	kW/cu in	0.25	0.27	0.30	0.28	0.29	0.30	0.27
Compression ratio		5.25:1	5.25:1	5.5:1	5.25:1	5.5:1	5.25:1	5.5:1
Bore	mm	70	70	75	70	83	71	81
	inches	2.75	2.75	2.94	2.75	3.25	2.81	3.19
Stroke	mm	102	108	102	108	121	108	121
	inches	4.0	4.25	4.0	4.25	4.75	4.25	4.75
Bore:stroke ratio		69%	65%	74%	65%	69%	66%	67%
Valve gear		L head	L head	L head	L head	L head	L head	L head
Carburettor		Schebler	Stromberg	Stromberg	Stromberg	Schebler	Schebler	Schebler
Main bearings		5	5	5	5	5	5	5

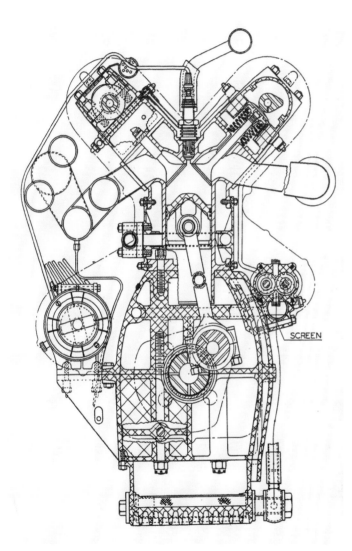

A transverse section through the engine of the Maserati 8CTF.

MASERATI
(ITALY)

Although Maserati never made a straight eight road car, it is ironic that the first car to bear the Maserati name was a straight eight.

When Alfieri Maserati was young, he had a successful career racing with a Tipo 20 Diatto. When he was 36, he was invited to join Diatto to help build a Grand Prix team to beat the all-conquering Fiat 2-litre straight eights. Unfortunately, the resulting GP Diatto 8C 2000s were not a success, and when the company was reorganised the racing team was abandoned. But Alfieri and his brother continued development of a GP car, and the resulting Maserati Tipo 26 was the first car to carry the name. It is possible that the Tipo 26 was in fact just the GP Diatto 8C 2000, virtually unaltered.

The straight eight engine was light, being constructed mostly of alloy. Originally the combustion chambers were lined with hemispherical steel shells, but these caused problems, so Maserati mounted the valves directly into the alloy head, a solution which worked well and became a feature of many subsequent models. The engine had a dry sump and just five main bearings, as was also used by Ballot. There were twin camshafts with the valves angled at 90 degrees. The engine was supercharged, with the Roots blower attached directly to the front of the engine delivering air to a single carburettor. Two features of the engine were unusual. Firstly, the connecting rods were tubular, a feature found on the aero engines from Isotta Fraschini and Hispano Suiza at the time. Secondly the cylinder head was secured by long bolts which went down through the block to the crankcase. With a displacement of 1,491 cc (91 cu in) the engine delivered a healthy 125 bhp (94 kW).

In 1927 a 2-litre version appeared, and in 1929 a tiny 1,078 cc (66 cu in) variant with an 11.4 psi boost was added. In 1938, the 8 CTF's straight eight engine was formed from two separate 'four' blocks sharing the same crankcase.

The 1940 8 CL marked a significant step forward, featuring four valves per cylinder and a 'square' format (bore the same as stroke) whereas most straight eights were heavily under-square to reduce the length of the engine. The supercharger boost was increased to 18.5 psi. There was also a three-litre version using two of the 4 CL models blocks.

To say there never was a road-going straight eight Maserati is not entirely true. Two two-seat Tipo 26 cars were constructed to compete in the Mille Miglia. These cars, known as Tipo 26, had to be road legal to compete in the race.

ABOVE: The Maserati Tipo 26, the very first car to carry the Maserati name.

LEFT: Alfieri Maserati at the wheel of a Diatto Type 30, the car which would evolve into the Maserati Tipo 26.

The Mathis business, founded by Emile Mathis, began life as a successful car dealership in Strasbourg, handling Fiat, de Dietrich and Panhard Levassor vehicles. In 1904 it started selling three models of car designed for Mathis by Ettore Bugatti (also Strasbourg-based) and marketed under the name Hermes. These were 28 hp, 40 hp and 98 hp Mercedes-like vehicles.

The first proper Mathis model appeared in 1910. This was followed just before the war by two smaller models, the Babylette of 1,100 cc (67 cu in) and the Baby of 1,300 cc (79 cu in) which were a great success. After the First World War the business grew rapidly, and

by 1927 it had become the fourth largest car company in France. Attempting to compete with Citroen, Mathis widened its range to include a 1,188 cc (72 cu in) 'six' in 1923 and an 'eight' in 1925. But this move was a mistake, and from 1927 the company followed a single model strategy initially with the four-cylinder side valve MY and then in 1928 the 2,288 cc (140 cu in) six-cylinder Emysix. A short-lived 3-litre straight eight appeared in 1931 called the FOH, followed by a more successful 1,445 cc (88 cu in) 'four' called the Emyquatre. There then followed another 'eight' the Emyhuit, but by then the company was in rapid decline, and the Mathis factories were closed.

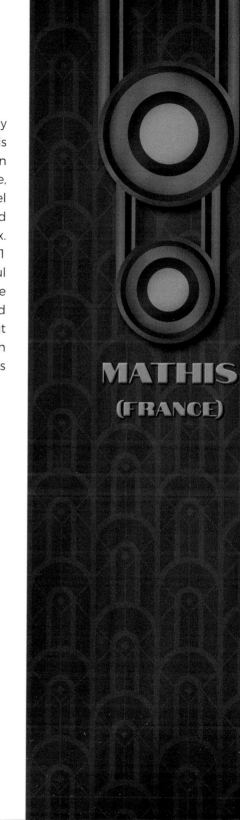

MATHIS
(FRANCE)

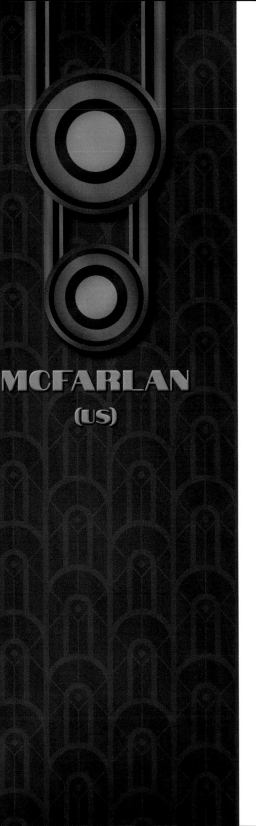

MCFARLAN

(US)

The McFarlan Carriage Company had been founded in 1856 by English-born John McFarlan (1822-1909). His grandson started the McFarlan Motor Corporation and it produced its first model in 1910. The younger McFarlan ran the business throughout its 19-year existence. In the early years it had moderate racing success, coming 19th in the 1912 Indy 500 and 25th in the 1911 race.

The road cars used off-the-shelf Lycoming side valve engines, both 'sixes' and 'eights'. The straight eight engine used throughout the 19 years of 'eight' production never changed and was the standard 4,712 cc (287.5 cu in) unit used by so many other manufacturers. It featured a bore of 81 mm (3.19 in), a stroke of 114.3 mm (4.5 in), a five bearing crank and a single Schebler carburettor. It was basic but sound.

McFarlan cars, especially the earlier 'sixes', were favoured by many celebrities including Jack Dempsey, Al Capone (who had two!) and Fatty Arbuckle.

In 1928 the company filed for bankruptcy.

ABOVE: The right side of the Lycoming engine in the 1927 McFarlan Boattail. **OPPOSITE:** The 'off the shelf' 4,712 cc (287.5 cu in) Lycoming engine, as used in all McFarlan cars. **INSET:** A 1927 McFarlan Boattail, a car favoured by many celebrities... and gangsters!

MERCEDES-BENZ (GERMANY)

The history of Mercedes-Benz is too well-known to require summarising here. Mercedes-Benz was an important player in the straight eight sector from 1928 until the Second World War, and even had a straight eight after the war in the shape of the sensational 300 SLR.

Aside from the SLR and the unusual six wheeled W31, there were four main 'families' of Mercedes-Benz straight eight cars:

◆ The Tipo 460/500 Nurburg series (W08)
◆ The Tipo 350 MannheiM-Series (W19, WS10)
◆ The 770 series (W07, W150)
◆ The 500K/540K series (W29)
◆ Tipo 460/500 Nurburg series (W08)

The Tipo 460 Nurburg, launched in 1928, was Mercedes-Benz first straight eight, and the series would remain in production until 1939, making it Mercedes longest running model series. Mercedes wanted a rival for the Horch 8 which was very successful at the 'top end' of the market. The rush to develop a rival meant that development work was limited, and at launch the 460 looked old fashioned beside the Horch. With its overhung chassis it was tall and staid, and was not a great success. It was said that it took Mercedes six years to sell off its stockpile of 460s. The car had a 4,622 cc (281 cu in) side valve engine, with a bore of 80 mm (3.15 in) and a stroke of 115 mm (4.53 in). With a compression ratio of just 5.0:1 and a single Zenith carburettor it developed a modest 79 bhp (59 kW) at 3,400 rpm. Torque was 175 ft lbs (237 Nm) at 1,200 rpm. Maximum speed was only around 63 mph (100 kph).

For 1929 the 460 Nurburg was given a major makeover. Mechanically it remained the same with the 4,622 cc (280.7 cu in) side valve engine, but the car had a much more up-to-date appearance with an under-slung chassis. Also, from 1929, an overdrive became an option, but there was still no synchromesh and it was still easily outsold by the Horch 8.

The 460 evolved in 1931 into the 500 Nurburg, with a larger nine bearing engine of 4,918 cc (300.1 cu in), a bore of 82.5 mm (3.25 in), a stroke of 115 mm (4.53 in) and a twin choke downdraft Solex carburettor. Power was up at 99 bhp (74 kW) at 3,100 rpm. Top speed was increased to a still modest 69 mph (110 kph).

In 1932 the Nurburg name was dropped and the car became just the Tipo 500. The engine remained the same, but slightly larger wheels gave a top speed of 75 mph (120 kph). In 1936, until the series ceased in 1939, power was increased to 108 bhp (81 kW) by virtue of an increase in the compression ratio from 5:1 to 6:1. The 500 could now achieve 76 mph (123 kph).

3,824 Tipo 460/500 were sold between 1928 and 1939. In contrast the Horch 8 sold over 12,000 in the same period. Annual sales of the 460/500 series declined from 87 in 1936 to just 51 by 1939.

TIPO 350 MANNHEIM-SERIES (W19, WS10, W22)

The MannheiM-Series of cars first appeared in 1929, equipped with a 3,689 cc (225.1 cu in) side valve 'six' engine. In 1932 the 380S (WS10) version appeared, powered by a 3,820 cc (233.1 cu in) side valve straight eight with a bore of 78 mm (3.07 in) and a stroke of 100 mm (3.94 in). Power output was 80 bhp (59 kW) giving a claimed top speed of 75 mph (120 kph).

The W19 380S was virtually the same as the WS10, but now had independent swing axle rear suspension. Slightly raised compression increased power to 84 bhp (63 kW)

The W22 380, which appeared in 1933, started life with the same 3,820 cc (233.1 cu in) engine of the WS10 but was equipped with overhead valves. A new twin carburettor was fitted, whilst a supercharger became an option. The least powerful non-supercharged version produced 89 bhp (66 kW) at 3,200 rpm. With a supercharger output increased to 118 bhp (88 kW) at 3,400 rpm and top speed rose to 81 mph (130 kph). The 'hottest' version, producing 138 bhp (103 kW), gained the 'K' suffix to denote the supercharger. The 380K could achieve up to 90 mph (145 kph).

770 SERIES (W07, W150)

The 770 series introduced in 1930, and often referred to as the Grosser Mercedes, was the successor to the 6,240 cc (380.8 cu in) six-cylinder 630 which first appeared in 1926. The first of the series, the W07, had a 7,655 cc (467.1 cu in) overhead cam engine with a bore of 95 mm (3.74 in), a stroke of 135 mm (5.31 in) and a compression ratio of 6.1:1. It produced 150 bhp (112 kW) at 2,800 rpm. With the optional Roots-type supercharger, which only engaged at full throttle, power was boosted to 200 bhp (149 kW) and the top speed was then 99 mph (160 kph). It had been found that the engine and cooling system could not cope with permanent supercharger engagement, so it only worked 'when needed'. 117 of this model were built.

An updated 770, the W150, came in 1938. This had essentially the same engine, but it was tuned for extra power. Without the

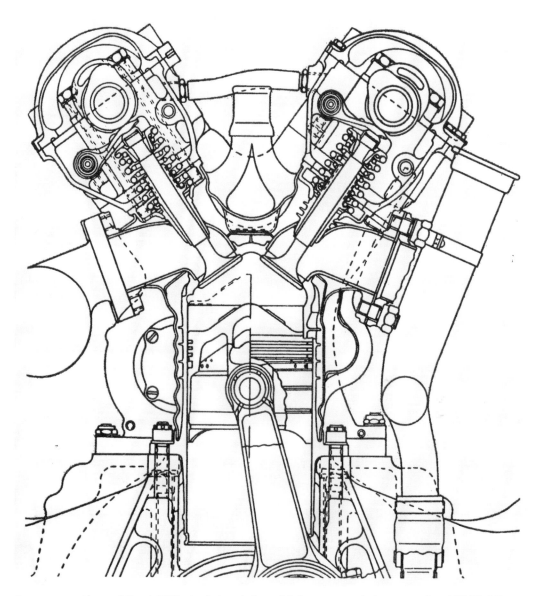

A cross section of the M125 straight eight which powered the amazing W125 GP car. With 5,660 cc and supercharger it delivered over 600 bhp.

supercharger it delivered 153 bhp (114 kW) at 3,000 rpm. With the optional supercharger engaged the output rose to 230 bhp (172 kW) at 3,200 rpm. This version of the 770 series was never on general sale, it being reserved for senior government and military staff, and was the favoured transport of senior Nazis. Only 88 were built.

500K/540K SERIES (W29)

The 500K, which appeared in 1934, effectively replaced the supercharged 380. It used the same independent rear suspension as the later 380s, and therefore had much better handling and was more comfortable than the earlier six-cylinder S/SS/SSK sporting models. The 5,018 cc (306.2 cu in) engine could, with the Roots-type supercharger engaged, deliver 160 bhp (120 kW) giving a maximum speed of 100 mph (160 kph), albeit at the expense of a fuel consumption of 9.4 mpg (7.8 US mpg). But the 500K was never for the impecunious! The engine had a bore of 86 mm (3.39 in), a stroke of 108 mm (4.25 in) and a fairly modest compression ratio of 5.5:1. It used a single Mercedes-made carburettor.

In 1936 the 540K appeared. The engine of the 500K was enlarged to 5,401 cc (329.6 cu in) by increasing both bore and stroke by around 2%, and with twin carburettors could deliver 115 bhp (86 kW). On the 540K the supercharger could be engaged manually (for short periods only) or by fully depressing the accelerator, at which the engine would deliver 180 bhp (130 kW) giving a top speed of 110 mph (170 kph). As with the 770 the engine could not be run with the supercharger permanently engaged because of cooling problems.

There was a prototype 580K produced in 1939 with an enlarged 5,800 cc (353.9 cu in) nine bearing engine delivering 197 bhp (142 kW) at 3,400 rpm, and torque of 324 ft lbs (439 Nm) at 2,200 rpm. The compression ratio was 6.5:1. Further development of this model was curtailed by the war.

W31 TYPE G4

The W31 was a specialised six-wheeled off-road vehicle produced from 1934. It was not a mundane 'jeep'-type vehicle, but rather a transport mode for the most senior ranks of the Nazi regime, as they were considered too expensive and exclusive for mere military use. Initially they had a 5,018 cc (306.2 cu in) straight eight delivering 100 bhp (74 kW). The top speed was only 42 mph (67 kph), this being limited to a large extent by the type of all-terrain tyres fitted. Just 11 examples were made. In 1937 a more powerful 5,252 cc (320.5 cu in) variant appeared, and a further 16 cars manufactured. In 1938 thirty more of an even more powerful version were built, with 5,401 cc (329.6 cu in) engines delivering 110 bhp (81 kW). These vehicles were used by Hitler and the Nazi staff for parades.

300 SLR

By 1955 the straight eight had almost become the Dodo of car engines. In the US, the home of the flathead straight eight, the straight eight was virtually dead, replaced by the more compact V8. Even Packard, one of the most loyal straight eight manufacturers, had abandoned this engine format by 1954. Yet in 1955 Mercedes announced the 300 SLR sports racer, with a straight eight of 2,982 cc (182 cu in) based on the W196 Formula One car, and delivering up to 310 bhp (230 kW). The 300 SLR was, in effect, a two-seat version of the F1 car. The choice of a straight eight format is, in hindsight, intriguing for such a car at a time when this type of engine seemed dead in the water. Yet, although the 300 SLR showed promise, the catastrophic accident at Le Mans in 1955, which killed 83 spectators and injured over 180 more when the car crashed and the magnesium alloy engine and bodywork caught fire, marked an end to the project.

OPPOSITE: The magnificent 1937 Mercedes-Benz 540K's engine came at a price in terms of fuel consumption, single digit mpg being the norm.

MERCEDES-BENZ EIGHT MODELS

Model		Type 460 W08	380S W19	770K	770 W07	500 Nurburg	380S WS10	380K	380 W22
Year introduced		1928	1929	1930	1930	1931	1930	1933	1933
Displacement	cc	4,622	3,820	7,655	7,655	4,918	3,820	3,823	3,820
	cu in	281	233.1	467.1	467.1	300.1	233.1	233.3	233.1
Power output	bhp (max)	79	84	200	150	99	80	138	89
	kW	59	63	149	112	74	59	103	66
	@ rpm	3,400	3,200	2,800	2,800	3,100	3,200	3,600	3,200
Specific output	bhp/litre	17.1	22.0	26.1	19.6	20.1	20.9	36.1	23.3
	bhp/cu in	0.28	0.36	0.43	0.32	0.33	0.34	0.59	0.38
	kW/litre	12.8	16.5	19.5	14.6	15.0	15.4	26.9	17.3
	kW/cu in	0.21	0.27	0.32	0.24	0.25	0.25	0.44	0.28
Compression ratio 5:1		6:1	4.7:1	4.7:1	5:1	5.6:1	5.54:1	6:1	
Bore	mm	80	78	95	95	82.5	78	78	78
	inches	3.15	3.07	3.74	3.74	3.25	3.07	3.07	3.07
Stroke	mm	115	100	135	135	115	100	100	100
	inches	4.53	3.94	5.31	5.31	4.53	3.94	3.94	3.94
Bore:stroke ratio		70%	78%	70%	70%	72%	78%	78%	78%
Valve gear		s/v 16v	s/v 16v	s/c ohc	s/c ohc	s/v	s/v 16v	ohv 16v	ohv 16v
Carburettor		1xZenith	2xSolex	1xMercedes	1xMercedes	1xSolex	2xSolex	s/c	1xMercedes

MERCEDES-BENZ EIGHT MODELS

Model		500	500K	Nurburg 500	540K	770 Grosser	580K	300 SLR
Year introduced		1934	1934	1936	1936	1938	1939	1955
Displacement	cc	4,918	5,018	4,918	5,401	7,655	5,800	2,982
	cu in	300.1	306.2	300.1	329.6	467.1	353.9	182
Power output	bhp (max)	99	160	108	180	153	197	310
	kW	74	120	81	130	114	147	230
	@ rpm	3,100	3,400	3,300	3,400	3,000	3,400	7,400
Specific output	bhp/litre	20.1	31.9	22.0	33.3	20.0	34.0	104.0
	bhp/cu in	0.33	0.52	0.36	0.55	0.33	0.56	1.70
	kW/litre	15.0	23.9	16.5	24.1	14.9	25.3	77.1
	kW/cu in	0.25	0.39	0.27	0.39	0.24	0.42	1.26
Compression ratio		6:1	5.5:1	6.6:1	5.2:1	6.1:1	6.5:1	9:1
Bore	mm	82.5	86	82.5	88	95	92	78
	inches	3.25	3.39	3.25	3.46	3.74	3.64	3.10
Stroke	mm	115	108	115	111	135	108	78
	inches	4.53	4.25	4.53	4.37	5.31	4.25	0.13
Bore:stroke ratio		72%	80%	72%	79%	70%	85%	100%
Valve gear		ohv 16v	ohv 16v	s/v 16v	ohv 16v	ohc	ohv 16v	dohc
Carburettor		1xSolex	1xSolex	1xSolex	s/c 2xMercedes	1xMercedes	s/c 2xMercedes	injection

A magnificent 1937 Mercedes-Benz 540K with concealed drophead. **INSET:** The supercharged 5,401 cc (329.6 cu in) engine in the 1937 Mercedes-Benz 540K, good for 180 bhp and 110 mph (170 kph) with the supercharger engaged.

A 1931 Mercedes-Benz 770, one of 117 built, and often called the 'Grosser Mercedes'. **TOP:** The massive 7,655 cc (467.1 cu in) engine of the 1931 Mercedes-Benz 770 with the part-time supercharger clearly seen at the front (left). The left side of the same 7.7-litre engine (right).

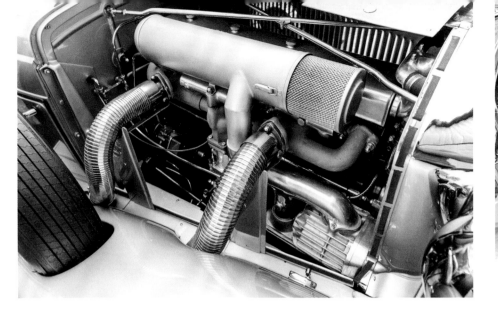

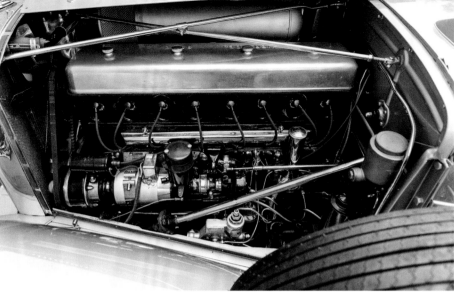

A 1936 Mercedes-Benz 500K, a genuine 100 mph car when the supercharger was engaged. **TOP:** The 5,018 cc (306.2 cu in) engine of the 1936 Mercedes-Benz 500K, showing the left side (top right).

A 1937 Mercedes-Benz 540K Cabriolet A with the more traditional 'bulky' folding roof. **TOP LEFT:** The range of ancillaries on the left side of the 540K Cabriolet A's engine. **TOP RIGHT:** The impressive exhaust system on the 1937 Mercedes-Benz 540K Cabriolet A, one to rival the Duesenberg SJ.

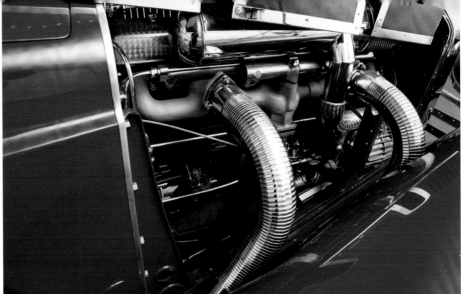

A 1935 Mercedes-Benz 500K with an unusually neat folding roof. **TOP LEFT:** The beautifully finished 5,018 cc (306.2 cu in) supercharged engine in the 500K. **TOP RIGHT:** The impressive inlet/exhaust (right side) of the 500K's engine.

Introduced in 1955 when the straight eight was almost extinct, the sensational Mercedes-Benz SLR was in effect a two-seat version of their W196 F1 car. The project was stopped after the tragic 1955 Le Mans incident when 86 were killed by an SLR 'flying' into the spectator stand.

1954 Mercedes W196 at the 2011 Goodwood Revival.

Mercedes W196R shown at the Mercedes-Benz Museum, Stuttgart, 2013.

Mercedes-Benz 300 SLR at the 2015 Pebble Beach Concours.

Mercedes-Benz 300 SLR at the 2015 Pebble Beach Concours.

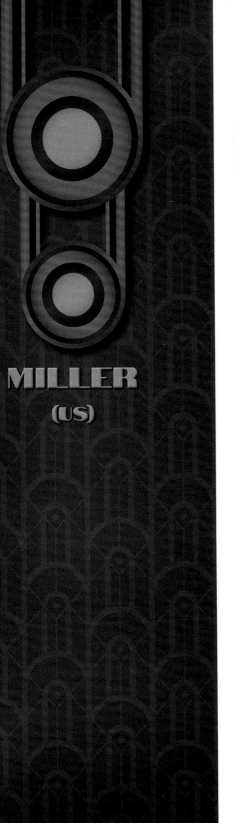

iller and Offenhauser are two names which are almost god-like in the world of North American racing. Offenhauser had worked for Miller before setting off on his own to build what might be seen as a variant of the Miller 'four', and develop the 'Offy' which is, arguably, the greatest racing engine of all time.

There was one big difference between Miller and Offenhauser. Whereas Fred Offenhauser only ever built four-cylinder engines, and indeed took the 'four' to levels probably never exceeded, Harry Miller spread his net wider and made four, six- and eight-cylinder engines.

Miller's first straight eight, the Miller 183, was developed at the request of two drivers, Tommy Milton and Ira Vail, who wanted an engine which would enable them to challenge the dominant Frontenacs and Duesenbergs of the day. Surprisingly these two makes only had three main bearings, and Miller decided to follow suit, with simple plain bearings in all the engines apart from the first two built. Nearly all the 183s had a non-detachable head, and the overhead camshaft was driven by a train of gears. The 183 was good for 125 bhp (94 kW) at 4,000 rpm which, at 42 bhp (32 kW)/litre was a record for a non-supercharged engine at the time.

For the subsequent 2-litre formula, Miller scaled down the 183 to create the 122, but changed from three plain bearings to five bearings, four plain and one ball. This smaller unit produced 120 bhp (90 kW) at 4,500 rpm, another record at 61 bhp (46 kW)/litre. In 1925 Miller

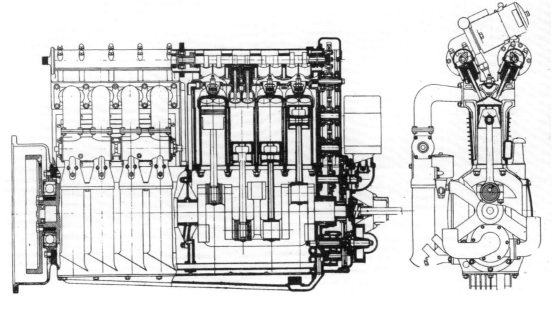

A longitudinal and cross section view of the Miller 183 engine.

added a centrifugal supercharger to the 122 to raise the power to 205 bhp (154 kW) at 5,800 rpm. This was 103 bhp (77 kW)/ litre, exceeded only by the contemporary Delage V12.

The 1926 Miller 91 was a further scaled down 122, which turned out 154 bhp (116 kW) at (for the time) an incredible 7,000 rpm. Miller experimented with a two-stage supercharged 91 which was rumoured to generate around 300 bhp (225 kW).

Miller engines were also fitted to a number of 'specials', including the Miller Locomobile Special and the 1937 Kirby-Deering Miller 8 Special shown in the photographs. The engine view of the 1.5-litre Kirby-Deering Special shows the centrifugal supercharger fitted.

Miller was successful in the Indy 500. In 1923, 1926, 1928, 1929, 1933 and 1934 it won with cars having both Miller engines and Miller chassis. In addition, in 1922, 1930, 1931, 1932, 1936 and 1938, cars powered by straight eight Miller engines but in different chassis saw victory.

MILLER EIGHT MODELS

Model		183	122	122 s/c	91
Year introduced		1921	1923	1924	1926
Displacement	cc	2,999	1,980	1,980	1,478
	cu in	183	121	121	90
Power output	bhp (max)	125-185	120-150	205-235	154
	kW	93-138	89-112	153-175	116
	@ rpm	4,000-4,400	4,500-5,000	5,800	8,000
Specific output	bhp/litre	42-62	61-76	104-119	104.0
	bhp/cu in	0.68-1.01	0.99-1.24	1.69-1.94	1.71
	kW/litre	31-46	45-58	80-91	78.0
	kW/cu in	0.51-0.75	0.74-0.93	1.26-1.45	1.29
Bore	mm	72	59	59	55.5
	inches	2.84	2.33	2.33	2.2
Stroke	mm	89	89	89	76.2
	inches	3.5	3.5	3.5	3
Bore:stroke ratio		81%	66%	66%	73%
Valve gear		dohc	dohc	dohc	dohc
Carburettor		4xtwin choke	4xtwin choke	4xtwin choke s/c	4xtwin choke s/c
Main bearings		5	5	5	5

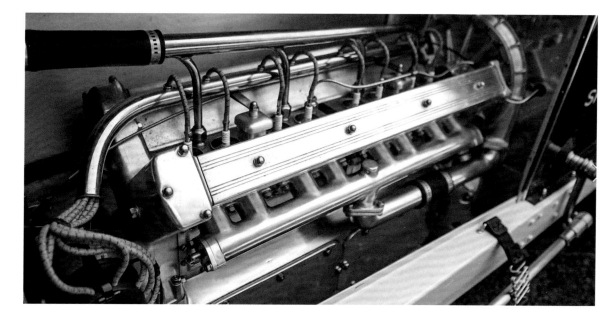

TOP: The induction side of the Locomobile Special's engine. This was tried with two stage supercharging whereupon power increased to an amazing 300 bhp. **BOTTOM:** The exhaust side of the engine. In naturally aspirated form, it produced 154 bhp at 7,000 rpm.

OPPOSITE TOP (BOTH): Two views of the 1937 Kirby Deering Miller 8 Special. **BOTTOM:** The 1926 Locomobile Junior 8 Special.

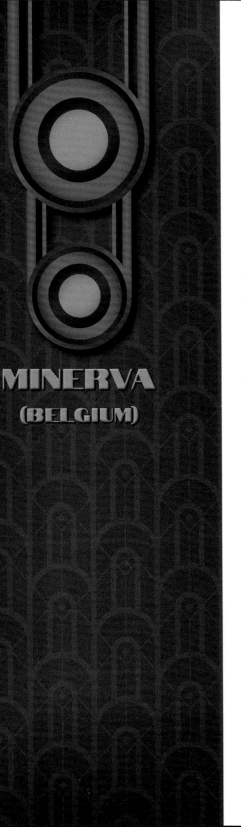

MINERVA
(BELGIUM)

A mongst 'players' in the straight eight market, Minerva was unusual in that its straight eights had sleeve valve engines.

Minerva started out as a bicycle manufacturer in 1897 before branching out into motorised bicycles. In 1902 the company started making cars, its first being a four-cylinder 6 hp model. By 1904 it had a range of automobiles, including two, three and four-cylinder models, and even a massive 8-litre model which won the 1907 Belgian Circuit des Ardennes.

A most significant development for the company was in 1908 when Minerva obtained a licence on the Knight

The inlet side of the Minerva Type AL 40CV showing the firing order of 1-6-2-5-8-3-7-4.

sleeve valve engine design. The Knight system, invented by Charles Knight, used double sleeves and was noted for running virtually silently. All Minervas after 1908 used sleeve valves.

During the First World War, Minerva was based in the Netherlands, but on moving back to Belgium in 1920 it restarted production of luxury cars, beginning with a 20CV 3.6-litre 'four' and a 30CV 5.3-litre 'six'. Two smaller models were introduced in 1923, the 15CV 2-litre 'four' and the 20CV 3.4-litre 'six'. In 1927 the 30CV was replaced by the 6-litre AK, and a new 2-litre 'four', the 12-14, was launched.

During the inter-war years Minerva built up a good reputation for making high-quality luxury cars, and in keeping with many other up-market motor car manufacturers in the 1930s it launched two straight eight models, the 6.6-litre AL and the 4-litre AP. The smaller 25CV AP's sleeve valve engine had a bore of 75 mm (2.95 cu in) and a stroke of 112 mm (4.41 in) giving a displacement of 3,958 cc (241.5 cu in). Power was 80 bhp (60 kW) at 4,000 rpm. Later a twin Zenith carburettor installation raised power to 104 bhp (78 kW). The larger AL had a 6.6-litre sleeve valve engine.

Sleeve valves enjoyed a fairly brief period of popularity. Whilst in theory a sound concept, the large area of metal-on-metal contact, combined with sometimes poor-quality oil, often led to major problems. Similar reliability issues were also found with aero engines, where the Napier Sabre never achieved its full potential.

The last Minerva was the 2-litre M4 in 1934. This model did not sell well, and whilst the name survived following a merger with Impéria in 1934, the last Minerva cars were produced in 1938.

MINERVA EIGHT MODELS

Model		AL	AP	AP (2)
Year introduced		1930	1930	1933
Displacement	cc	6,625	3,958	3,958
	cu in	402.8	241.5	241.5
Power output	bhp (max)	125	80	104
	kW	93	60	78
	@ rpm	4,000	4,000	4,000
Specific output	bhp/litre	18.9	20.2	26.3
	bhp/cu in	0.31	0.33	0.43
	kW/litre	14.0	15.2	19.7
	kW/cu in	0.23	0.25	0.32
Bore	mm	94	75	75
	inches	3.7	2.95	2.95
Stroke	mm	139	112	112
	inches	5.51	4.72	4.72
Bore:stroke ratio		68%	67%	67%
Valve gear		sleeve	sleeve	sleeve
Carburettor		1xZenith	1xZenith	2xZenith
Main bearings		9	9	9

A 1934 Minerva Type AL 40CV, unusual in having a sleeve valve engine.

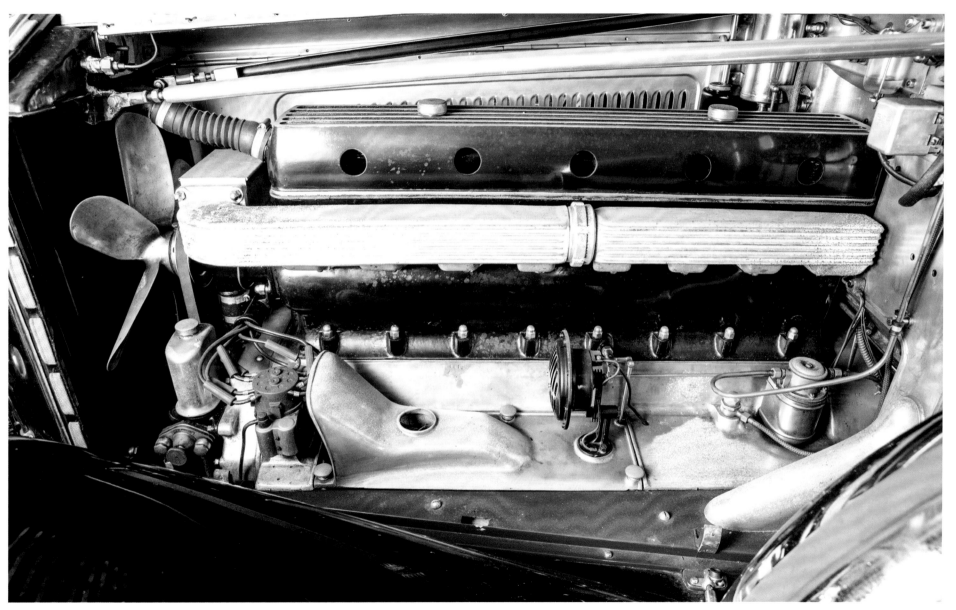

The neat exhaust side of the Type AL 40CV's 6.6-litre sleeve valve engine.

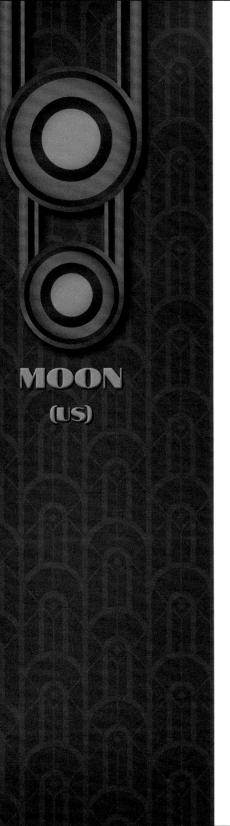

The Moon Motor Car Company was founded in St. Louis, Missouri, US by Joseph Moon, and produced its first car in 1906. This was powered by a Rutenber four-cylinder engine, Rutenber being notable for being the first designer and manufacturer of four-cylinder petrol engines in the United States. Between 1907 and 1913 cars were produced with either a Moon-produced engine, or an 'off the shelf' Continental unit. After 1913 all Moon cars were Continental powered.

The Moon business was a little convoluted, in that for the year 1908 the cars were also sold under the name Hol-Tan, whilst from 1925-28 there was a subsidiary company making the Diana models, and from 1929-30 another company making Windsor cars. These were all similar and used the proprietary Continental engines.

Moon produced straight eights with Continental engines for the model years 1928 and 1929, these being the 8-75 and the 8-80. The 8-80 had a 4,403 cc (268.6 cu in) Continental L-head engine with a bore of 76 mm (3 in), a stroke of 121 mm (4.75 in), and a single Stromberg carburettor, producing 86 bhp (64 kW) at 3,200 rpm.

The business closed in 1930. It is interesting that when the company started in St. Louis, Missouri in 1905 there were nearly one hundred automobile manufacturers based in the city.

ABOVE: Moon radiator emblem for the 1928 Aerotype Model 8-80.

Nash Motors was founded in 1916 by Charles Nash, formerly president of General Motors, after he had acquired the Thomas B Jeffery Company which manufactured the Rambler model.

Nash established a reputation for high quality for the price. Until 1930 the company concentrated on four and six-cylinder models, which incorporated many innovative features such as 'flow through' ventilation and fully-reclining seats. Then in 1930 the company followed the trend of the moment and decided to go 'up market' launching a straight eight model.

The 1930 Advanced Eight was indeed an advanced motor car, with twin spark plugs, overhead valves and a nine-bearing crankshaft. Initially it was called the Nash

The engine in the 1934 Nash Ambassador had overhead valves, but did not retain the twin plugs from the earlier Advanced Eight. Note the 'quick release' valve cover.

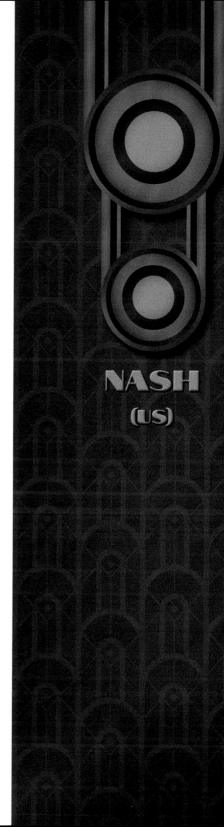

NASH

(US)

NASH EIGHT MODELS

Model		8-90	1070	1080	1090
Year introduced		1930	1932	1932	1932
Displacement	cc	4,895	4,056	4,275	5,279
	cu in	298.6	247.4	260.8	322
Power output	bhp (max)	100	85	100	125
	kW	75	47	75	93
	@ rpm	3,200	3,200	3,400	3,600
Specific output	bhp/litre	20.4	21.0	23.4	23.7
	bhp/cu in	0.33	0.34	0.38	0.39
	kW/litre	15.3	11.6	17.5	17.6
	kW/cu in	0.25	0.19	0.29	0.29
Compression ratio		5.25:1	5.1:1	5.25:1	5.25:1
Bore	mm	83	76	80	86
	inches	3.25	3.00	3.13	3.38
Stroke	mm	114	111	108	114
	inches	4.50	4.38	4.25	4.50
Bore:stroke ratio		73%	68%	74%	75%
Valve gear		ohv	s/v	ohv	ohv
Carburettor		Marvel	Stromberg	Stromberg	Stromberg
Main bearings		9	9	9	9

Twin Ignition Eight on account of the twin plugs, but in 1931 the name was simplified to the Eight-90 model or Advanced Eight. The company entered 1932 with four new models, the 1060, 1070, 1080 and 1090. The 1060 was a flathead six, the 1070 a flathead eight, whilst the 1080 and 1090 continued with the ohv 'twin spark' eight. The 1932 models included synchromesh, automatic centralised lubrication, a freewheel system and suspension adjustable from inside the car. The 1070 had a 4,056 cc (247.4 cu in) engine outputting 85 bhp at 3,200 rpm. The 1080 had a 4.275 cc (260.8 cu in) engine delivering 100 bhp (75 kW) at 3,400, whilst the 1090 had a 5,279 cc (322 cu in) unit delivering 125 bhp (93 kW) at 3,600 rpm. Later models would revert to the slightly smaller 4,261 cc (260 cu in) 100 bhp (74 kW) engine first seen in the Advanced Eight.

The Nash straight eight models came to use the name 'Ambassador', creating a 'sub-brand' for Nash's top models, although the first use of the Ambassador name was in 1927 for an up-market version of the Nash Advanced Six, or Model 267. The Ambassador remained part of the 'six' range until 1930 when the name was applied to the new straight eight.

When production at Nash restarted after the war the eight was no longer included in the model line-up, but the Ambassador name lived on.

The straight eight Nash Ambassador is a rare car, and this 1934 example is a restoration project. The name Ambassador was rather confusingly used for a 'six' model up until 1930.

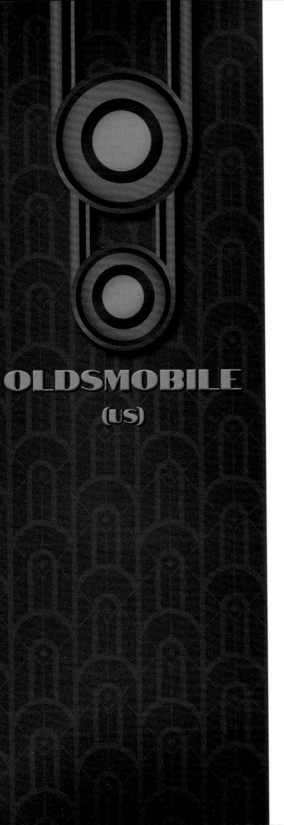

OLDSMOBILE (US)

The Olds Motor Vehicle Company was founded in 1897 by Ransom E Olds. By 1901 the company was turning out over 600 Olds automobiles a year, making it the first high volume manufacturer of petrol-driven cars in the US, although some steam and electric vehicle manufacturers had a higher output. Following a dispute Olds left the company and founded the REO Motor Car Company.

The cars made by the Olds Motor Vehicle Company were officially known as 'Olds automobiles', but they were generally referred to by the public as 'Oldsmobiles', and over time this name stuck and was eventually officially adopted.

1910 marked a significant event for Oldsmobile when it launched its first prestige model, the Limited Touring, which at $4,600 cost more than a typical three-bedroom house. On becoming part of General Motors in the late 1920s Oldsmobile as a brand was positioned in the up-market segment behind Cadillac.

As a premium brand it was natural that it would develop a straight eight variant in the 1930s. From 1932 until 1948, when the new V8 Rocket engine was introduced, the same basic design of side valve straight eight would power its top models. During this period the eight-cylinder cars were referred to as the 'L Series', whilst the six-cylinder cars were called the 'F Series'.

The first Oldsmobile 8 launched in 1932 had a 3,940 cc (240.4 cu in) engine with a bore of 76.2 mm (3.0 in), stroke of 108 mm (4.25 in) and a five-bearing crank. It was of a relatively straight-forward side valve design, with a single carburettor, and produced 87 bhp (65 kW) at 3,350 rpm.

In 1933 the engine gained a higher compression ratio of 6.2:1 and a shorter stroke of 104.8 mm (4.13 in), whilst the bore remained at 76.2 mm (3.0 in). Displacement decreased from 3,940 cc (240.4 cu in) to 3,823 cc (233.3 cu in), but power was up by 3 bhp to 90 bhp (67 kW) at 3,350 rpm. Carburettion and crank bearings were unchanged.

1937 saw another change in engine dimensions, with the bore of 82.6 mm (3.25 in) and the stroke of 98.4 mm (3.87 in) making the engine much more 'square' than most straight eights. The new engine had an increased displacement of 4,213 cc (257.1 cu in) giving a power output of 110 bhp (82 kW) at 3,600 rpm. The shorter stroke increased the engine speed for maximum power. Torque was 210 ft lb at 2,000 rpm. The compression ratio of this variant was later increased to 7.0:1, boosting power by a further 5 bhp and torque by 8 ft lbs.

In 1939 Oldsmobile changed the model names. The L Series 8 became the Series 80, but the engine remained the same 4,213 cc (257.1 cu in) unit. The following year,

The 1942 Oldsmobile Cutlass was a very late in-line eight.

The engine in the Cutlass was a simple 4,213 cc (257.1 cu in) side valve unit, looking rather lost in the engine bay!

the same engine was only used in the new, larger, Series 90, there being no Series 80. Names were given to models, and the 90 became the Custom Cruiser 90. In 1941 both eight and six-cylinder engines were offered in the same bodywork, the varieties being distinguished by the second digit, the eight becoming the 98 and the six being the 96. The top model was now called the Custom Cruiser 98. The six-cylinder variety was dropped from the Series 90 in 1942, leaving just the Custom Cruiser 98.

From 1942 to 1948 the Custom Cruiser 98, with the same 4,213 cc (257.1 cu in) engine remained the top model until the straight eight unit was replaced by the V8 Rocket in 1949.

OLDSMOBILE EIGHT MODELS

Model		L Series 8	L Series 8 ii	L Series 8 iii	Series 90
Year introduced		1932	1933	1937	1940
Displacement	cc	3,940	3,823	4,213	4,213
	cu in	240.4	233.3	257.1	257.1
Power output	bhp (max)	87	90	110	110
	kW	65	67	82	82
	@ rpm	3,350	3,350	3,600	3,600
Specific output	bhp/litre	22.1	23.5	26.1	26.1
	bhp/cu in	0.36	0.39	0.43	0.43
	kW/litre	16.5	17.5	19.5	19.5
	kW/cu in	0.27	0.29	0.32	0.32
Compression ratio		5.9:1	6.2:1	6.2:1	6.2:1
Bore	mm	76.2	76.2	82.6	82.6
	inches	3.00	3.00	3.25	3.25
Stroke	mm	108	104.8	98.4	98.4
	inches	4.25	4.13	3.87	3.87
Bore:stroke ratio		71%	73%	84%	84%
Valve gear		s/v 16v	s/v 16v	s/v 16v	s/v 16v
Main bearings		5	5	5	5

pel's only attempt to launch an up-market car, a straight eight called the Opel Regent, was completely scuppered by General Motors when, in March 1929, it acquired 80% of the shares of the Opel business. Afraid of competition with its existing Cadillac and Buick models, the company bought back all 25 Regents that had been sold and destroyed them. None exist today, and even photographs are rare.

The Regent, launched in November 1928, had a 5,972 cc (364.4 cu in) side valve straight eight with a bore of 89 mm (3.5 in) and a stroke of 120 mm (4.72in). It delivered 108.5 bhp (81 kW) at 3,200 rpm, and torque of 174 ft lbs (236 Nm) at 2,800 rpm. It was capable of a top speed of 81 mph (130 kph).

It is clear the car had potential, but Opel would never again compete in the top echelons of the market.

Even photographs of the Opel Regent are extremely rare, since General Motors, upon acquiring the majority of the company in 1929, had all 25 Regents built destroyed, fearing internal competition with their Cadillac and Buick brands. This rare photograph was taken at the 1928 IAA Exhibition, and ironically the Opel appears in front of the Cadillac stand!

Packard occupies a unique position in the story of straight eights, and deserves greater coverage here than most other manufacturers. The company launched its first straight eight, appropriately called the Eight, in 1925. This was powered by a fairly basic 'flathead', two valve per cylinder, side valve engine. Although Packards were always at the premium end of the market, the engine remained virtually unchanged, apart from displacement, until Packard's last straight eight model launched as late as 1954. To some extent this simplicity enabled the company to weather the financial ups and downs of the 1930s. The only significant change was that from 1935, when the smaller engined 120 was launched, the least expensive Packards had a five-bearing engine rather than the nine-bearing unit in the more expensive ones.

Packard produced its first cars in 1899, and its last Detroit-built model, a concept car called the Packard Predictor, in 1956. Packard bought Studebaker in 1953 and from 1957 Packards were essentially just badge-engineered Studebakers built at the Studebaker plant in South Bend, Indiana.

From the outset Packards were firmly aimed at the top of the market, competing against other premium makes such as Peerless and Pierce Arrow. The three companies were often referred to as the 'The Three P's'. Packard was a major exporter, selling in 61 countries in the 1920s and '30s, and exporting more premium sector cars than any other US manufacturer.

In spite of not having the backing of a large conglomerate, as Cadillac had with General Motors, or Lincoln with Ford, Packard survived the Great Depression much better than most premium brands, with Peerless, Franklin, Marmon, Ruxton, Stearns-Knight, Stutz, Duesenberg and Pierce Arrow all disappearing by 1938. Packard's survival was partly due to its adherence to simple, standardised, engines which allowed interchange between models, and enabled it to use a single production line, giving significant savings in costs. In addition, a more affordable car was introduced in the medium price range, the 120 being the company's first car under $1,000. Sales tripled in 1935, the year the 120 was launched, and doubled again in 1936. But the cheaper 120 did damage the company's premium image, and the launching in 1937 of the first new six-cylinder model since 1928 did not help to restore it.

After the Second World War Packard relaunched the pre-war mid-range Clipper model as a 'new' 1948 range, but the premium range was not revived. Other mistakes, like launching a taxi model, eroded Packard's premium image even further. From 1951 new up-market models, the 250, 300 and 400 Patricians, were launched but most sales were still of the mid-range 120-based models. From 1957 no more Packards were built in Detroit, and Packards became badge-engineered Studebakers. In 1959 the Packard name disappeared from the Studebaker-Packard range, and in 1962 Packard was removed from the company's name completely.

The tables below list the 'technological' variants by decades; within which there were over 400 separate models listed using the same engines.

The photographs show Packard engines ranging from 1936 to 1951, and whilst the coachwork changed dramatically, the engine hardly changed at all.

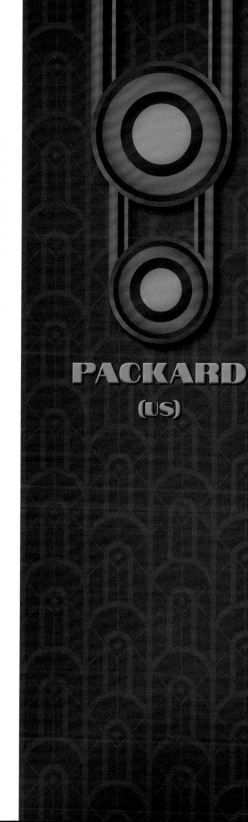

PACKARD
(US)

PACKARD ENGINES

Year	Variants	Displacement	Power Output	Bore	Stroke	Compression
1925	Eight	5861cc 357.7 cu in	80 bhp (60kW)	85.7mm 3.37in	127.0mm 5.0in	
1928	Eight & Custom Eight	6306cc 384.8 cu in	109 bhp (81kW)	88.9mm 3.50in	127.0mm 5.0in	
1929	Standard Eight	5230cc 319.2 cu in	90 bhp (67kW)	81.0mm 3.19in	127.0mm 5.0in	
	Custom Eight	6306cc 384.8 cu in	105 bhp (78kW)	88.9mm 3.50in	127.0mm 5.0in	
	Speedster Eight	6306cc 384.8 cu in	145bhp (108kW)	88.9mm 3.50in	127.0mm 5.0in	
1930	Standard Eight	5230cc 319.2 cu in	90 bhp (67kW)	81.0mm 3.19in	127.0mm 5.0in	
	Speedster Eight	6306cc 384.8 cu in	145bhp (108kW)	88.9mm 3.50in	127.0mm 5.0in	
1931	Standard Eight	5230cc 319.2 cu in	100bhp (75kW)	81.0mm 3.19in	127.0mm 5.0in	
	Custom Eight	6306cc 384.8 cu in	120bhp (89kW)	88.9mm 3.50in	127.0mm 5.0in	
1932	Light Eight	5230cc 319.2 cu in	110bhp (82kW)	81.0mm 3.19in	127.0mm 5.0in	
	De Luxe Eight	6306cc 384.8 cu in	135bhp (101kW)	88.9mm 3.50in	127.0mm 5.0in	
1933	Eight	5230cc 319.2 cu in	120bhp (89kW)	81.0mm 3.19in	127.0mm 5.0in	
	Super Eight	6306cc 384.8 cu in	145bhp (108kW)	88.9mm 3.50in	127.0mm 5.0in	
1934	Eight	5230cc 319.2 cu in	120bhp (89kW) @ 3200rpm	81.0mm 3.19in	127.0mm 5.0in	6.0:1
	Super Eight	6306cc 384.8 cu in	145bhp (108kW) @ 3200rpm	88.9mm 3.50in	127.0mm 5.0in	6.0:1
1935	120	4213cc 257.1 cu in	110bhp (82kW) @ 3800rpm	82.6mm 3.25in	98.4mm 3.87in	6.5:1
	Eight	5235cc 319.4 cu in	130bhp (97kW) @ 3200rpm	81.0mm 3.19in	127.0mm 5.0in	6.5:1
	Super Eight	6306cc 384.8 cu in	150bhp (112kW) @ 3200rpm	88.9mm 3.50in	127.0mm 5.0in	6.3:1

The engine in the 1940 Packard Super Eight 160 is 'standard Packard', a design which hardly changed over many years. In the Super Eight 160 it's a 5,835 cc (356 cu in) unit delivering 160-165 bhp (119-123 kW). **INSET:** This 1940 Packard Super Eight 160 is a fine example of the four-door drophead style which was popular in the 1940s.

The engine in this 1941 Packard 180 looks virtually identical to that in the 1951 250, launched ten years later. **INSET:** This 1941 Packard 180 reflects the rather 'patrician' style we normally associate with Packard.

Year	Variants	Displacement	Power Output	Bore	Stroke	Compression
1936	120 B	4622cc 282.1 cu in	120bhp (89kW) @ 3800rpm	82.6mm 3.25in	108.0mm 4.25in	6.5:1
	Super Eight	5230cc 319.2 cu in	135bhp (101kW) @ 3200rpm	81.0mm 3.19in	127.0mm 5.0in	6.0:1
1937	120 C, CD & 138CD	4622cc 282.1 cu in	120bhp (89kW) @ 3800rpm	82.6mm 3.25in	108.0mm 4.25in	6.5:1
	Super Eight	5230cc 319.2 cu in	135bhp (101kW) @ 3200rpm	81.0mm 3.19in	127.0mm 5.0in	6.0:1
1938	Eight	4622cc 282.1 cu in	120bhp (89kW) @ 3800rpm	82.6mm 3.25in	108.0mm 4.25in	6.6:1
1939	120	4622cc 282.1 cu in	120bhp (89kW) @ 3800rpm	82.6mm 3.25in	108.0mm 4.25in	6.41:1
1940	120	4622cc 282.1 cu in	120/125bhp (89/93kW) @ 3600rpm	82.6mm 3.25in	108.0mm 4.25in	6.41/6.85:1
	Super 8 160	5835cc 356 cu in	160/165bhp (119/123kW) @ 3500 rpm	88.9mm 3.50in	117.5mm 4.63 in	6.41/6.85:1
	Custom Super 8 160	5835cc 356 cu in	160/165bhp (119/123kW) @ 3500 rpm	88.9mm 3.50in	117.5mm 4.63 in	6.41/6.85:1
1941	120	4622cc 282.1 cu in	120/125bhp (89/93kW) @ 3600rpm	82.6mm 3.25in	108.0mm 4.25in	6.41/6.85:1
	Clipper 8	4622cc 282.1 cu in	125bhp (93kW) @ 3600rpm	82.6mm 3.25in	108.0mm 4.25in	6.85:1
	Super 8 160	5835cc 356 cu in	160/165bhp (119/123kW) @ 3500 rpm	88.9mm 3.50in	117.5mm 4.63 in	6.41/6.85:1
	Custom Super 8 160	5835cc 356 cu in	160/165bhp (119/123kW) @ 3500 rpm	88.9mm 3.50in	117.5mm 4.63 in	6.41/6.85:1
1942	Clipper 8 & Coupe 8	4622cc 282.1 cu in	125bhp (93kW) @ 3600rpm	82.6mm 3.25in	108.0mm 4.25in	6.85:1
	Super 8 160 & Super Clipper 160	5835cc 356 cu in	165bhp (123kW) @ 3500 rpm	88.9mm 3.50in	117.5mm 4.63 in	6.85:1
	Custom Super 8 160 & Custom Super Clipper 180	5835cc 356 cu in	165bhp (123kW) @ 3500 rpm	88.9mm 3.50in	117.5mm 4.63 in	6.85:1

Year	Variants	Displacement	Power Output	Bore	Stroke	Compression
1946	Clipper Eight & Deluxe	4622cc 282.1 cu in	125bhp (93kW) @ 3600rpm	82.6mm 3.25in	108.0mm 4.25in	6.85:1
	Super Clipper & Custom Super Clipper	5835cc 356 cu in	165bhp (123kW) @ 3500 rpm	88.9mm 3.50in	117.5mm 4.63 in	6.85:1
1947	Clipper Eight & Deluxe	4622cc 282.1 cu in	125bhp (93kW) @ 3600rpm	82.6mm 3.25in	108.0mm 4.25in	6.85:1
	Super Clipper & Custom Super Clipper	5835cc 356 cu in	165bhp (123kW) @ 3500 rpm	88.9mm 3.50in	117.5mm 4.63 in	6.85:1
1948	Standard & Deluxe Eight	4720cc 288 cu in	130bhp (97kW) @ 3200rpm	88.9mm 3.50in	95.3mm 3.75 in	7.0:1
	Super Eight	5359cc 327 cu in	145bhp (108kW) @ 3600rpm	88.9mm 3.50in	107.9mm 4.25in	7.0:1
	Custom Eight	5834cc 356 cu in	160bhp (119kW) @ 3600rpm	88.9mm 3.50in	117.5mm 4.63 in	7.0:1
1949	Standard & Deluxe Eight	4720cc 288 cu in	135bhp (100kW) @ 3200rpm	88.9mm 3.50in	95.3mm 3.75 in	7.0:1
	Super Eight & Super Eight Deluxe	5359cc 327 cu in	150bhp (112kW) @ 3600rpm	88.9mm 3.50in	107.9mm 4.25in	7.0:1
	Custom Super Eight	5834cc 356 cu in	160bhp (119kW) @ 3600rpm	88.9mm 3.50in	117.5mm 4.63 in	7.0:1
1950	Standard & Deluxe Eight	4720cc 288 cu in	135bhp (100kW) @ 3200rpm	88.9mm 3.50in	95.3mm 3.75 in	7.0:1
	Super Eight & Super Eight Deluxe	5359cc 327 cu in	150bhp (112kW) @ 3600rpm	88.9mm 3.50in	107.9mm 4.25in	7.0:1
	Custom Eight	5834cc 356 cu in	160bhp (119kW) @ 3600rpm	88.9mm 3.50in	117.5mm 4.63 in	7.0:1
1951	200 & 200 Deluxe	4720cc 288 cu in	135bhp (100kW) @ 3200rpm	88.9mm 3.50in	95.3mm 3.75 in	7.0:1
	250 & 300	5359cc 327 cu in	150bhp (112kW) @ 3600rpm	88.9mm 3.50in	107.9mm 4.25in	7.0:1
	Patrician 400	5359cc 327 cu in	155bhp (116kW) @ 3600rpm	88.9mm 3.50in	107.9mm 4.25in	7.8:1
1952	200 & 200 Deluxe	4720cc 288 cu in	135/138bhp (100/102kW) @ 3200rpm	88.9mm 3.50in	95.3mm 3.75 in	7.0/7.5:1

The 1951 Packard 250 was one of the last in-line eight models, this engine format being dropped in 1954. Packard used essentially the same simple side valve engine design throughout all their straight eight models. This is the variant in the 1951 Packard 250.

Year	Variants	Displacement	Power Output	Bore	Stroke	Compression
1952	250 & 300	5359cc 327 cu in	150/155bhp (112/116kW) @ 3600rpm	88.9mm 3.50in	107.9mm 4.25in	7.0/7.8:1
	Patrician 400	5359cc 327 cu in	150/155bhp (112/116kW) @ 3600rpm	88.9mm 3.50in	107.9mm 4.25in	7.0/7.8:1
1953	Clipper & Commercial	4720cc 288 cu in	150bhp (112kW) @ 4000rpm	88.9mm 3.50in	95.3mm 3.75 in	7.7:1
	Clipper Deluxe & Commercial	5359cc 327 cu in	160bhp (119kW) @ 3600rpm	88.9mm 3.50in	107.9mm 4.25in	8.0:1
	Cavalier, Mayfair & Caribbean	5359cc 327 cu in	180bhp (134kW) @ 3600rpm	88.9mm 3.50in	107.9mm 4.25in	8.0:1
	Patrician	5359cc 327 cu in	180bhp (134kW) @ 3600rpm	88.9mm 3.50in	107.9mm 4.25in	8.0:1
1954	Clipper Special & Commercial	4720cc 288 cu in	150bhp (112kW) @4000rpm	88.9mm 3.50in	95.3mm 3.75 in	7.7:1
	Clipper Deluxe & Super	5359cc 327 cu in	165bhp (123kW) @ 3600 rpm	88.9mm 3.50in	107.9mm 4.25in	8.0:1
	Cavalier	5359cc 327 cu in	180bhp (134kW) @ 4000rpm	88.9mm 3.50in	107.9mm 4.25in	8.0:1
	Patrician, Pacific & Caribbean	5883cc 359 cu in	212bhp (158kW) @ 4000rpm	90.4mm 3.56in	114.3mm 4.5in	8.7:1

This 1934 Packard Eight 1101 carries most elegant two-door drophead coachwork.

The Eight 1101's engine is a 5,230 cc (319.2 cu in) variant of the standard Packard design delivering 120 bhp (89 kW).

Packard's first 'eight' was launched in 1925, and this 1928 Packard Custom Eight 4-43 is a fine example of their second model.

The 1928 Packard Custom Eight's engine is a 6,306 cc (384.8 cu in) delivering 109 bhp (81 kW). It is an enlarged version of the company's first 'eight' launched in 1925.

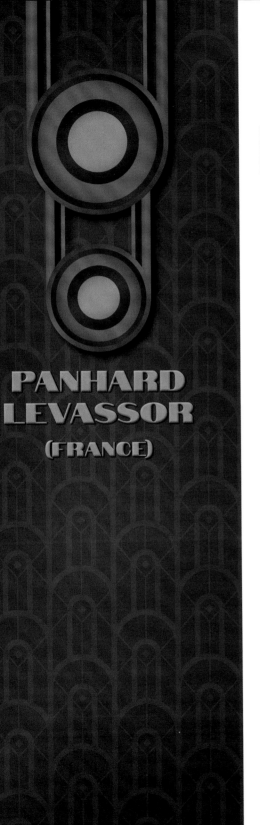

PANHARD LEVASSOR

(FRANCE)

Panhard was one of the earliest car companies, having been established in 1887 in France. The first car was sold in 1890, this being propelled by an engine made under a Daimler licence. The first all-Levassor design appeared in 1891, which in many ways set the design format for future cars, being four-wheeled, with an engine and radiator at the front. For the 1894 Paris-Rouen Rally, one was fitted with a steering wheel rather than a tiller, believed to be the first ever used in a car.

Panhard mainly developed small/medium-sized cars, and certainly post World War Two, Panhards were noted for being very light with small, but relatively powerful, engines. But in 1931 there had been a complete departure from this format in the shape of the 8DS X67, which had a 5,084 cc (310 cu in) 125 bhp straight eight sleeve valve engine capable of propelling the car to 69 mph (110 kph). Only 43 of the eight-cylinder models were made, and it is not known if any survive. Even photographs are rare and not of high quality.

Panhard had started developing sleeve valve engines in 1910, and from 1910 to 1924 most models were offered with sleeve or poppet valves. But from 1924-40 all models used sleeve valve engines.

Panhard Levassor was noted for small and medium sized vehicles which were light and relatively powerful. The 8DS, with its 5,084 cc (310 cu in) sleeve valve engine was a complete departure for the company. Even photographs of the 8DS are rare.

Peerless Motors was founded in 1900 in Cleveland, Ohio and started assembling De Dion Bouton cars under licence. The first Peerless branded automobile appeared in 1902, and the 35 hp Green Dragon of 1904 competed fairly successfully in endurance races. From 1905 to 1907 the business expanded rapidly and began focusing on 'high-end' luxury vehicles. In 1915 it announced its first V8, designed in-house, and intended to compete against the likes of Cadillac. This car remained the main model until 1925.

In 1929 the entire range was redesigned to compete against Marmon and Stutz. Sales increased and in 1930 the in-house-designed V8 was dropped in favour of a cheaper Continental side valve straight eight to save costs. The same engine was used until the end of production, and was a 5,279 cc (322 cu in) Continental 13K L-head with a bore of 86 mm (3.38 in) and a stroke of 114 mm (4.5 in). With a compression ratio of 5.0:1 and a single Schebler carburettor it produced 120 bhp (89 kW) at 3,200 rpm. But the Great Depression took its toll of the business, and the last Peerless, an over ambitious V16, appeared in 1931.

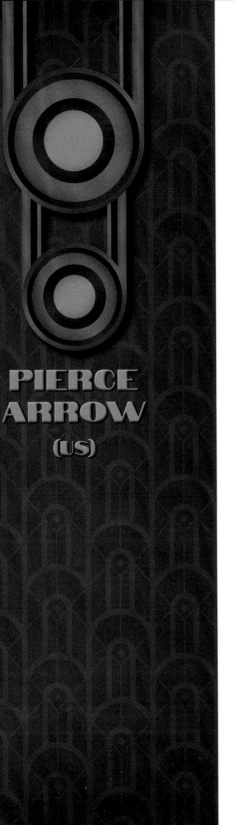

Pierce Arrow is almost unique in that it only ever addressed the top end of the luxury car market. Also, in so doing, its advertising and media work almost played down the car itself in favour of selling a 'lifestyle', something so modern it is hard to think that it was doing this in the late 1920s and early '30s. In contemporary advertisements the car was often in the background, the main image being of the high-class lifestyle customers are assumed to lead. It almost suggested that 'if you wish to know the details of our car, you are not our sort of customer'!

The Pierce Arrow business dated back to 1865 with a company called Heinz, Pierce and Co which made household items, especially fancy bird cages. In 1872 George Pierce bought out his partners and decided to branch out, first into bicycles and then into automobiles. Until 1928 the company manufactured a series of four and six-cylinder cars, always aimed at the top of the market.

Then, in 1928, Studebaker took control of the business, and Pierce Arrow gained access to a large dealer network. The company retired its range of elderly six-cylinder models and launched a side valve straight eight model which, with a bore of 88.9 mm (3.5 in) and a stroke of 127 mm (5.0 in), displaced 6,317 cc (385.5 cu in). With two valves per cylinder, a compression ratio of 6.4:1 and a single Stromberg carburettor, it produced 150 bhp @ 3,400 rpm. This engine remained virtually unchanged until 1937.

The Pierce Arrow business lasted until 1938. In its final few years it introduced in 1933 an even more up-market car, the V12 Silver Arrow, in a final attempt to appeal to New York's mega-rich. But at $10,000, $194,500 in today's money, it was simply far too expensive even for the rich in a period of such financial turmoil. Just five of this model were sold, and the company was declared bankrupt in 1938.

Pierce Arrow only ever aimed at the top of the market, and this 1934 Pierce Arrow 840A is a fine example.

The straight eight engine remained virtually unchanged throughout the life of the company, being a 6,317 cc (385.5 cu in) side valves unit. The firing order 1-6-2-5-8-3-7-4 is seen on the inlet manifold.

Pierce Arrow 840A also produced fixed head coupes, such as this 1934 example. **INSET:** The extremely tidy engine compartment of the 1934 fixed head coupe.

The inlet/exhaust side of the 1934 Pierce Arrow 840A's 6,317 cc (385.5 cu in) engine, a simple but neat design.

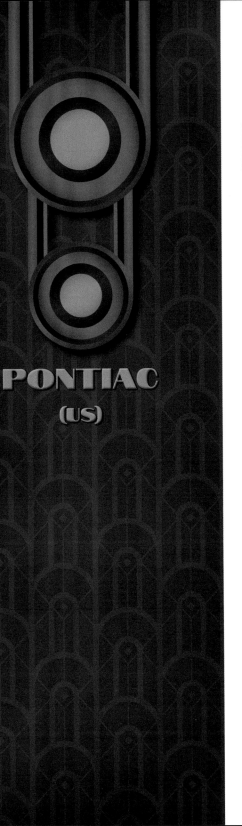

PONTIAC (US)

Pontiac was one of the most loyal advocates of the straight eight format. The company introduced its first straight eight in 1932 for the 1933 model year, and continued using this engine format all the way through to 1954, by which time it was eclipsed by the V8s from sister divisions of General Motors, Cadillac, Buick and Oldsmobile. By 1954 the flathead eight, whilst smooth and quiet, with all the valve gear contained within the block, was antiquated and Pontiac finally switched to V8 power the following year. But Pontiac heralded the end of its straight eights in style, by displaying at the General Motors Motorama in 1954 the Bonneville Special, equipped with a 230 bhp (170 kW) engine, the highest power its straight eight engine ever produced. Only two Bonneville Specials were made.

Over its 22-year life the Pontiac straight eight engine evolved gradually rather than through any major step changes. The original 1933 engine replaced the flathead V8 used until 1932, which was in fact an Oakland unit. It would take 22 years for the company to revert to a V8. The 1933 engine had a bore of 81 mm (3.19 in) and a stroke of 88.9 mm (3.5 in), surprisingly 'square' for a straight eight. The displacement was 3,661 cc (223.8 cu in) and with a compression ratio of 5.7:1 it delivered 77 bhp (57 kW) at 3600 rpm. This enabled a top speed for the Eight of 78 mph (125 kph).

For 1934 the dimensions of the engine were unchanged but quoted power was up at 84 bhp as a result of an improved Carter carburettor. Torque was given as 153 ft lbs at 1,600 rpm, reflecting real low speed pulling power. The same specification was used in 1935, but in 1936 capacity increased slightly to 3,806 cc (232.2 cu in) and compression was increased to 6.2:1. These changes raised the power output to 87 bhp (65 kW) at 3800 rpm. In 1937 capacity was again increased to 4,079 cc (248.9 cu in) and power output was now up to 100 bhp (75 kW) at 3800 rpm.

This engine specification was used through 1938 and 1939, although three extra horsepower was quoted. The specification then remained at 103 bhp (75.8 kW) and 4,079 cc (248.9 cu in) until 1947. When the Hydra-Matic Drive option was introduced in 1948, the cars with the automatic box had a higher compression ratio of 7.5:1 giving 106 bhp (78 kW) whilst the manual box cars remained at 103 bhp with a compression ratio of 6.5:1.

The next change came in 1950 when the engine was bored out to give 4,395 cc (268.4 cu in), whilst power output for the manual shift models increased to 108 bhp (79 kW) and the automatic versions delivered 113 bhp (83 kW). Power continued to slowly increase, and by 1954, the last year of the straight eight, it was 122 bhp (89 kW) for the manual cars and 127 bhp (93 kW) for the automatics.

All through the 22-year run, the engines had five main bearings and Carter carburettors. They were noted for their long life and reliability, many covering 100,000 miles with no problems.

Pontiac was one of the most loyal advocates of the straight eight, using essentially the same design for 22 years. This is the 4,395 cc (268.4 cu in) engine in the 1951 Pontiac Eight. A simple straight-forward side valve unit.

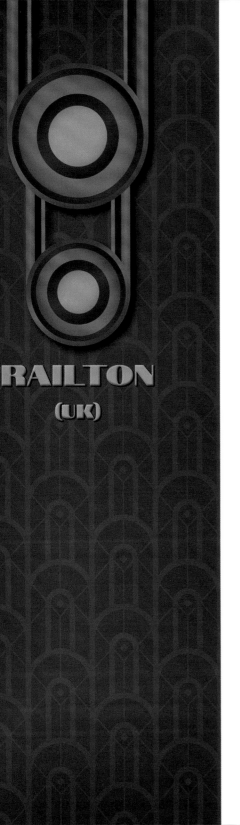

RAILTON

(UK)

The Railton was one of the more successful Anglo-American hybrids of the 1930s. Manufactured by the Fairmile Engineering Company in Cobham, Surrey, UK the car was the brainchild of the company's founder, Noel Macklin. He had sold his Invicta car company in 1933 and was seeking a new venture. The Invicta had proved too expensive and Macklin wanted to make a more affordable 'supercar'.

The first Railton, the Terraplane, was basically a Hudson Terraplane fitted with lighter British-built coachwork. The engine was the straight-forward 16 valve Hudson unit with a bore and stroke of 75 mm x 114 mm (2.95 in x 4.49 in) giving a displacement of 4,010 cc (244.7 cu in). Fed by a single downdraft Carter carburettor, and with a compression ratio of 6.5:1, it delivered 94 bhp at 3,600 rpm. This was sufficient to give excellent performance for the time, 0-60 taking 13 seconds with a top speed of 90 mph (145 kph). It cost £499 (£33,280 at 2020 values) making it a relatively affordable 'supercar'.

The first change came in 1935 when the Hudson Terraplane chassis was replaced by the Hudson Eight chassis, and the engine was enlarged to 4,168 cc (254.5 cu in) by increasing the bore from 75.0 mm to 76.2 mm. The name also changed from Terraplane to Railton Eight. Power output increased to 113 bhp (84 kW) at 3,800 rpm. A lightweight version was available which could achieve 0-60 mph in (for the 1930s) a staggering 8.8 seconds. In 1937 power output increased to 124 bhp at 4,200 rpm with the addition of a twin choke carburettor. An optional alloy head was also available. In total 1,379 were manufactured.

In 1939 Macklin sold the business to Hudson and switched to power boats. During the Second World War, six Railtons were built for use by the Metropolitan Police in London, and after the war four more were completed from spare parts. A new Railton was shown at the 1949 Motor Show in London but at £5,000 (£173,000 at 2020 values) it was far too expensive for the post-war market and did not go into production.

1946 Railton Eight.

OPPOSITE: The simple Hudson engine in the 1946 Railton Eight.

1936 Railton Eight Mk 2. **OPPOSITE:** The 4,168 cc (254.5 cu in) engine in the 1936 Railton Eight Mk 2.

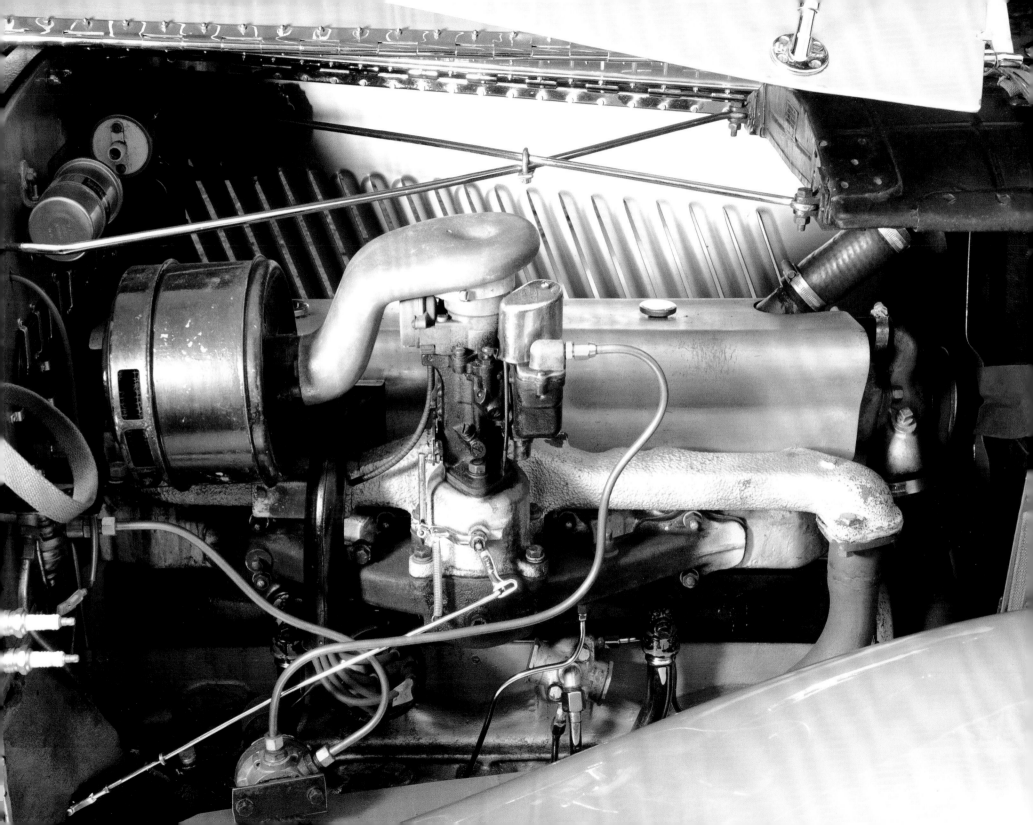

1939 Railton Eight Fairmile. **OPPOSITE:** The simple side valve Hudson engine in the 1939 Eight Fairmile.

RALLY

(FRANCE)

Automobiles Rally was a small company based in Colombes in northwest Paris specialising in building small, powerful, sporting cars. The company was founded by Eugène Affovard Asnière and his first vehicle was a cycle car with a 989 cc Harley Davidson engine.

Typical of his later cars was the 1926 Grand Sport with a supercharged 1,093 cc Chapuis-Dornier engine delivering 70 bhp (51kW) and capable of 110 mph (180 kph), a very fast car for its day. The cars were noted for their fine sporting appearance.

In 1927 the company launched the Type R, with a 1,478 cc (90.2 cu in) dohc straight eight engine with a bore of 56 mm (2.2in) and a stroke of 75 mm (2.95in) which delivered 59 bhp (44 kW) at 4,500 rpm, a fast engine speed for the time. As well as twin camshafts, it had twin carburettors. It is not certain whether this was just a prototype, or whether it was a limited production model.

In any case, the company could not survive the Great Depression, and closed in 1933 after just twelve years.

oday Renault is noted for small to medium-sized cars. What is not common knowledge is that between 1930 and the Second World War the company also made high-end luxury cars designed to compete against vehicles produced by Delage and Delahaye, and even against Rolls-Royce, Hispano Suiza and Isotta Fraschini. In many cases these cars sported expensive coachwork from top designers, and they were often entered in Concours d'Elegance competitions, and frequently won prizes.

Most of these top-end Renaults after 1929 were powered by straight eight engines. Prior to 1929 the cars used large six-cylinder power units, the Renault 40 of 1911-1928 having a choice of a 7.5-litre or a 9.1-litre engine. Also, in 1927, the company produced two new

high-end models, the luxury 'Type RA' and the simpler 'Type PG' with a 3,180 cc (194.1 cu in) engine. These became known as the Vivasix range, and would remain in production until 1930. They were supplemented in 1929 by the more luxurious Vivastella, a 3,620 cc/4,085 cc six-cylinder 'executive' car which lasted in the model range until 1939.

It was also in 1929 that Renault started a new assault on the top end of the market, with the launch of the Reinastella, the largest car the company had made to date. Also, significantly, it was the first Renault to have the radiator in front of the engine. The engine was a fairly standard side valve straight eight, with a bore of 90 mm (3.54 in) and a stroke of 140 mm (5.51 in) giving a displacement of 7,125 cc (434.8 cu in). With

The 4,825 cc (294.4 cu in) engine of the Renault Nervastella Type TG2, with its single Stromberg carburettor.

RENAULT

(FRANCE)

RENAULT EIGHT MODELS

Model TGS		Reinastella	Nervastella	Nervastella ZD2	Nervastella ABM6	Reinesport	Nervasport
Year introduced		1929	1930	1933	1935	1933	1932
Displacement	cc	7,125	4,241	4,825	5,448	7,125	4,241
	cu in	434.8	258.8	294.4	332.5	434.8	258.8
Power output	bhp (max)	108.5	99	99	108	108.5	99
	kW	81	74	74	81	81	74
	@ rpm	2,800	3,300	3,300	3,300	2,800	3,300
Specific output	bhp/litre	15.2	23.3	20.5	19.8	15.2	23.3
	bhp/cu in	0.25	0.38	0.34	0.32	0.25	0.38
	kW/litre	11.4	17.4	15.3	14.9	11.4	17.4
	kW/cu in	0.19	0.29	0.25	0.24	0.19	0.29
Bore	mm	90	75	80	85	90	75
	inches	3.54	2.95	3.15	3.35	3.54	2.95
Stroke	mm	140	120	120	120	140	120
	inches	5.51	4.72	4.72	4.72	5.51	4.72
Bore:stroke ratio		64%	63%	67%	71%	64%	63%
Valve gear		s/v 16v	s/v 16v	s/v 16v	s/v 16v	s/v 16v	s/v 16v
Carburettor		1xStromberg	1xStromberg	1xStromberg	1xStromberg	1xStromberg	1xStromberg

RENAULT EIGHT MODELS

Model		Suprastella	Nerva Grand Sport	Nervahuit
Year introduced		1938	1934	1931
Displacement	cc	5,448	5,448	4,241
	cu in	332.5	332.5	258.8
Power output	bhp (max)	110	108	79
	kW	82	81	59
	@ rpm	2,800	3,300	2,600
Specific output	bhp/litre	20.2	19.8	18.6
	bhp/cu in	0.33	0.32	0.31
	kW/litre	15.1	14.9	13.9
	kW/cu in	0.25	0.24	0.23
Bore	mm	85	85	75
	inches	3.35	3.35	2.95
Stroke	mm	120	120	120
	inches	4.72	4.72	4.72
Bore:stroke ratio		71%	71%	63%
Valve gear		s/v 16v	s/v 16v	s/v 16v
Carburettor		1xStromberg	1xStromberg	1xStromberg

one Stromberg carburettor it delivered 108.5 bhp (81 kW) at 2,800 rpm. Depending on coachwork, it was good for around 84 mph. The Reinastella remained in production until 1933.

In 1930 the slightly smaller, but more technologically advanced, Nervastella was launched, also with a straight eight engine, albeit slightly smaller. Initially with a bore of 75 mm (2.95 in) and a stroke of 120 mm (4.72 in) the total displacement was 4,241 cc (258.8 cu in). With its single Stromberg carburettor, the Nervastella produced 99 bhp (74 kW) at 3,300 rpm. The engine size was increased twice during its production period, to 4,825 cc (294.4 cu in) in 1933 with the Nervastella ZD2, and 5,448 (332.5 cu in) cc in 1935 with the Nervastella ABM6. Surprisingly, the company did not claim any increase in power output for the 1933, and added just 9 bhp (7 kW) with the 1935 upgrade.

Alongside the Reinastella and Nervastella, Reinesport and Nervasport versions were produced from 1933 and 1932 respectively, these being lighter and more economical versions of the larger models, but sharing the same engines.

In addition, a reduced specification model appeared in 1931, this sharing the smallest Nervastella engine, the 4,241 cc (258.8 cu in) unit, and was called the Nervahuit

In 1938 the Nervastella was replaced by the Suprastella, which shared the same 5,448 cc (332.5) engine as the last Nervastellas, now rated at 110 bhp (82 kW) at 2,800 rpm. Depending on coachwork, the Suprastella was capable of between 84 mph (135 kph) and 90 mph (145 kph). The Suprastella continued until 1942, after which Renault no longer competed in the luxury sector.

REO

(US)

The REO Motor Car Company was the second car company founded by Ransom E Olds. Olds had founded the Olds Motor Vehicle Company in 1897, but left in 1905 and set up the new venture in Lansing, Michigan.

REO's most significant models were the six-cylinder Reo Flying Cloud and the eight-cylinder Reo Royale (note that the company's name has been written both as 'REO' and 'Reo' even in the company's own literature). The strategy of trying to cover a broad range of the market, at the time of the Great Depression, proved too much for the business and, like many other companies which had ventured into the straight eight sector, it abandoned motor car manufacturing in 1936. But it continued making lorries and buses.

The Reo Royale was quite a trendsetter, with semi-streamlining, one-shot centralised lubrication, thermostatically operated radiator shutters and (in later examples) REO's own semi-automatic transmission, the Self-Shifter. But the straight eight 8-30 engine was a perfectly conventional nine bearing side valve unit. With a bore of 76.2 mm (3.0 in) and a stroke of 120.7 mm (4.75 in), it had a displacement of 4,403 cc (268.7 cu in). With a single carburettor and two valves per cylinder it delivered 90 bhp (67 kW). The Royale was also offered as a Royale 8-35 with a larger 5,866 cc (358 cu in) engine delivering 125 bhp (93 kW).

When sales remained disappointing, the company added additional straight eight variations to its range, including the Royale 8-31, Flying Cloud 8-25 and a new 90 bhp (67 kW) eight about the same size as the 'sixes'. None of this helped prevent the company's inevitable demise.

RIGHT: The right side of the REO 8-35's engine is very neat. **INSET:** The engine in the 1932 Reo Royale 8-35 Convertible Coupe was a 5,866 cc (358 cu in) side valve unit. The colour coordination between block and coachwork was a nice touch. **OPPOSITE:** The 1931 REO Royale Victoria Coupe was an advanced car, with a semi-automatic gear box, central lubrication and thermostatically controlled radiator slats. But inside was a conventional 4,403 cc (268.7 cu in) flathead engine.

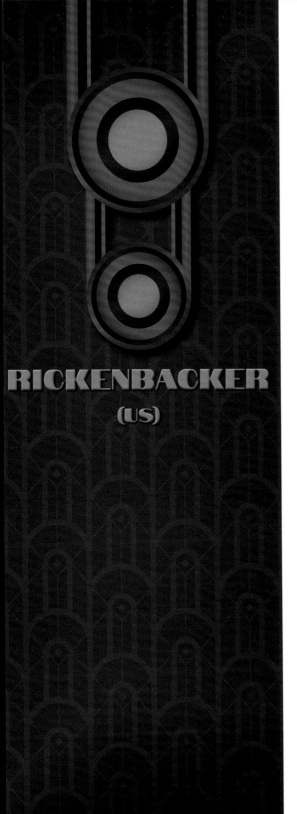

RICKENBACKER
(US)

The Company was founded in 1922 by Eddie Rickenbacker who used his WW1 Squadron emblem of a top hat inside a ring as his car's badge. His early cars were six-cylinder models, but in 1925 he introduced a straight eight model called the Vertical Eight Super Fine which referred to the advanced proprietary engine and high quality of his cars.

This first 'eight' was a 5166cc side valve unit with a bore of 82.6mm, a stroke of 120.7mm, and two valves per cylinder. It produced 90 bhp at 3000 rpm. It had a nine bearing crank and was fed by two Zenith carburettors.

1927 saw two new S8s, the 8-80 and 8-90, which differed from the previous side valve model by utilising overhead valves. The engine used the same block as the previous model but had a slightly smaller bore of 69.9mm giving a displacement of 3699cc. This ohv unit delivered 80 bhp at 3000 rpm, and retained the two Zenith carburettors of the previous model.

Rickenbacker cars were too expensive for the time, and sales were poor. By the time the Company closed down in 1927 a total of 35,000 cars had been sold. The manufacturing equipment was sold to a Danish entrepreneur who also bought the Audi business in 1928. Audi then built a new model with a Rickenbacker engine. This is covered in the chapter on Audi.

RICKENBAKER EIGHT MODELS

Model		Eight	8-80/8-90
Year introduced		1926	1927
Displacement	cc	5,166	3,699
	cu in	315.2	225.7
Power output	bhp (max)	90	80
	kW	67	60
	@ rpm	3,000	3,000
Specific output	bhp/litre	17.4	21.6
	bhp/cu in	0.29	0.35
	kW/litre	13.0	16.2
	kW/cu in	0.21	0.27
Bore	mm	82.6	69.9
	inches	3.25	2.75
Stroke	mm	120.7	120.7
	inches	4.75	4.75
Bore:stroke ratio		68%	58%
Valve gear		s/v 16v	s/v 16v
Carburettor		2xZenith	2xZenith
Main bearings		9	9

A 1926 Rickenbacker 8 Supersports, one of the company's earliest 'eights'. The engine in the 1926 8 Supersports was a 5,166 cc nine bearing side valve unit fed by two Zenith carburettors. The following year the company would switch to overhead valves.

327

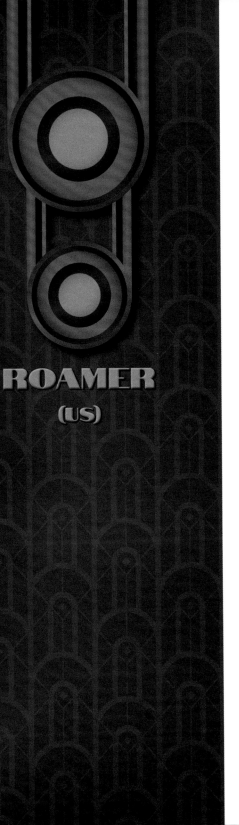

ROAMER

(US)

The Roamer was a car manufactured between 1916 and 1929 by the Barley Motor Car Company. In the early days it had some success with models using six-cylinder Rutenber and four-cylinder Rochester-Duesenberg engines. Roamer advertised its cars as 'America's smartest car', emphasising quality by using a radiator grille almost exactly the same as that on a Rolls-Royce.

Unfortunately, the supply of Duesenberg engines came to an end, and the company switched to 'off the shelf' power units such as those supplied by Lycoming. Launched in 1925, the side valve straight eight came in three different power ratings; the model names, 8-78, 8-80 and 8-88 reflecting the power output.

The top model, the 8-88, had an engine with a bore of 81 mm (3.19 in) and a stroke of 114.3 mm (4.5 in) giving a displacement of 4,712 cc (287.5 cu in). It had a five-bearing crankshaft and a single Schebler carburettor. A slightly enlarged version with a 4,892 cc (298.6 cu in) Lycoming engine was introduced before the company folded.

In total around 12,000 Roamers were made, but sales slipped badly after 1924 and the 'eights' could not save the company, which closed its doors in 1929.

Röhr Auto A.G. was founded in Germany in 1926 by Hans Gustav Röhr. Car production began in 1927, and of its six models before production ceased in 1934, five were straight eights. A feature of the make was fully independent suspension.

The first straight eight model was the 1927 8 8/40. The 1,980cc (120.8 cu in) engine produced 40 bhp (29 kW) allowing a modest top speed of 56 mph (90 kph).

The next model, the 8 Type R 9/50, launched in 1928, brought an enlarged engine of 2,246cc (137.1 cu in) with a bore of 60 mm (2.36 in), a stroke of 100 mm (3.94 in) and a nine-bearing crankshaft. Power increased to 50 bhp (37 kW) at 3,200 rpm, giving a top speed of 63 mph (100 kph). The engine was fed by a single Solex carburettor. The 8 Type R was a success and was manufactured at the rate of ten per day and by 1928 the company employed 800 people.

In 1930, during the Great Depression, Röhr Auto A.G. ran into trouble and filed for bankruptcy. Production stopped in early 1931, and the company was taken over, re-emerging as Neue Röhr A.G. in April the same year.

The 8 Type RA 10/55 was launched In 1931 with a slightly larger 2,494cc (152.2 cu in) engine with output raised to 54 bhp (40 kW). It still had a nine-bearing crankshaft and a single Solex carburettor.

In 1933, the 8 Type RA 10/55 was replaced by the 8 Type F 13/75 with a twin-Zenith carburetted 3,287cc (200.6 cu in) engine producing 75 bhp (55 kW) at 3,200 rpm allowing a top speed of 75 mph (120 kph).

The final incarnation of the Röhr was the 1934 Olympian Type FK, with the same engine as the Type RA but tuned up to 100 bhp (74 kW) giving a top speed of 84 mph (135 kph). Unfortunately, the rise of the National Socialists in 1934 put great pressure on the financial sector in Germany, and without support from the banks the Röhr business became unsustainable, and the company finally closed.

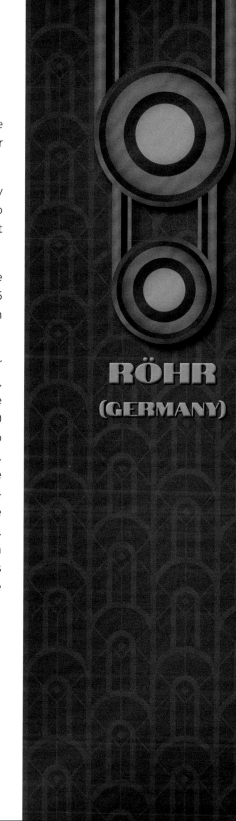

RÖHR

(GERMANY)

RÖHR EIGHT MODELS

Model		8 Type R	8 Type RA	8 Type F	Olympian
Year introduced		1928	1931	1933	1934
Displacement	cc	2,246	2,494	3,287	2,494
	cu in	137.1	152.2	200.6	152.2
Power output	bhp (max)	50	54	75	100
	kW	37	40	55	74
	@ rpm	3,200	3,200	3,200	3,200
Specific output	bhp/litre	22.3	21.7	22.8	40.1
	bhp/cu in	0.36	0.35	0.37	0.66
	kW/litre	16.5	16.0	16.7	29.7
	kW/cu in	0.27	0.26	0.27	0.49
Bore	mm	60	63	69.6	63
	inches	2.36	2.48	2.74	2.48
Stroke	mm	100	100	108	100
	inches	3.94	3.94	4.25	3.94
Bore:stroke ratio		60%	63%	64%	63%
Valve gear		s/v	s/v	s/v	s/v
Carburettor		1xSolex	1xSolex	2xZenith	1xSolex
Main bearings		9	9	9	9

OPPOSITE: The 1928 Röhr Type R 9/50 had a 2,246 cc (137.1 cu in) engine fed by a single Solex carburettor. It was advanced for 1928 in having full independent suspension.

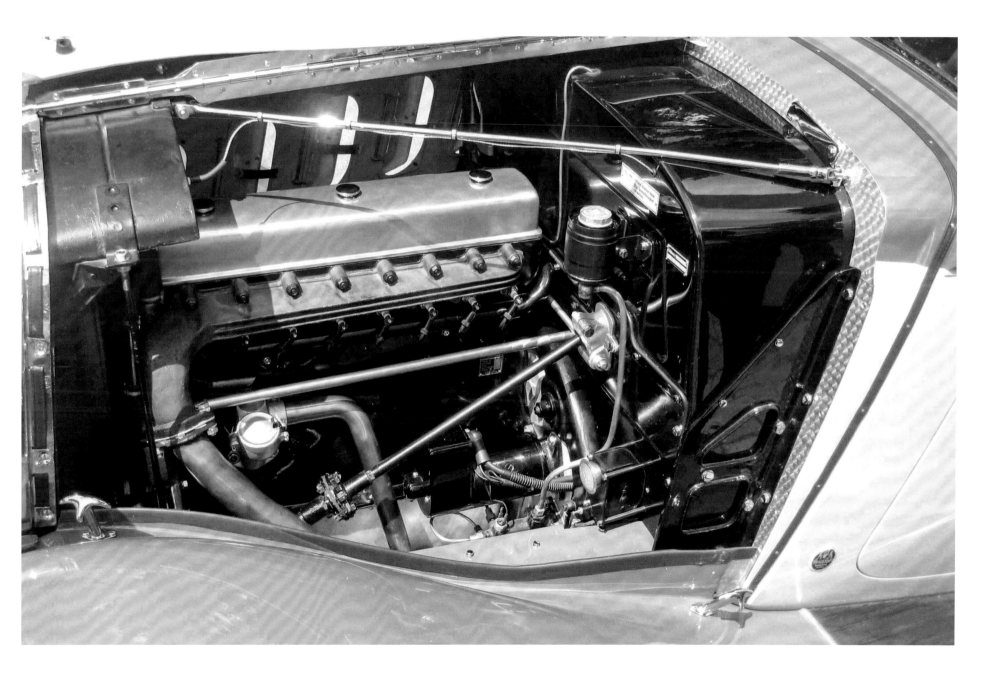

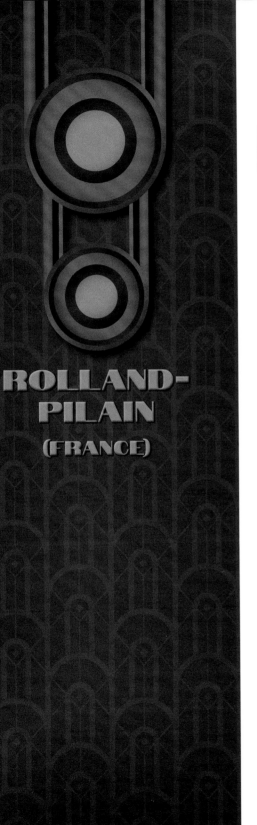

ROLLAND-
PILAIN
(FRANCE)

Rolland-Pilain started manufacturing cars in France in 1907 following a few years as car repairers. Until 1922, only four and six-cylinder engines and road cars, ranging from 1,924 cc (117.4 cu in) to 3,969 cc (242.2 cu in) displacement, were built.

In 1921/22 three highly advanced racing cars for the 1922 Grand Prix season were constructed. The design was unique amongst contemporaries in that the cylinder block and upper half of the crankcase were a single alloy casting in which dry liners were inserted. Two different twin cam cylinder heads were used, both with two valves per cylinder and made of cast iron. One design was conventional with valves at 90 degrees and finger-like cam followers. The other was revolutionary in having desmodromic valves inclined at 160 degrees in order to get the biggest diameter valves possible with a hemispherical combustion chamber. Unlike the earlier Delage with such valves the Rolland-Pilain did away with the small springs designed to complete valve closure. This clearly required extremely accurate design and manufacturing of the cams.

The crankshaft was made in thirteen pieces and sat in five main bearings, whilst the connecting rod bearings were roller bearings. The use of magnesium pistons halved their weight in comparison with conventional aluminium ones. The engine utilized four carburettors.

Unfortunately, their racing career was not a success, and it appears as though the desmodromic valves were abandoned at some point. The poor success on the track did little to stimulate sales of the S8 3-litre Type Grand Sport (as it was known) to the public. Only three Grand Prix cars were made.

Production of all vehicles ceased in 1927 after around 5,000 cars had been built.

OPPOSITE: The 1922 Rolland-Pilain Grand Prix was a highly advanced car with twin cams and desmodronic valves. Photographs are rare.

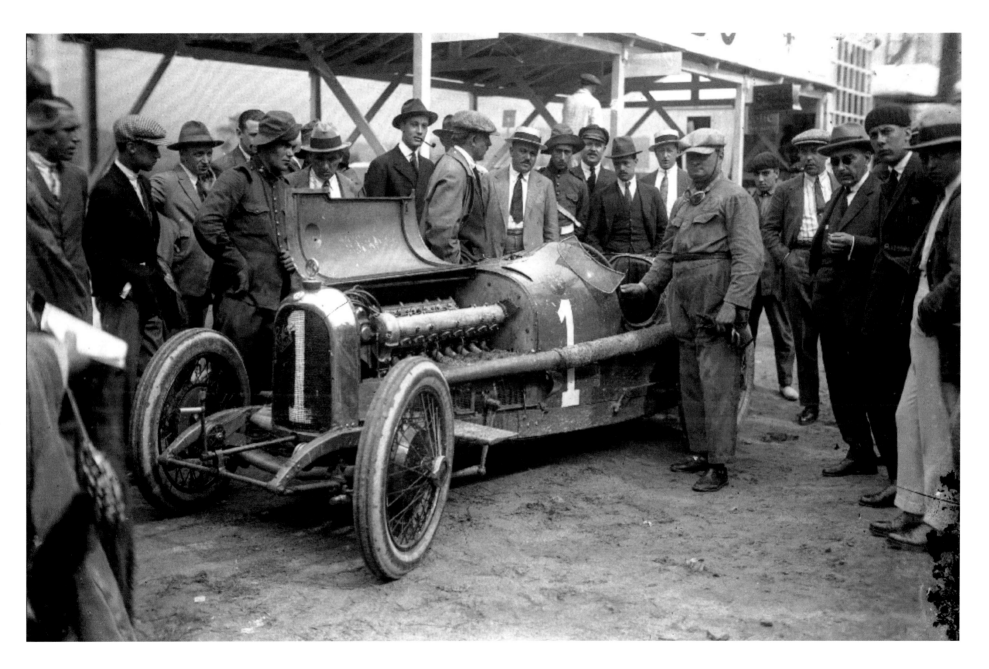

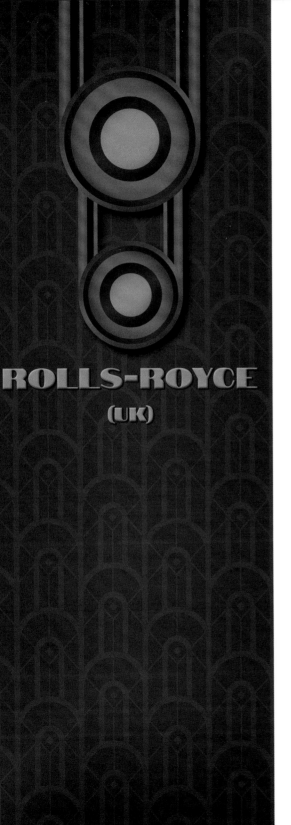

ROLLS-ROYCE

(UK)

Rolls-Royce has been producing eight-cylinder models for a long time. Indeed, the first V8 road car in the world was a Rolls-Royce in 1905. The company produced two versions, the Landaulet Par Excellence and the Legalimit, powered by a 3,535 cc 90-degree V8. Since the Silver Cloud II, launched in 1959, the V8 format has been the Rolls-Royce engine of choice. But the company did produce one straight eight, the exclusive Phantom IV in 1950.

The story goes that, post-war, Rolls-Royce had not planned to continue the series of 'big' Phantoms which had culminated in the glorious V12 Phantom III. The Phantom III engine was extremely complex, including hydraulic tappets which worked well at first but often failed through poor quality lubricating oil or inadequate maintenance. Many PIIIs were converted to solid tappets to avoid these issues. Then in 1937 a project had been started to reduce manufacturing costs by rationalising components across engines. Several prototypes were developed, but the most significant one appeared in 1939 in the form of a Bentley Mark V chassis fitted with a 6.3-litre straight eight Rolls-Royce engine. Although officially called Comet, it was commonly known as The Scalded Cat because of its scorching performance. In 1948 Prince Philip heard about the car and was able to borrow it. He was so impressed he decided to 'order' one, even though it was not a production model. That was the start of a car, the Phantom IV, which was so exclusive it was only sold to heads of state.

From 1943 the engine used in The Scalded Cat was developed into the B-Range of engines used in four, six-and eight-cylinder forms to power a range of military and commercial vehicles during the war. The eight-cylinder version powered the 18 Phantom IVs produced between 1950 and 1956. Two versions of this engine were used; the first 15 cars had the 5,675 cc (346 cu in) B80 version, whilst the last three had the 6,516 cc (397 cu in) B81. Both engines shared the same stroke of 114 mm (4.5 in), whilst the 89 mm (3.5 in) bore of the B80 was increased to 95 mm (3.75 in) for the B81. Maximum power output was 160bhp (119 kW) for the smaller version and 185 bhp (138 kW) for the larger one. Both versions had overhead inlet and side exhaust valves, a compression ratio of 6.4:1 and a single Stromberg carburettor.

There was a high degree of rationalisation across the range. For example, the eight-cylinder variant used two sets of oil bath air filters and exhaust manifolds from the four-cylinder version, and pistons, connecting rods, valves, spring liners were fully interchangeable across the range until the B81 was introduced; even then there was still a high degree of commonality. In military applications this interchangeability was an enormous benefit.

The photographs show the 1953 Phantom, which belonged to Queen Elizabeth, together with images of both sides of the engine which emphasise its fairly mundane appearance.

This 1953 Rolls-Royce Phantom IV is one of just eighteen produced between 1950 and 1956. This royal car is distinguished by having no number plate and having the distinctive small blue light above the windscreen. Royal cars are the only vehicles apart from the emergency services to be permitted to have forward facing blue lights. The engine in the 1953 Phantom IV was derived from the B-Range of military engines. The first fifteen Phantom IVs had the 5,675 cc B80 version, whilst the last three had the larger 6,516 cc B81.

In 1929 New Era Motors of New York announced the launch of the front wheel drive Ruxton, designed to be a direct competitor to Cord. Production began in June 1930 at both the Moon and Kissel factories. Unfortunately, extended legal wrangles led to the venture being terminated just four months after it started. In total 96 cars were made in that short production period. The engine was a 4,408 cc (269 cu in) L-head straight eight Continental 18S engine driving a three-speed front wheel drive transaxle on De Dion suspension. Power output was 100 bhp (74.6 kW)

The Ruxton was notable for being just 135 cm (53 in) tall, when the typical American car was 183 cm (72 in) tall. The absence of a drive shaft to the rear wheels allowed the bodywork to sit low down. Of the 96 Ruxtons produced, just nineteen are known to survive.

This is a 1930 example of the Ruxton Model C, a car noted for being only 53 inches in height. This the benefit of its front wheel drive.

The engine in the Ruxton Model C was a straight-forward 4,408 cc (269 cu in) Continental 18S. **INSET:** The 'business side' of the Continental engine with the single updraft carburettor and quite tidy 'plumbing'.

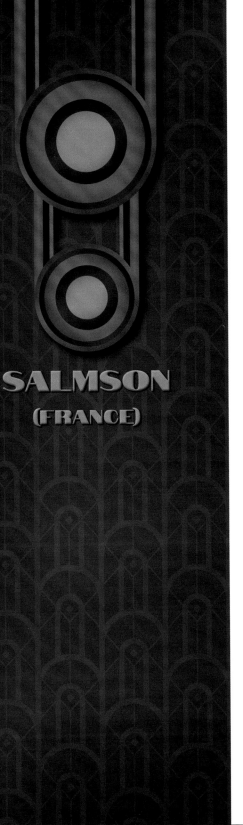

SALMSON

(FRANCE)

The French firm of Emile Salmson, Ing was founded in Paris in 1890 by Emile Salmson as a manufacturer of centrifugal pumps and steam-driven compressors for use by the military and the railways. In 1896 it was renamed Emile Salmson et Cie and began focusing on petrol engine applications, and became one of the first companies to manufacture purpose-built aero engines, which it did throughout The First World War. Using the expertise developed during the war, the company began manufacturing cars and continued to do so until 1957.

The first vehicles were British GN cycle cars built under licence, but from 1921 Salmson produced its own designs, the first using an unusual four-cylinder engine where one pushrod worked both inlet and exhaust valves in turn. This was the work of engineer Emile Petit. Surprisingly this engine only had two main bearings.

Petit, keen to explore racing opportunities, developed the basic 'four' to include twin cams driven by skew gears and a vertical shaft. These little 1,100 cc and 1,200 cc twin cam racing engines were potent and light and sold by the thousands. Salmson only ever made small engines, and perhaps the most spectacular of all was the supercharged twin cam straight eight of just 1,100 cc

Salmson's Eight.

produced in 1928 and aimed at competing against the highly successful twin cam Amilcar. This tiny 'eight' produced 140 bhp (104 kW) at 7,200 rpm, a high engine speed for the time. An output of 127 bhp/litre (95 kW/litre) was extremely impressive for 1928.

An interesting feature of this engine was the drive to the camshaft which rose as a sequence of spur gears between the two four-cylinder blocks. This was exactly the solution later used by Alfa Romeo for its 8C 2300 in 1931, though whether this was directly copied from Salmson is not clear. Unfortunately, at this time the company decided to abandon racing ventures to concentrate on its small engine cars, so the spectacular straight eight was not developed further.

Although today associated mainly with small and medium sized cars, mostly based on similar Volkswagen models, Škoda has in the past strayed into the upper echelons of the car market, even producing chauffeur-drive limousines.

Škoda cars originate with the company Laurent and Klement, founded in 1895, but the company experienced financial problems and was taken over by Škoda Works in 1925, and at the same time it took the brave step of launching a straight eight, the 860. Its 3,880 cc (236.8 cu in) side valve engine was basically two four-cylinder engines joined together. The nine bearing crankshaft and a chain-driven camshaft located in the crankcase on the left of the engine gave a smooth performance. With 59 bhp (44 kW) it could achieve 80-85 mph. In some ways it was advanced, with aluminium pistons and Dural cranks.

But the 860 was not a success with just 47 being made and, it is rumoured, only 23 were sold. Fortunately, at least one, the car in the photograph, survives. The mid to late 1920s was not a good time to launch a luxury limousine.

1932 Škoda 860.

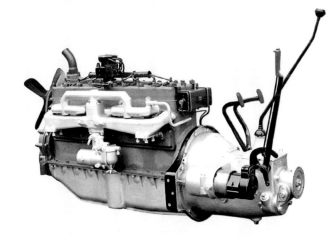

The 3,880 cc (236.8 cu in) engine in the 1932 Škoda 860.

ŠKODA
(AUSTRIA-HUNGARY NOW CZECH REPUBLIC)

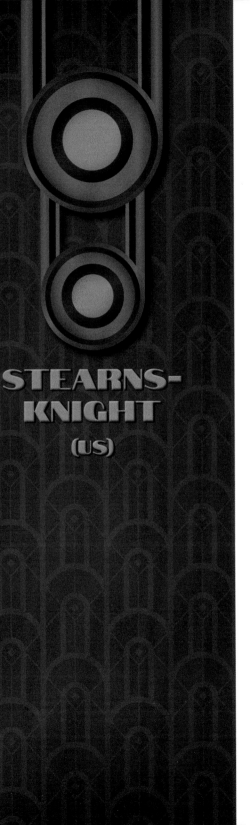

STEARNS-KNIGHT (US)

Stearns-Knight had a reputation for being amongst the finest automobiles in the world at the time, claimed by many to be on a par with the likes of Rolls-Royce, Duesenberg and Isotta Fraschini.

Frank Stearns was an interesting and colourful character. Born into a wealthy family, he left school at 17 to build cars converting the basement of his family's large house into a machine shop. Stearns was a prodigious inventor, designer and constructor. Starting with a single cylinder engine in 1896, he was producing twin cylinder engines by 1902, 'fours' by 1905, and by 1909 his line-up consisted of the four-cylinder 15-30 and 30-60, together with the 45-90 'six'. In 1911 he came out with a sleeve valve engine based on the invention of Charles Yale Knight, the engine and the car being referred to as the Stearns-Knight, the name having to be hyphenated as part of the agreement with Knight. The company was offering a 6.8-litre straight eight by 1914, and a V8 by 1917, one of the few offering a V8 at that time.

The 1927 straight eight 8-90 is considered to be the pinnacle of the Stearns business, and after that model there were no new developments until the company closed in 1929. The 8-90 had a 6.3-litre (357 cu in) double sleeve valve engine with nine main bearings delivering 112 bhp and giving the potential for 100+ mph performance. There were small variations in engine size, with a 6.8-litre (385 cu in) unit, having a bore of 89 mm (3.5 in) and a stroke of 127 mm (5.0 in), being the largest and delivering an extra 8 bhp.

The Stearns-Knight 'eight' was always an exclusive and expensive car, and in its last year just 295 were made. A bare chassis to go to a coachbuilder cost around $8,500 ($125,000 in today's terms) and coachwork could easily double that cost.

ABOVE: A 1929 Stearns-Knight 8-90. The 8-90 was the pinnacle of Stearns' business, and is considered on a par with Rolls-Royce. The company closed in 1929 just after this example was made. **OPPOSITE:** The 6.3-litre (357 cu in) engine in the 1929 Stearns-Knight 8-90 had double sleeve valves and nine main bearings allowing near silent running.

STOEWER
(GERMANY)

The first Stoewer company was founded in 1896 by Emil and Bernhard Stoewer to manufacture sewing machines. In 1899 they branched out into car production, forming Gebruder Stoewer, Fabrik fur Motorfahrzeugen. Their first car was the 6.5 hp Grosser Motorwagen, or large motor car, but it was with the 1908 G4, of which 1,070 were built, that the company became successful. In the 1920s a new class of car was introduced, the D-Types, with the four-cylinder D3, D9 and D10, and six-cylinder D5, D6 and D12 models.

As with many other car manufacturers, Stoewer introduced more up-market straight eight models at just the wrong time. In 1928 it launched the S8, with a 1,991 (122 cu in) cc engine, and the G14 with a 3,633 cc (222 cu in) unit. These were quickly followed by even grander models, the Gigant G15 with a 3,974 cc (242 cu in) 80 bhp (59 kW) engine, the Repräsentant P20 with 4,906 cc (299 cu in) and the M12 Marschall powered by a 2,963 cc (181 cu in) straight eight. They were all 2-valve 'flathead' units fed by a single carburettor.

The worldwide economic problems in the late 1920s limited the appeal of the larger Stoewers, and production of the straight eights ceased after 2,274 had been produced. The table below shows some statistics for these cars. As can be seen from the table the survival rate of Stoewers is extremely low, only eleven known to survive, just 0.5% of those made.

After the Second World War, during which Stoewer made 13,000 FWD off-road cars for the Wermacht, the factory was seized by the Red Army, the plants dismantled and sent to the Soviet Union.

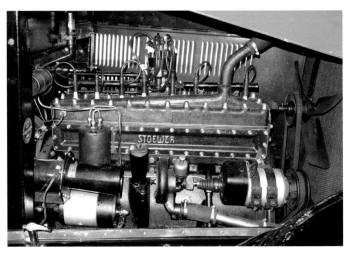

A rare 1928 Stoewer S8 from the Stoewer Museum collection. **RIGHT:** The small 2-litre side valve 'eight' engine in the Stoewer S8.

STOEWER EIGHT MODELS

Model		S8	G14	S10	G15 Gigant	Representat 20	M12 Marschall
Year introduced		1928	1928	1928	1928	1930	1930
Displacement	cc	1,991	3,633	2,464	3,974	4,906	2,963
	cu in	122	222	151	242	299	181
Power output	bhp (max)	45	70	52	80	100	60
	kW	33	52	38	59	74	44
	@ rpm	2,600	2,450	3,500	3,500	3,200	3,500
Specific output	bhp/litre	22.6	19.3	21.1	20.1	20.4	20.2
	bhp/cu in	0.37	0.32	0.34	0.33	0.33	0.33
	kW/litre	16.6	14.3	15.4	14.8	15.1	14.8
	kW/cu in	0.27	0.23	0.25	0.24	0.25	0.24
Bore	mm	60	70	62	72	80	68
	inches	2.36	2.76	2.44	2.83	3.15	2.68
Stroke	mm	88	118	102	122	122	102
	inches	3.46	4.65	4.02	4.80	4.80	4.02
Bore:stroke ratio		68%	59%	61%	59%	66%	67%
Valve gear		s/v 16v	s/v 16v	s/v 16v	s/v 16v	s/v 16v	s/v 16v
Carburettor		single	single	single	single	single	single
Number made		380	150	790	650	24	280
Number surviving		1	0	4	5	1	0

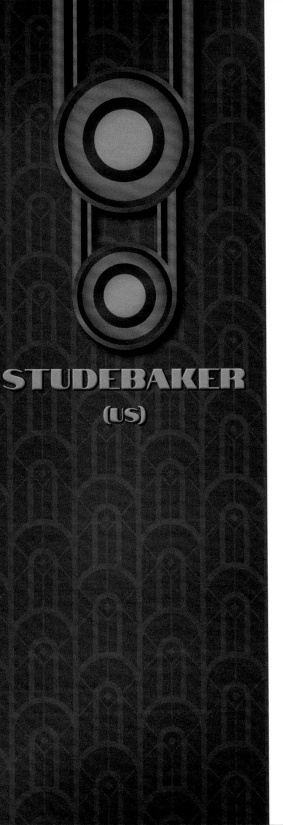

STUDEBAKER
(US)

The Studebaker Brothers Manufacturing Company was founded in 1852 and made wagons for farmers, the military and miners. It began manufacturing vehicles in 1902 with electric cars, and started making petrol-driven vehicles in 1904.

Until 1928 the top of the range Studebaker was the six-cylinder 5,800 cc (354 cu in) 'Big Six' model. In 1926 the name of this model was changed to President until the new straight eight President was launched in 1928. Upon the 'eight' appearing the top 'six' was renamed Dictator, a name which did little for sales outside the United States!

The straight eight President had a slightly smaller side valve engine than the Big Six, with a bore of 85.7 mm (3.37 in) and a stroke of 111.1 mm (4.37 in) giving a displacement of 5,121 cc (312.5 cu in). The new engine delivered 100 bhp (75 kW) at 3,200 rpm. The crankshaft was drilled to provide lubrication direct to the five bearings. By 1932 the engine had an increased bore of 88.9 mm (3.5 in) giving a displacement of 5,517 cc (336.7 cu in) and an increase in power to 122 bhp (91 kW).

In 1929 a smaller straight eight engine of 3,622 cc (221 cu in) was offered as an option on the smaller Dictator model. The President was discontinued in 1942.

An elegant and compact 1931 Studebaker President drophead two-seater.

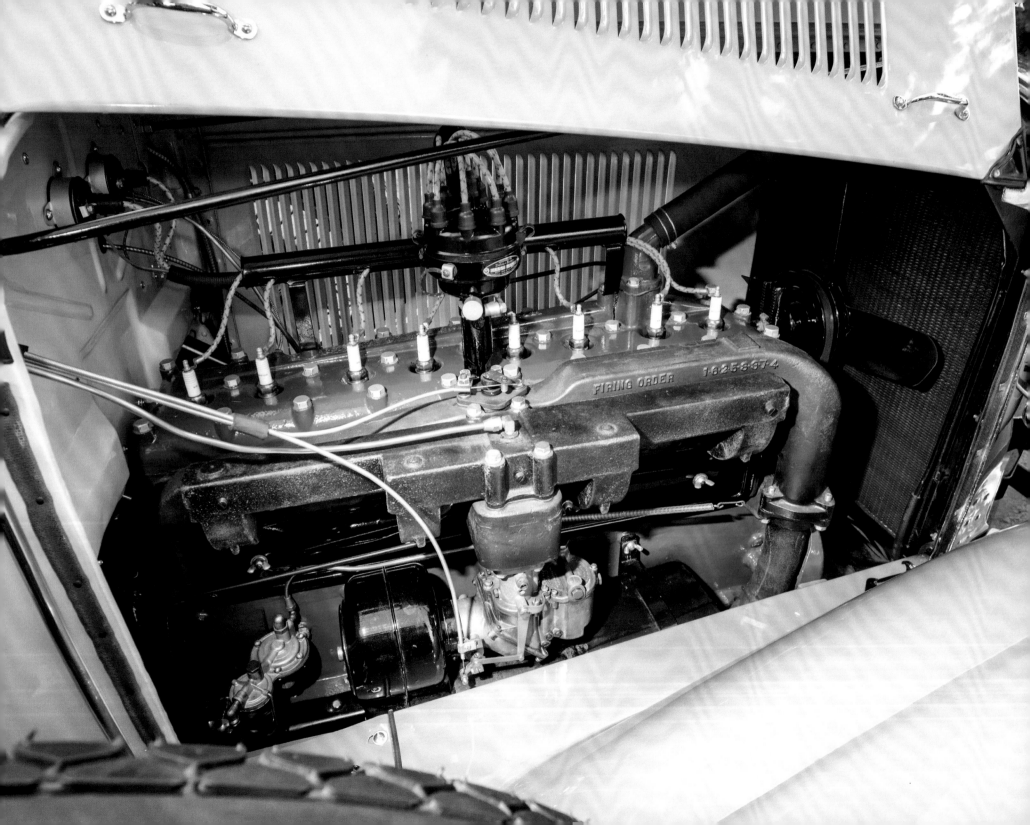

The 1931 Studebaker President had a straight-forward 5,121 cc (312.5 cu in) nine bearing side valve engine (above). To aid lubrication, the crankshaft was drilled. The inlet/exhaust size of the President's engine (opposite), showing a firing order of 1-6-2-5-8-3-7-4. The wiring to the plugs is very neat.

STUDEBAKER EIGHT MODELS

Model		President 8	President 8	Dictator 8
Year introduced		1928	1932	1929
Displacement	cc	5,130	5,517	3,622
	cu in	313	336.7	221
Power output	bhp (max)	100	122	81
	kW	75	91	60
	@ rpm	3,200	3,200	3,200
Specific output	bhp/litre	19.5	22.1	22.4
	bhp/cu in	0.32	0.36	0.37
	kW/litre	14.6	16.5	16.6
	kW/cu in	0.24	0.27	0.27
Compression ratio		5.1:1	5.1:1	5.0:1
Bore	mm	85.7	88.9	77.8
	inches	3.37	3.5	3.06
Stroke	mm	111.1	111.1	95.3
	inches	4.37	4.37	3.75
Bore:stroke ratio		77%	80%	82%
Carburettor		1xStromberg	1xStromberg	1xStromberg
Main bearings		5	5	5

In the 1930s Stutz was at the forefront of technological sophistication in the American car industry. Unlike in Europe, where many models had dual overhead cams, in the US only Stutz and Duesenberg produced cars for sale to the public with dohc. The vast majority of American cars at the time were flatheads, even amongst upmarket models from the likes of Packard and Lincoln. In the straight eight sector Stutz and Duesenberg had dohc models, possibly the result of their involvement in racing.

Stutz's first venture into straight eights was the Vertical Eight in 1926, which featured an engine with a single overhead cam, nine main bearings, a cross flow head, two valves and two spark plugs per cylinder. It had been designed by Charles Greuter, who did not work at Stutz at the time, but was employed by the Excelsior Motor Company in Chicago. However, he joined Stutz and set to work on an improved version of the Vertical Eight, which became known as the Series AA Vertical Eight. The main change was the use of a 'silent' chain to power

A 1930 Stutz M-Series with very elegant two-door drophead coachwork.

the single overhead cam, replacing the noisy train of bevel gears. This engine developed 92 bhp (69 kW) @ 3,200 rpm from its 4712cc (287 cu in). By 1930 the Vertical Eight had evolved into the M-Series cars with an enlarged 5,275 cc (321.9 cu in) engine, still with a single overhead camshaft and two valves per cylinder. The final stage of evolution came in 1931 when the engine was given twin overhead camshafts and four valves per cylinder, and renamed the DV 32 (DV standing for 'dual valve', and the 32 referring to the total number of valves), giving greatly improved breathing capacity, up by around 60%. Its larger displacement delivered 156 bhp (116 kW) at 3,900 rpm, which was just marginally less than the complex 'flathead' V12s from Packard and Lincoln, and only 20 bhp (16 kW) less than the V16 ohv Cadillac. It became known as the Bearcat, or Super Bearcat, a resurrection of the name of the famous model from 1913/14.

In parallel with the DV32, the earlier sohc unit, renamed the SV16 (SV for single cam, and 16 for the number of valves) was still available, delivering a more modest 113 bhp (84 kW) at 3,300 rpm.

The DV32 made a good impression on the motoring press, especially in Europe. But the car was extremely expensive. The LeBaron sedan sold for $5,295 ($88,090 in 2020 values), which was more than the V16 Cadillac. It proved too expensive for the market, and sales were slow, with just 700 being sold in total. In 1934 the production of Stutz cars came to an end, at least until the 'revival' of the name in 1971, when the Blackhawk appeared and remained on sale until 1987.

STUTZ EIGHT MODELS

Model		Vertical 8	M-Series	DV32	SV16
Year introduced		1926	1930	1931	1931
Displacement	cc	4,712	5,275	5,275	4,894
	cu in	287.5	321.9	321.9	298.7
Power output	bhp (max)	92	113	156	113
	kW	69	84	116	84
	@ rpm	3,200	3,300	3,900	3,300
Specific output	bhp/litre	19.5	21.4	29.6	23.1
	bhp/cu in	0.32	0.35	0.48	0.38
	kW/litre	14.6	15.9	22.0	17.2
	kW/cu in	0.24	0.26	0.36	0.28
Compression ratio		4.8:1	5.0:1	5.0:1	6.25:1
Bore	mm	81	85.7	85.7	82.6
	inches	3.19	3.37	3.37	3.25
Stroke	mm	114	114	114	114
	inches	4.5	4.5	4.5	4.5
Bore:stroke ratio		71%	75%	75%	72%
Valve gear		sohc 16v	dohc 32v	dohc 32v	sohc 16v
Carburettor		2xZenith	1xZenith	1xSchebler	2xZenith
Main bearings		9	9	9	9

The exhaust side of the M-Series' 5,275 cc (321.9 cu in) sohc engine.

The inlet side of the Stutz M-Series engine with its single updraft carburettor.

A 1929 Stutz Vertical
Eight 'restoration job'.

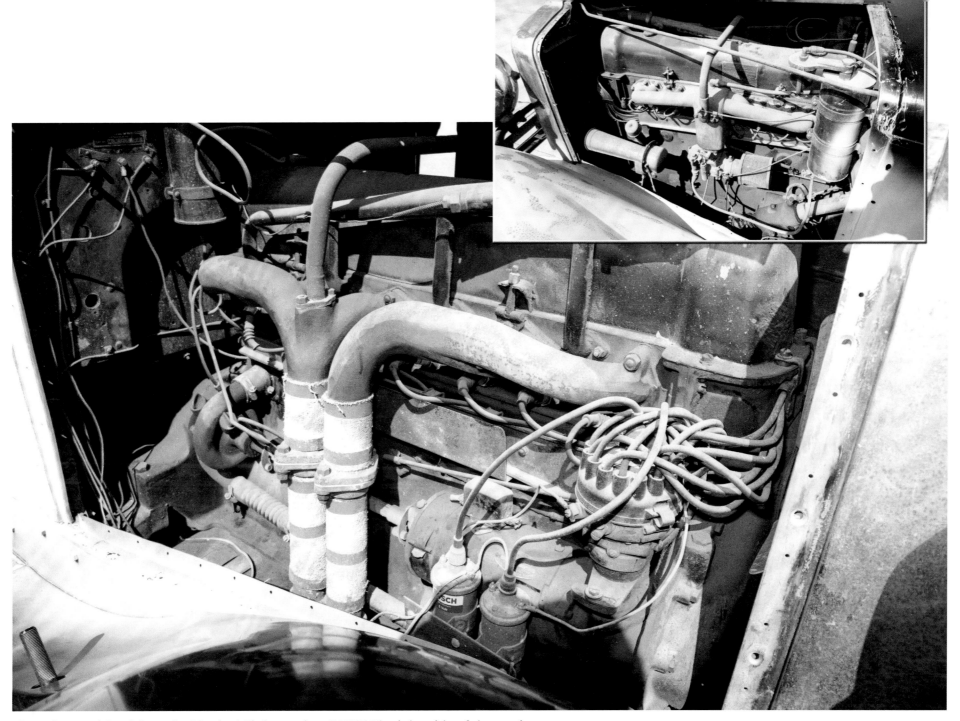

The exhaust side of the sohc Vertical Eight engine. **INSET:** The inlet side of the engine.

unbeam's main involvement with straight eight engines was in Grand Prix and Voiturette racing, although it did produce some road cars, albeit in limited numbers.

After the First World War Sunbeam combined with Talbot and Darracq to form the STD combine which became a major player in Grand Prix and Voiturette racing, as well as land speed record attempts, albeit with mixed results. In late 1920 the STD Experimental Department began development of a new Grand Prix chassis and a new straight eight engine. The design of the engine was strongly influenced by Ernest Henry's pre-war work for Peugeot and post-war work at Ballot.

During the 1920s STD used two engine formats for racing, a 4.9-litre straight six and a 3-litre straight eight. The straight eight had a bore of 65 mm (2.6, in) and a stroke of 112 mm (4.4 in) giving a displacement of 2,973 cc (181.4 cu in). The alloy cylinder block was cast as two units of four with a non-detachable head cast in one unit. The alloy block had shrunk-in steel liners, and the phosphor bronze valve seats were screwed in. The crankshaft had five plain bearings and sat in a dry sump. As the crank throw was counterbalanced there was no flywheel. Twin camshafts were driven by a train of straight cut bevel gears at the front of the engine and there were four valves in each cylinder inclined at 60 degrees to each other. The compression ratio varied from 5.7:1 to 6.3:1, and the maximum output was 112 bhp (84 kWs) at 4,700 rpm.

Carburettion varied and included four horizontal Claudel Hobson carburettors (the company was a subsidiary of STD) and four Zenith carburettors. Two firing orders were used: 1-3-4-2-8-6-5-7 and 1-8-3-6-4-5-2-7. The first pattern is akin to two 'fours' working almost independently, whilst the second pattern reflect a central 'four' with a split 'four' making up the ends.

Away from the track, Sunbeam launched the 30/98 straight eight in 1926, which was available with either a 4,825 cc (294 cu in) or a 5,028 cc (307 cu in) engine. These engines had nine main bearings, and a single Claudel Hobson carburettor. In 1927 the road cars became the 4,828 cc (295 cu in) '30' and the 5,447 cc (332 cu in) '35'. These cars were produced in limited numbers, only around 65 being sold in total.

In 1936 Sunbeam showed a new straight eight at the Olympia Motor Show. This was based on a Humber chassis and featured a 4,503 cc (275 cu in) engine which developed 150 bhp (112 kW) at 4,500 rpm. But a decision was made not to produce this, and the four completed cars were broken up.

Triumph never manufactured a production straight eight, but the 1934 Dolomite deserves special mention in this book even though just three were made at the time. Some spare engines and chassis were later assembled into complete cars by a London company called High Speed Motors (HSM), and total production is believed to be around six.

In 1934, Donald Healey performed unexpectedly well in the Monte Carlo Rally driving a modified Triumph Gloria, and as a result the Triumph Company decided to enter the sports car field. The result was the Dolomite, which was a virtual copy of the Alfa Romeo 8C 2300. The engines were almost identical, with the drive for the twin camshafts positioned between two sets of four-cylinders, a signature feature of the 8C. By dividing the camshafts in two, the torsional issues of a long shaft were halved. The main difference between the two cars was the swept volume. By reducing the bore from the

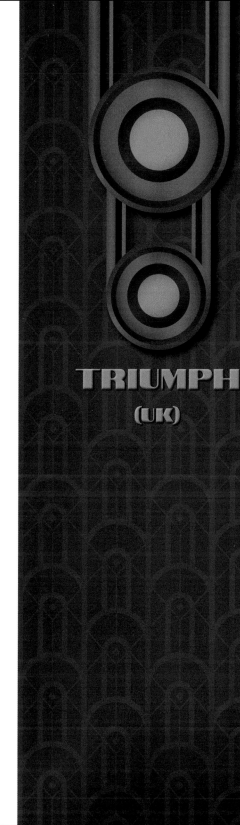

TRIUMPH
(UK)

A contemporary photograph of the 1934 Triumph Dolomite's 1,991 cc engine showing the perfectly balanced exhausts.

Alfa's 65 mm (2.6 in) to 60 mm (2.4 in) the displacement was reduced to 1,991 cc (121 cu in). The engine was good for 140 bhp (104 kW) at 5,500 rpm. They were intended to carry a chassis-only price of £1000, and a 100 mph guarantee, a prototype having lapped Brooklands at just under 120 mph. The photographs show the elegant exhaust system, which was not an Alfa copy, nor was the oil reservoir at the front of the car.

The car never went into full production partly because of financial issues at Triumph, and possibly also the realisation that demand for the car may never match expectations.

ABOVE: The inlet side of the Triumph Dolomite engine showing the central drive to the twin overhead camshafts, the supercharger and finned inlet manifold. It was almost a copy of the Alfa Romeo 8C 2300, with a smaller displacement.

RIGHT: This and the following six images are pages from the Triumph Dolomite brochure.

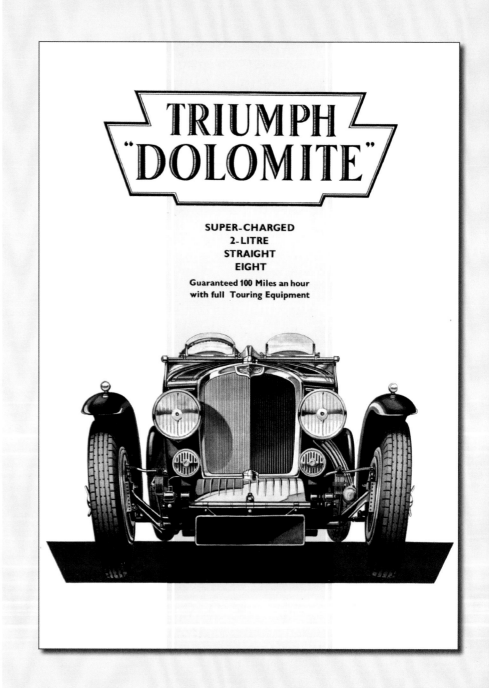

ENGINE (Induction Side).

This illustration clearly shows the 8-cylinder, super-charged power unit and the accessibility of all the components. The induction pipe is of electron, and has been designed to ensure 100 per cent. efficiency. The steering box, also of electron, has a 2-point suspension direct to the engine crankcase, and is of the worm and wheel type with ball bearings throughout. The neat and accessible mounting of the super-charger will be noted, and forward of this is the carburetter and air intake. In this view too, the Armstrong Siddeley Wilson self-change gearbox and the method of control can be seen.

FRONT WHEEL ASSEMBLY.

Note the clean and robust stub axle. The ample brake drums have separate adjusting units for each shoe. These adjusting units are mounted on each side of the top end of the swivel pin and make brake adjustment instantaneous. No tools whatever are required. An air scoop is fitted to carry heat away from the brakes as quickly as possible. The steering arm and solid eyed front road springs are points that will appeal.

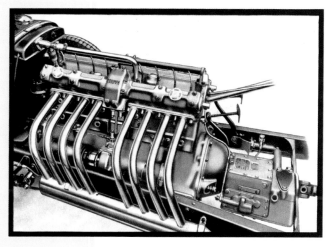

ENGINE (Exhaust Side).

The exhaust system is prominent in this photograph. It will be noted that the dynamo is gear-driven from the centre of the crankshaft, and is most accessibly placed. Forward of the engine the vertically-driven magneto can be seen. The position of this unit results in a very neat layout for the ignition leads which are entirely insulated. This view also shows the Armstrong Siddeley Wilson gearbox and further details of the gear control are noticeable. The whole engine and gearbox are remarkable for their clean layout and accessibility.

BRAKE ASSEMBLY.

This photograph shows the exceptionally robust R.R. Hiduminium alloy brake shoes, the cam adjusters for these shoes can also be observed. The reverse side of the closely fitting aluminium back plate is shown, together with the Lockheed cylinder. The whole of this brake assembly is of the most rigid construction and yet, by reason of the materials and design, it is remarkably light and efficient.

TRIUMPH "DOLOMITE"

TRIUMPH 'DOLOMITE' 8-CYLINDER CHASSIS SPECIFICATION.

ENGINE. 8 Cylinders in Line.
R.A.C. Horse Power Rating ... 17·85
Bore ... ... 60 m/m.
Stroke ... ... 88 m/m.
1,990 c.c.
Capacity / Max. R.P.M. 5500
B.H.P. 140
Cylinder block and Head detachable, constructed of R.R. Hiduminium aluminium alloy with steel alloy valve seats. Crankcase and sump Elektron. Cylinders fitted with Nitrogen hardened cast-iron liners. 10 Bearing Crankshaft in full dynamic balance. Vibration Damper incorporated. Twin overhead Camshafts operating directly on valves, which are fitted with triple valve springs. These Camshafts are gear-driven from centre of Crankshaft, thus preventing torsional stress on crankshaft. Pistons of R.R. Hiduminium alloy of special design.

LUBRICATION. Dry sump. High pressure pump feed to all bearings, sump scavenged by low pressure pump to auxiliary oil tank —capacity 3 galls.

CARBURATION. By twin body Downdraught Carburetter with single float chamber.

SUPERCHARGER. Gear-driven Roots Type of "Triumph" design and manufacture.

IGNITION. By coil or Magneto optional, driven from front end of Crankshaft.

COOLING. Centrifugal water circulating pump and sloping "V" type radiator with specially efficient type core.

GEAR BOX. Special Armstrong Siddeley Wilson type 4-speed self changing type with double oil pump. Pre-selector control mounted on steering column. Gear ratios:—
1st ... ... 3·10 to 1
2nd ... ... 1·85 to 1.
3rd ... ... 1·23 to 1.
4th ... ... Direct.
Reverse ... ... 3·42 to 1.

TRANSMISSION. Open tubular Propeller Shaft, short and stiff, mounted on needle roller bearing universal joints.

REAR AXLE. Semi-floating. Pressed steel casing and spiral bevel drive.

FRAME. Special Nickel Steel, deep section upswept over rear axle.

SPRINGING. Front and rear semi-elliptic springs, mounted outside chassis frame very close to wheel centres, ensuring stability. Adjustable shock absorbers.

STEERING. Of worm and nut type. Elektron steering box. High ratio 1·75 turns from one lock to another. Wheel position adjustable for angle and height.

BRAKES. Hydraulic four-wheel brakes, operating Ferodo-lined shoes of R.R. Alloy in Elektron drums of 16in. diameter with steel liners. Correct proportioning of braking between front and rear maintained by larger operating cylinders in front brakes. Hand brake operating direct on rear wheels.

WHEELS. Racing Rudge-Whitworth wire wheels.

TYRES. Dunlop Fort, 19-5·25in.

REAR AXLE RATIO. 4·5 to 1 or 4 to 1, as ordered.

USEFUL DATA.
Chassis Weight ... ... 14 cwt.
Complete Car (unladen) ... 19 cwt.
Turning Circle... ... ... 37 feet.
Minimum Ground Clearance 8 inches.
Track ... ... 4ft. 6in.
Wheel Base ... ... 8ft. 8in.
Petrol Capacity ... ... 20 galls.
Oil Capacity ... ... 3 galls.
Annual Tax (After Jan. 1st, 1935) £13 10 0

EQUIPMENT. 12v. Electrical System. Twin batteries at rear of chassis. Constant voltage control dynamo. Electric starter. Electric petrol gauge. Oil and water temperature gauges. Oil and supercharger pressure gauges. Ammeter, clock and revolution counter. High frequency electric horns. Dipping head lamps, side lamps, "Stop" tail lamp.

CHASSIS PRICE. 1,000 Guineas. (at Works).

The prices and specification printed in this leaflet are subject to alterations without notice.

TRIUMPH COMPANY LIMITED - - COVENTRY
Telephone : 4191 Coventry   Telegrams : Triumfcar, Coventry
LONDON : 218, GREAT PORTLAND STREET, W.I
Telephone : Museum 3951   Telegrams : Cyclothure, Wesdo, London

P 122

TRIUMPH "DOLOMITE"

The Triumph "Dolomite" has been designed to fill a gap which has long existed in the ranks of British cars. British Manufacturers, as designers and producers are second to none, but for the last few years singularly little attention has been given by them to the "ultra-performance" type of motor car. Continental manufacturers have had a clear field in this direction and have made good use of their opportunities.

The Triumph "Dolomite" is introduced as the "ultra-performance" car of to-day, a super-charged, 2-litre straight eight, each standard car being delivered with a guarantee that it has covered a flying mile at a speed in excess of 100 miles an hour, with full touring equipment. This in itself is unique.

The Triumph "Dolomite" will not be produced as a racing car, but a guarantee of performance for a standard car as detailed above ensures that, suitably developed, it will be capable of a definite challenge to any car of a similar capacity produced in Europe or elsewhere. It is a car which, in the hands of those with the necessary knowledge and skill, is capable of upholding British prestige in a class which for the last few years has been so successfully exploited by foreign cars. Production is strictly limited, and each car is built and tested under the personal supervision of Mr. Donald Healey, who will welcome all purchasers at the Works, and place at their disposal all technical data and information that they may desire.

PRICE (Complete) :
£1,225
Chassis only, 1,000 Guineas

OFF-SIDE VIEW OF THE CHASSIS.

Here is the perfectly proportioned chassis, with the power unit placed well back in the frame, giving ideal weight distribution, with the resultant outstanding road-holding qualities. This set-back radiator is not only attractive, but it represents the last word in efficiency. This view also shows the downswept side members and cross members. The short, stiff propeller shaft is noticeable, the universal joints being of the needle roller bearing type.

NEAR-SIDE VIEW OF THE CHASSIS.

The exhaust system is designed to ensure the unrestricted get-away of exhaust gasses and complete absence of back pressure. The rigid front cross member, behind which is housed the cast aluminium oil tank, will be noted. The 20 gallon petrol tank is fitted on rubber mountings direct to the chassis, and is insulated from vibration and road shocks. Oil tank, radiator and petrol tank caps are all of the " quick action " type. This photograph illustrates very clearly the dimensions of the brake drums in relation to the wheel size. The clean aluminium dash and the gear control of the Armstrong Siddeley Wilson box can also be seen.

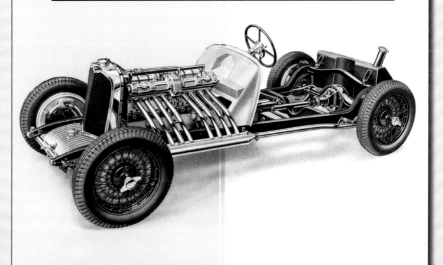

359

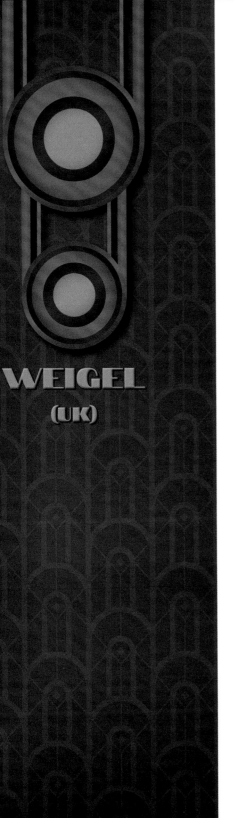

WEIGEL

(UK)

eigel was a British car manufacturer active between 1907 and 1910 in London. The company is notable for two reasons. It built the first British cars ever to compete in a Grand Prix, the 1907 French Grand Prix at Dieppe. Secondly it was one of the first manufacturers to build a straight eight. These two facts are intimately linked. The Grand Prix cars were powered by a straight eight of a formidable 14,866 cc (907 cu in) made by joining two 40 hp engines in tandem. The engines had an unusual firing order, where pairs of cylinders fired at the same time in the sequence 1+8, 4+5, 2+7 and 3+6. The Weigel was also unusual for the time in having shaft drive to the rear axle, whereas the majority of Grand Prix cars at the time used chains.

The cars were not a success, and the business carried on producing its four-cylinder models until 1911, when it went out of business.

The Weigel with Mr. D. M. Weigel at the wheel.

Weigel at the 1908 French Grand Prix at Dieppe, the driver was Pryce Harrison.

W indsor was a subsidiary of the Moon Motor Car Company and produced side valve straight eight models similar to Moon's. The 8-82 was made in 1929, the 8-85 in 1930, and the larger 8-92 in 1929 and 1930. All models were sold under the name Windsor White Prince. The Windsor brand was introduced in the hope of saving the business, as the linked Diana Motors had failed and Moon sales were falling. It did not work. The Windsor business folded in 1930.

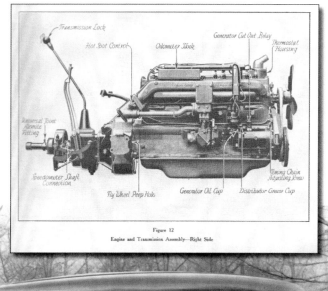

Figure 12
Engine and Transmission Assembly—Right Side

WINDSOR
(US)

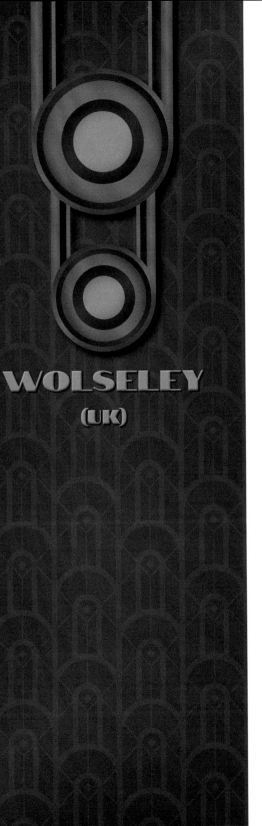

WOLSELEY

(UK)

Wolseley's foray into the world of straight eights seemed completely out of character, lasting just four years, with its two models having limited success.

Two luxury models were made, the 21/60 and the 32/80. Although certainly luxury cars, they were definitely owner-driver vehicles, no limousine version being produced. The first and smaller of the two was the 21/60, with a 2.7-litre (165 cu in) ohc straight eight engine, with a single SU carburettor, replacing the usual straight six in this chassis. Ten main bearings promised smooth running. The engine had a bore of 65 mm (2.6 in) and a stroke of 101 mm (4.0 in), giving a fairly low bore:stroke ratio of 64%. The cars were certainly not cheap, but were more affordable than many other straight eight offerings. A chassis without coachwork was priced in 1927 at £550, which equates to £32,100 at 2020 prices. Complete with a touring or two-seater body the 21/60 could be had for £695 (£40,450 at today's prices), and the full saloon for £750 (£43,650 at 2020 values). Wolseley advertised the 21/60 as '...offering luxury motoring at moderate cost...'. A limited number of car buyers liked the offering, and 560 were sold. But today it is a very rare car.

In 1929 the larger 32/80 was produced initially as a prototype. This had a 4,022 cc (245 cu in) straight eight. This larger engine was not related directly to the smaller 21/60, but was similar in having an ohc, ten main bearings and one SU carburettor. The larger unit was unusual in having roller bearing rockers. The 32/80 was said to be capable of a respectable 75 mph. Following the prototype four others were made, and one of these,

built in 1930, certainly existed in 2006 and was sold but without its engine. The list price of the larger model is not recorded, as it was not for general sale.

The 21/60 and 32/80 models only lasted into 1930, the global depression not helping sales of these 'moderately expensive eights'. After these two models Wolseley never again built cars in the 'luxury' category, focusing instead during the 1930s and post war years to cars in the 'upper middle' price bracket.

ABOVE: A contemporary photograph of the now very rare Wolseley 21/60 with its 2.7 litre (165 cu in) ohv straight eight engine.

OPPOSITE: The 4-litre ohc engine from one of the five Wolseley S8 32/80s made in 1929/30.

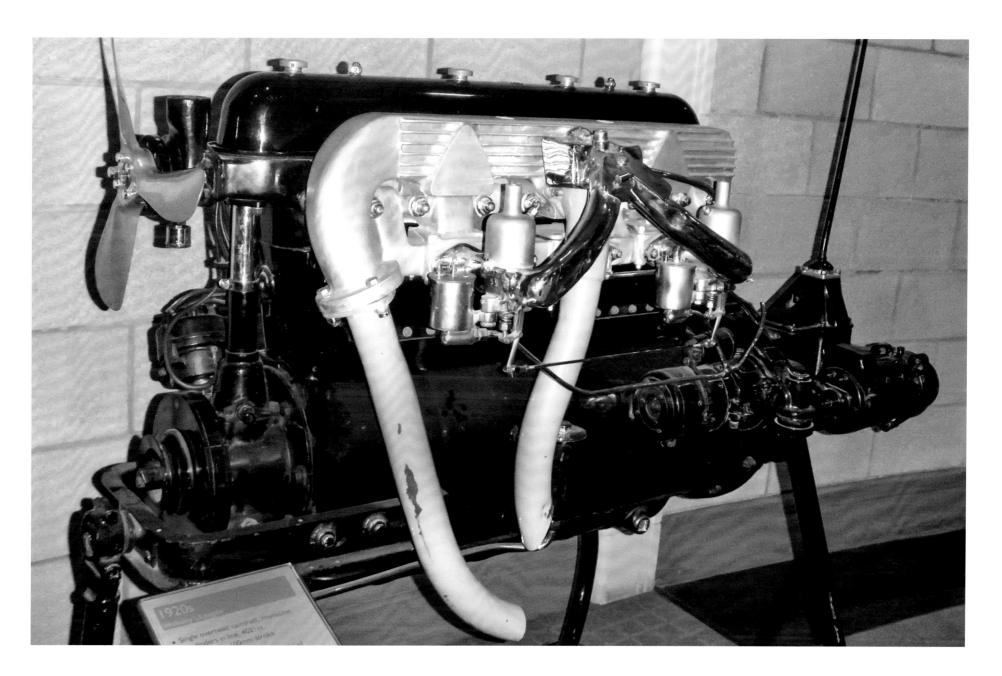

1920s

• Single overhead camshaft, monobloc
• Four-cylinder in-line, 4021cc
• 100mm stroke

ZIS/ZIL
(USSR NOW RUSSIA)

The early history of the Russian ZIS/ZIL is steeped with mystery and false rumours, the most common being that the cars were mere copies of contemporary Buicks and Packards. Whilst there was undoubtedly a strong link between the early cars and some American models, there is no evidence of direct copying. It is more likely that the Packards and Buicks were respected as quality cars, and Russia saw them as 'role models' for its own top vehicles.

ABOVE: The simple 5,750 cc (350.8 cu in) side valve engine of the ZIS-101. **OPPOSITE:** The 1936 ZIS-101, and whilst showing close similarity to contemporary Packards it was not, as was widely believed, a copy.

The first Soviet luxury car was called the L-1 and appeared in 1933. It was indeed similar to the 1931 Buick 90, and used a 5,650 cc (344.7 cu in) straight eight engine which was basically a variant of John Dolza's Buick power plant. With a low compression ratio of 4.4:1 the engine produced a claimed 105 bhp (78 kW). This appears to be an optimistic figure as its successor, the ZIS-101, was said to produce 90 bhp (67 kW). Production began in Leningrad, in a factory mainly producing heavy industrial equipment called Krasny Putilovjets. In order to increase the capacity for this heavy equipment, the car production was transferred to Moscow.

The decision was then taken to produce a new model, as the L-1 was considered old fashioned in appearance, and the result was the ZIS-101 which appeared in 1936. Dies for pressing the body panels were ordered from the United States and manufactured by Briggs in Detroit. Despite the strong US link, the panels were not copies of Packard panels, being designed by A. Vachinski in Moscow.

The engine of the ZIS-101 was a bored-out version of the straight eight unit in the L-1, giving a displacement of 5,750 cc (350.8 cu in). Cast iron cylinders were retained, as was the twin-choke American Marvel carburettor. The output was a modest 90 bhp (67 kW) at 2,800 rpm giving a top speed of around 68 mph. Alloy pistons were under development at the time, and by 1940 aluminium pistons were used, along with a domestically produced carburettor, which together with an increased compression ratio of 5.5:1 boosted power output to 110 bhp (82 kW). The compression ratio was limited by the low octane petrol at the time. The model was developed through ZIS-101 A and ZIS-101 B variants.

Production of a second generation ZIS began in August 1945, which was a few months before Packard launched its Twenty-First Series, so claims that the ZIS was a copy have little foundation, although it was similar in many ways. A higher-octane petrol was made available for the senior Soviet officials who used the cars, and a higher compression ratio increased power output to 140 bhp (104 kW) from its 6-litre engine, allowing a top speed of around 87 mph. The ZIS continued to be made for the next twelve years, although from 1956 it became known as the ZIL-110, the 'L' standing for Lenin, as Stalin had fallen out of favour.

The ZIL-110 was the last model with a straight eight engine. The new ZIL-111 introduced in 1958 would be very different. Although the old straight eight had been developed to produce 182 bhp (136 kW), it was decided that the engine was out of date, and a new V8 unit was used thereafter.

In total around 2,038 ZIS/ZIL cars were produced.

OPPOSITE: A contemporary sectional drawing of the ZIS engine.

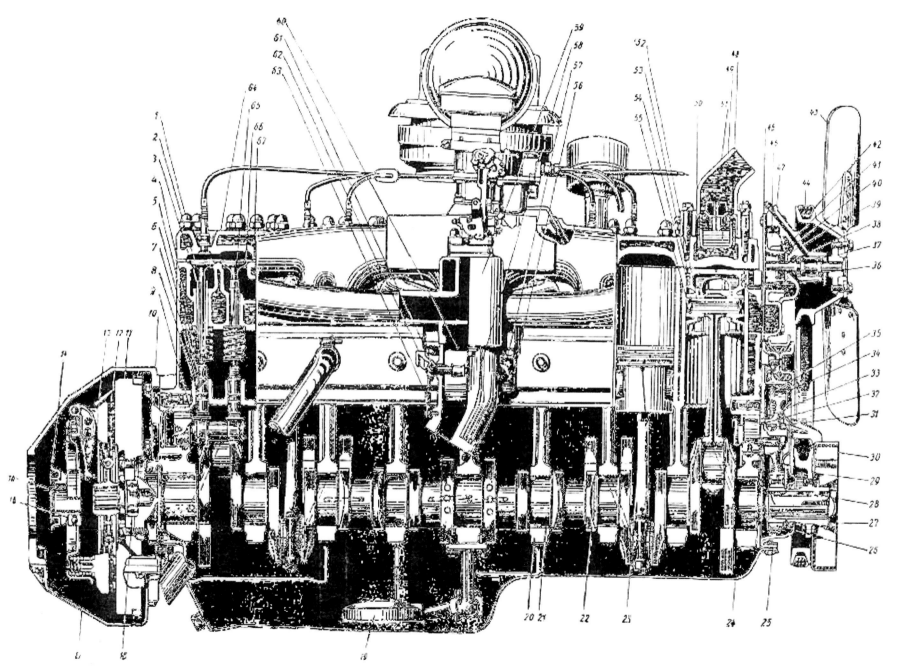

STRAIGHT EIGHTS
IN THE AIR AND
ON THE WATER

There is a tendency to think of straight eight engines entirely in the context of the motor car, but this engine format also saw business both at sea and in the air, and on the ground in warfare.

There is a fundamental difference between the nature of the power requirements of planes and boats, and those of the motor car, and these differences work in favour of the straight eight format. Whereas engines in road vehicles are constantly changing their speed of rotation, those in boats and aircraft normally operate for long periods at a fairly constant rate of rotation. As a result the torsional vibration in both the crankshaft and the camshaft, inevitable to some extent in all piston engines, is significantly reduced. The same is not true for ground military applications, but straight eights have seen many applications in ground armies.

STRAIGHT EIGHTS IN THE AIR

One of the problems of early aero engines was reducing the rotational speed of the engine in order to drive the propeller at the optimum speed. If the propeller rotates too quickly 'cavitation' can occur unless the pitch is low, but low pitch means inefficiency. Also with a large propeller rapid rotation can result in the blade tips exceeding the speed of sound, with the laws of fluid dynamics fundamentally changing. But reduction gears to reduce the rotational speed of propellors were too large and heavy for the aircraft of the time. William Beardmore Ltd, a Glasgow-based engineering company with diversified interests including aero engines, suggested a different solution; low speed engines, but these had to have very large displacement to generate the required power at low revs. Beardmore experimented with both petrol and diesel variants of low speed aero engines, some of straight eight format. One advantage of straight engines in the air is their low cross-sectional profile, and hence lower air resistance, when compared to V or radial engines.

One such straight eight was the Beardmore Tornado diesel engine. This was notable as being the engine chosen for the ill-fated airship, the R101, which crashed near Beauvais, France on the 4th October 1930 on her maiden flight, and which had five Tornados. The design combined two four-cylinder railcar engines together. It was intended to give an output of 700 bhp (520 kW) at 1000 rpm, but in practice had a continuous operational rating of 585 bhp (436 kW) and a safe maximum of 650 bhp (484 kW). There were two critical vibration frequencies which limited maximum sustainable revs to 935 rpm, hence the reduced power. Eventually a solution was found in the form of spring couplings between the crank and the propeller, but this was too late for the R100 which used petrol engines. There were also problems with the big end bearings which were found to be prone to early failure. The Tornado engines used Ricardo petrol starting engines. Details of the Tornado are as follows:

FUEL diesel heavy oil
BORE 210 mm (8.25 in)
STROKE 304.8 mm (12.0 in)
DISPLACEMENT 84,125 cc (5,130.8 cu in)
POWER (MAXIMUM) 650 bhp (480 kW) at 935 rpm (max revs)
POWER (CRUISING) 475 bhp (350 kW) at 825 rpm (cruise)
COMPRESSION RATIO 12.25:1
FUEL CONSUMPTION 0.429 lb/bhp/hr (max) 0.421 lb/bhp/hr cruise

Another example from Beardmore was the Simoon, which was made in both petrol and diesel versions. This was essentially its 'inverted' six-cylinder Typhoon engine with two extra cylinders added. With a bore of 217.5 mm (8.56 in) and a stroke of 305 mm (12 in) its displacement was 90,600 cc (5,528 cu in). With a 5.25:1 compression ratio in petrol form, it produced a normal output of 1,100 bhp (820 kW) at 1,250 rpm, and 1,200 bhp (895 kW) could be achieved at 1,350 rpm. The Simoon was installed in the second Blackburn T.4 Cubaroo replacing a Napier Cub. But none of Beardmore's slow revving 'eights' was a success, and few were made.

Whilst the engines in the R101 are perhaps the best known aerial straight eights, there were straight eights in the sky long before 1929. The Green Engine Company, established in London by Gustavus Green, was a prolific manufacturer of aero engines in the First World War, noted for a wide variety of engine formats and high-quality workmanship. The company did develop an overhead cam straight eight of a relatively modest 11,837 cc (722 cu in) with a bore of 116 mm (4.6 in) and a stroke of 140 mm (5.5 in). This engine developed 82 bhp (61 kW) at 1,100 rpm, but for such a modest output it was too heavy and was not a success.

Five other companies and designers were active before or during the First World War with straight eight cylinder aero engines. These were:

◆ SPA (Societa Piemontese Automobil) in Turin
◆ Isotta Fraschini in Milan
◆ Wolseley Tool and Motor Car Co. Ltd
◆ Daimler-Motoren AG
◆ Otto Hieronymus (as a designer) using the brand name 'Hiero'

Founded in 1906 SPA produced a six-cylinder Type 6A aero engine in quantity from 1916, and also produced an eight cylinder version of 20,048 cc (1,223 cu in) which, with a compression ratio of 5.3:1 could turn out 300 bhp (228 kW) at 1,600 rpm.

Also in Italy, a similar strategy was followed by Isotta Fraschini who added two cylinders to its tried and tested V-4B to create the V-5 straight eight of 19,130 cc (1,167 cu in). With twin carburettors this produced 200 bhp (149 kW) at 1,400 rpm. This engine was later enlarged to 20,182 cc (1,232 cu in) and produced 290 bhp (216 kW) at 1,600 rpm. It was moderately successful and was also built under licence by other companies in Italy.

In Britain Wolseley was building straight eight marine engines in the first decade of the 20th century with some success. A boat called 'Wolseley-Siddeley', powered by two 207 bhp Wolseley engines, won the Prix de Monte Carlo in 1908, and had several more successes in subsequent years. The same design of engine was used to propel the first British rigid airship, the Mayfly, which carried three of the Wolseley engines. But the craft was not a success, the power to weight ration being too low.

In Germany, in the years leading up to the First World War, development started on designing and building rigid airships for military use. The first airship, the SL 1, required two powerful but light engines, each sitting in a suspended gondola. Daimler-Motoren AG was approached for a solution and decided to follow the well-trodden track of placing two four-cylinder units in tandem on the same crankcase and sharing a crankshaft. Joining two of its J4L engines together produced a 31,750 cc (1,937 cu in) 'eight' turning out 246 bhp (182 kW) at 1,200 rpm. But the engines were heavy at 780 kg (1,720 lbs), although fuel economy was reported to be good. Weight would be more critical for the next aviation 'eight', as it was destined for aeroplanes. Daimler's six-cylinder Mercedes DIII developed 170 bhp (127 kW) and was durable and reliable, so following the same path two cylinders were added to create the eight-cylinder DIV. Adding cylinders was easy because the DIII had separate cylinders with individual water jackets. The DIV did include an important innovation. With most 'two fours in tandem' engines at the time the two sets of four-cylinders ran as 'separate' fours with their cranks offset by 90 degrees. For the DIV a different arrangement was used. The centre four-cylinders behaved like a 'four', whilst cylinders 1, 2, 7 and 8 acted like a 'split four' but also with a 90-degree displacement. This became known as a 2-4-2 arrangement.

The last of the five manufacturers mentioned above was Otto Hieronymus, an engine designer who worked for Laurin and Klement before setting up on his own to build 'Hiero' engines. In 1914 he introduced a straight eight engine developing up to 220 bhp (164 kW), but it was not widely adopted, the 'sixes' being more popular.

Ultimately the straight eight would fall out of favour with aircraft manufacturers on weight grounds, larger bore 'sixes' delivering similar power and a weight saving.

STRAIGHT EIGHTS ON THE WATER:

Today enormous in-line 'straight' diesel engines are the mainstay of most of the world's large vessels. Wartsila, one of the leading marine engine manufacturers, makes these engines ranging from straight 'fours' and 'sixes' right through to straight 14s, and with almost every possible number of cylinders in between (including straight eights). The 14-cylinder version of the RTA96-C is the largest engine of any sort ever built, with a bore of 965 mm (38 in) and a stroke of 2489 mm (98 in) delivering 109,000 bhp (81,200 kW). Large container vessels just need one of these units to operate competitively. These large engines often turn at a constant very low speed for hours, or even days, on end and under these circumstances, issues like torsional vibration of the enormous crankshaft are absolutely minimal.

But the marine straight eight is not just a recent phenomenon. Straight eight engines were important power plants for fast boats for racing, record breaking and patrolling in the first two decades of the 20th century. The first manufacturer of a straight eight for use on the water was Fabbrica di Automobili Florentia, based in Florence, Italy. The company opened a shipyard on the Gulf of Genoa to build powerboats and fast patrol boats, and produced a straight eight following the 'standard route' by joining two 'fours' together.

One of the Beardmore Tornado diesel engines from the airship R101.

371

Two other manufacturers were significant producers of marine straight eights before the First World War. Wolseley was mentioned earlier in the context of airships. The other was the Sterling Engine Company based in Buffalo in New York State. By 1912 Sterling was able to boast in its marketing material about many racing successes by boats using its 150 bhp (111 kW) straight eight engine. This engine was 21,024 cc (1,238 cu in) and was gradually developed until it produced 180 bhp (133 kW). Sterling straight eights were still being produced in the 1930s and powered many of the American landing craft on D-Day.

The photographs show examples of marine straight eights dating from the 1920s, the Wolseley eight cylinder and the Burmeister and Wain eight. Into the 1940s Chrysler produced the Royal series of engines (e.g. M8 in the late 1940s and the M48 in the 1950s) for marine use, as did Packard with its Marine Eight.

ABOVE: The eight-cylinder Burmeister & Wain diesel engine for MS Glenapp built in 1920. **OPPOSITE:** A Wolseley eight-cylinder marine oil engine, with the cylinders in pairs.

STRAIGHT EIGHT ADVERTISEMENTS

The golden age of straight eight cars was, without doubt, the 1930s; and this fortunately coincided with another golden age, that of Art Deco-style advertising. The 1930s also saw massive growth in land, sea and air travel. The glamour of the new Trans-Atlantic liners, and the increasing affordability of air travel, saw large marketing investments in the travel sector, which in turn attracted gifted artists to design posters and magazine advertisements. The same was true for land travel, with railway posters reaching their zenith, and advertisements for the automobile often selling not just cars but a glamorous lifestyle. And so much of this was in the amazing Art Deco style.

The sample of posters and advertisements shown here reflect a spectrum of contemporary media themes and strategies. In particular:

◆ Selling a life style rather than just a brand. This concept is remarkably contemporary, although even today it is rarely applied to selling cars.

◆ Leveraging racing success. Obviously some manufacturers, such as Bugatti and Mercedes, would take advantage of their track success in selling road cars

◆ Personal endorsements. Using personal recommendations from, presumably, well known people of the day, is not something we are familiar with today

◆ Residual value. It is rather surprising to find residual value used as a benefit by really up-market manufacturers like Pierce Arrow and others

◆ Safety. Even back in the 1930s safety was seen as a marketing advantage

◆ High Art Deco style. Some manufacturers really went for the high end of Art Deco design

◆ Very conservative delivery. However some manufacturers maintained a low-key, serious, technical theme to their marketing

375

LE PUR SANG DE L'AUTOMOBILE

LE PUR-SANG DES AUTOMOBILES

ALSACE   MOLSHEIM   BAS·RHIN

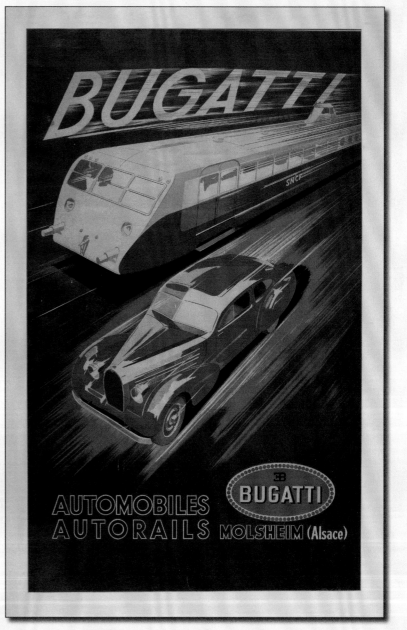

The GIFT

THE SILVER ANNIVERSARY

BUICK

THE GIFT SUPREME—the gift that combines thrilling happiness, practical convenience and healthful recreation—the gift that makes Christmas last for thousands of miles—is this finest and most fashionable of motor cars, the new Buick with Masterpiece Body by Fisher. Make your family genuinely happy on Christmas day. Give them a Buick!

WHEN BETTER AUTOMOBILES ARE BUILT...BUICK WILL BUILD THEM

CHANDLER

YOUTH PICKS THE ROADSTER

Sixteen or sixty—youth in years or in spirit—youth picks the roadster. Youth has a natural flair for controlled power, liquid flexibility, speed, snap, stamina, split-second performance— in other words, *youth picks the Diana Light Straight Eight.*

Youth, too, insists on style, color lines, eye appeal. And here's America's smartest roadster, Palm Beach, Biarritz—American sturdiness with the touch of Europe's best.

Here's *elastic* speed, etc., range varying from 2 to 77 miles an hour—acceleration, 5 to 25 miles an hour in 2 seconds.

But Diana Eight is more than a brilliant performer, more than a great automobile—*it's a fraternity, it's a club, it's a cult, and it spans the whole country north and south, east and west. It's everywhere.*

SIMPLIFIED CONTROL AND THE EASIEST STEERING IN AMERICA

DIANA

The LIGHT STRAIGHT "8"

$1795
F.O.B ST.LOUIS

SPECIFICATIONS: Eight Cylinders; 73 Horsepower; 16 miles to the gallon of fuel; Lanchester Dampener; Purolator Oil Filter; Air Cleaner; Simplified Control; Hydraulic 4-wheel Brakes; Balloon Tires (Shimmy Proof); Finest Quality Leather Upholstering; Sport Top with Boot to match; Body of latest European Arrowhead Design; Front seat accommodates Three Passengers, Rumble Seat holds Two; Special Compartment for Golf Sticks; Finish is two-tone Double Duco (tested by violet rays); Natural Wood or Disc Wheels.

Built by the MOON MOTOR CAR COMPANY for the DIANA MOTORS COMPANY
Stewart McDonald, President, St. Louis

One Hundred Eighty-six

DUESENBERG

STRAIGHT EIGHTS

Holds Sixty-Six Official A. A. A. World's Records

Jimmy Murphy, "San Francisco Boy," with his Duesenberg Straight Eight on July 25th this year WON the French Grand Prix, setting for all time Duesenberg claims the WORLD'S CHAMPION AUTOMOBILE

"Built to outclass, outrun, and outlast any car on the road"

Exclusive Features of the Duesenberg

Duesenberg "Straight-Eight" World's famous motors.
100 Horse Power at 3,000 R. P. M.
Weight of complete automobile only 3,000 pounds.
Duesenberg Special Improved Four Wheel Oil Brake.
3 to 90 miles per hour on high gear.
20 miles per gallon of gasoline.

A. W. RAWLING COMPANY
NORTHERN CALIFORNIA DISTRIBUTORS
Telephone Lakeside 581
2838-2840 Broadway

MAY, 1935   VANITY FAIR

She drives a
Duesenberg

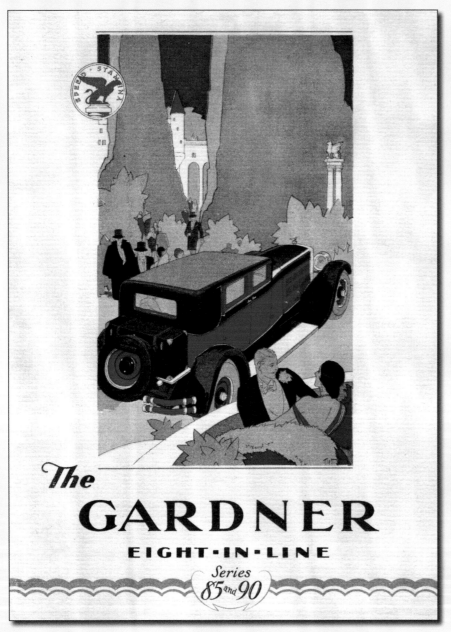

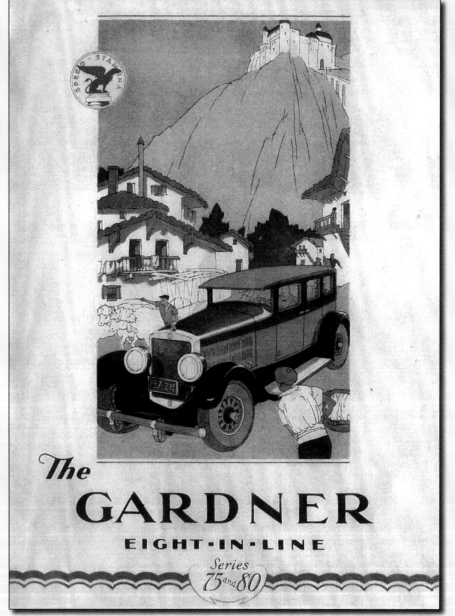

Customs Series "120" Supercharger — 4 Door Sedan, 120 W.B.

Cavalier Series "95" Coupe, 116 W.B.

THE ONLY ENGINE
built with protection for
**ZERO WEATHER
STARTING**
GRAHAM DOES IT FIRST
The most impressive engineering development of the year is the new Graham instantaneous cylinder wall lubrication for cold weather starting. The first movement of the starting motor lubricates cylinder walls, preventing piston scuffing and all abnormal wear.

You Can Afford a Graham
Prices start as below:
Crusaders $902
Cavaliers $1120
Superchargers $1336
Delivered Windsor, Ontario, completely equipped.
Nothing to add but freight and license.
GRAHAM-PAIGE MOTORS (Canada) Ltd. - Windsor, Ont.

◆ You want power . . . you want economy . . . you get them both in GRAHAM! You want dashing beauty, a gliding ride and comfort, to the *nth* degree. Yes, you get them all in GRAHAM.

Look back over the years . . . see how GRAHAM has been one step ahead without fail. True streamlining, full water-jacketing, high compression aluminum head, chemically plated pistons and pins, perfected hydraulic brakes, shatterproof glass, outboard springs, the supercharger and now "non-scuff" instantaneous lubrication: Every one of them *first* in GRAHAM. Truly, GRAHAM is *the* pioneer in beauty and engineering achievements.

Graham

Introducing...

The
Graham-Paige Eight

Five chassis—sixes and eights—prices ranging from $860 to $2445. Illustrated is Model 835, 5-passenger Sedan, with 4-speed transmission, $2285. All prices f. o. b. Detroit.

It is our purpose that Graham-Paige owners shall be served by representatives who possess the fundamental three "C's" — Character, Capability, Capital. Illustrated is the home of the Graham-Paige Company of Michigan.

WITH the introduction of the 835, a straight eight with four speeds forward (standard shift), the new line of Graham-Paige motor cars is complete. Only by personal experience can you adequately appreciate the beauty, smoothness, swiftness, and substantial value of these motor cars.

Joseph B. Graham
Robert C. Graham
Ray A. Graham

GRAHAM-PAIGE

HUDSON *Terraplane* · HUDSON *Six* · HUDSON *Eight*

WITH SIX STAR MOTOR

MEET HUDSON FOR 1938

Original Design is the keynote · of this distinctive beauty!

HERE ARE motor cars to capture your heart!

For here are cars original in their advanced styling . . . amazingly different in riding qualities and performance . . . because they are different in *basic* design.

Those clean, graceful lines that set Hudson so apart from the crowd flow naturally from Hudson's exclusive "step-down" design with its recessed floor, which makes possible the lowest-built car of them all.

But your pleasure has only begun when you *see* a Hudson. New wonders unfold as you drive, for this truly low-built car provides America's lowest center of gravity; yet with full road clearance and more head room and seating room than in any other car. And you know instinctively that with this low-built beauty comes the tenacious road-hugging stability that makes Hudson America's best-riding and safest car.

So for a motoring experience to be long remembered, accept your Hudson dealer's invitation to try "The New Step-Down Ride" . . . and discover *all* the delightful advantages of Hudson's original design. Hudson Motor Car Company, Detroit 14.

"DREAM"—ORIGINAL DRESS DESIGN FROM
CHRISTIAN DIOR'S AMERICAN COLLECTION
AS INTERPRETED BY CAROLE EDMUNDSON

HUDSON
NOW . . . 3 GREAT SERIES
Lower-Priced Pacemaker * Famous Super * Custom Commodore

Here's the car they said was years away!

the only car you step

<u>down</u> into..a new type of automobile no one else

in America is prepared to build today!

HUDSON is the only American-built motor car you step *down* into when entering, not *up* on.

This new development in automobile design and construction brings you many sensational advantages—among them, newly streamlined beauty and a breath-taking flow of low-built lines that would otherwise be impractical.

This new kind of motor car is only five feet from ground to top, yet by stepping down, you get *more* head room and *roomier* seats than in any other mass-produced car built today—and there's good road clearance, too!

Because you step down, Hudson's new, all steel Monobilt body-and-frame* completely encircles you, even outside the rear wheels, with a rugged, box-steel foundation frame—and this brings you a new measure of added safety.

You ride within this frame—cradled between axles—not on top of a frame as in the past. Hudson's new, lower center of gravity and rugged basic structure give this car delightful roadability —a hug-the-road way of going, especially on curves, that is so safe, so serene, so smooth, it is unlike anything you've known before!

Hudson dealers invite you to enjoy this ride—to thrill to the eager power of Hudson's all-new Super-Six engine—the most powerful six built today—or the masterful Super-Eight. You're invited to experience automatic gear-shifting in forward speeds as provided by Hudson's "Drive-Master" transmission.

This is the motor car they said was years away, but the nearest Hudson dealer will show it to you now! Hudson Motor Car Company, Detroit 14.

* Trade-mark and patents pending

This time it's Hudson

Eight body styles in Super and Commodore Series. Your choice, 121 h.p. new Super-Six or 128 h.p. improved Super-Eight engine. New, low-pressure, Super-Cushion tires. Ten body colors. Two special colors or five two-tone combinations—white sidewall tires—at slight extra cost.

Collier's, *The National Weekly*

THE SILVER ANNIVERSARY HUPMOBILE

Five-Passenger Victoria (Series 321) . . $1060 (Standard Equipped) at Factory

STILL THE CAR OF THE CAREFUL INVESTOR

For 25 years Hupmobile has been "the car of the careful investor." The choice of the man who buys a car as he would a bond — who wants just a bit more for his money. Who recognizes that Hupmobile's keener engineering, finer workmanship, closer inspection, better materials, mean extra dividends of longer life, bigger trade-in value, less money spent on operation and repairs.

Now . . . in the Silver Anniversary Series, Hupmobile has outdone itself. Exceeded its own 25-year record. Added to Hupmobile's recognized dependability, a new and lavish luxury—new refinements of finish and design, new brilliance in power, speed and performance. Celebrated its Silver Anniversary with a new car . . . and a new value! A better investment than ever.

The 1933 Series have these latest improvements: Doors of unusual shape and width—for style, for convenience. Automatic thermostatic shock absorbers. Rigid X-frame. Chassis torsional stabilizer. Tubular front axle. Underslung springs. Synchro-silent free-wheeling transmission. Hypoid rear axle. Extreme lowness for safety and riding comfort. Form-fitting fenders. New full-chromium radiator of aero-dynamic design. Chromium plated dual horns. Longer hood with narrow cowl and door type louvers. Increased horse power and speed. Safety glass windshields.

Three chassis (Series 321, 322, 326)
Four body styles on each

Hupmobile

Sedan / prices $995 to $1445 at factory

THE SATURDAY EVENING POST

HUPMOBILE · THE CAR OF THE CAREFUL INVESTOR

Hupmobile Eight (Series 222) 5-Passenger Sedan . . . $1295 (Standard Equipped) at the Factory

We are frequently asked why comparatively few Hupmobiles are listed in used-car advertisements. The situation is probably without parallel. The explanation is interesting and important. Most automobile dealers have "Hupmobile waiting lists." Knowing exactly where used Hupmobiles can be resold, these dealers do not need to advertise them. Such marked preference can come from only one source—recognition of performance, dependability, and all-around ruggedness that years of use cannot impair, and of style so true that it stays in. Naturally, this favorable attitude of discriminating used-car purchasers contributes immeasurably to Hupmobile's reputation as "the car of the careful investor."

Hupmobile

SIXES AND EIGHTS $795 AND UP, *at the Factory*

Improved second series six-cylinder cars now on display

L'automobile "Suprema" di domani pronta per la consegna di oggi !

Se volete possedere un'automobile veramente superiore e raffinata, fermate la vostra scelta su una ISOTTA FRASCHINI.
Dopo 24 anni di primato indiscusso, la ISOTTA FRASCHINI vi offre oggi la vettura suprema;
carrozzeria insuperabile per "comfort" con un nuovo accurato molleggio
su un chassis della massima potenza.

Le ISOTTA FRASCHINI

sono il prodotto combinato di provetti meccanici e di brillanti artisti.

JORDAN

What More Could You Ask?

COMPACT—Good Looking—Balanced —Weight hung hammock-like between the springs.

Easy to steer. Easy to park. A joy to handle in the traffic. A thrill to step-on in the open country. Fleet of foot. Silent—Smooth-powered—as only an eight can be.

A new type of body—all-steel and patented. You feel as if you were riding in an observation car.

Beauty—Safety—Comfort—Economy—and performance. That's the Jordan Line Eight Sedan—$1945.

Victoria for four $1945. Playboy $1845.

JORDAN MOTOR CAR COMPANY, Inc., CLEVELAND, OHIO

Prices f. o. b. Cleveland.

The blue sky overhead—
the green turf flying by—a
thousand miles of open road
—then a quiet inn for dinner.

Marmon

'78

$1965

Above, New Series Marmon 78 Speedster for six passengers

IMPORTANT NEW DEVELOPMENTS IN NEW SERIES 68 AND 78

LARGER motor—more power—in the "68"; even smoother operation in both cars. New colors. New interior harmonies. Double chromium plating of exposed metal parts—radiator, lamps, etc. (requires no polishing). New body styles as exemplified by smart Six-Passenger "78" Speedster, illustrated above. New, more massive front end appearance. New and effective ensemble of radiator, lamps and lamp mountings. New conveniences such as coincidental lock on instrument board which simultaneously locks both ignition and transmission. Horizontal louvres and "piano-type" hood hinges. New development in carburetion which has tendency to "super-charge" gas mixture. New instrument panels with large numerals, legible from the tonneau. New bumpers of individual Marmon design. New flush type lock and carrier when wheels are carried forward. *Prices*, New Series 68 (Standard Sedan), $1465. New Series 78 (Standard Sedan), $1965. All prices f.o.b. factory, de luxe equipment at moderate extra cost. Convenient time-payment plan.

$1465

68

The New Series Marmon 68 Five-Passenger Sedan

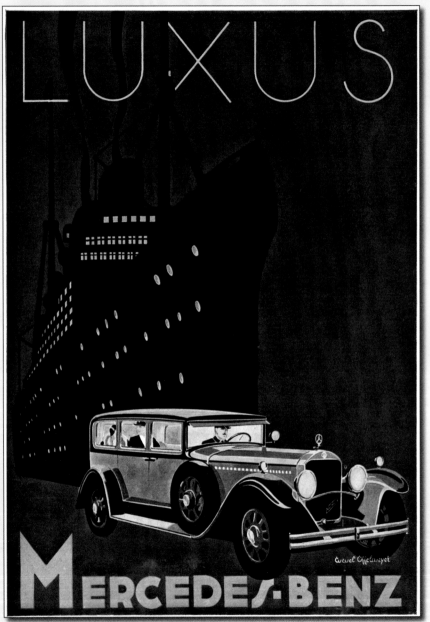

AUGUST 22, 1931   THE LITERARY DIGEST

Ask the man who owns one

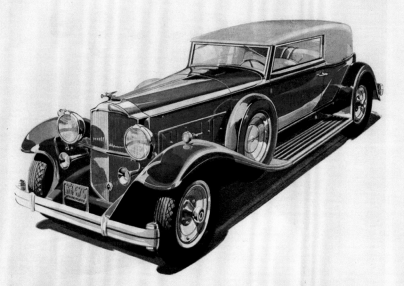

IN THE new Convertible Victoria for five Packard has anticipated the desires of a discriminating clientele. Preference in body styles in the past has swung from open cars to closed—but now open car smartness combined with closed car comfort is meeting with wide appreciation. And so Packard offers the Victoria, which, with the Coupe-Roadster for two or four and the Sedan for five, provides an unusual choice of convertible models to buyers of either the Packard Eight or Packard Eight De Luxe. ¶ In all, the new Continental Packard Eights are available in a complete range of twelve body types. All have longer wheelbases, wider tread, lower and roomier bodies.   Power is greater, smoother, quieter. Four-speed, synchro-mesh transmission provides greater driving ease. While the exclusive Packard *Ride Control*—dash-adjustable shock absorbers—insures supreme riding comfort whatever the road, load or temperature. The new Packard cars are more beautiful, more distinguished, more luxurious than ever before—and their riding ease is unmatched throughout the world of fine cars.

PACKARD

Top up...top down...it's tops!

Even standing still, it makes an action picture!

For this glamorous new Packard is America's first all-new convertible—completely new from tires to top—and every exciting line suggests the wonderful things it can do.

Beneath its low and massive Free-Flow styling is a special-engineered chassis . . . foundation for the quietest, most restful ride in all motordom.

Beneath its proud bonnet is a brand-new, 145-horsepower Packard Super Eight engine . . . brilliantly responsive, silky smooth . . . precision-built by the men who handled wartime America's most exacting power assignments.

And in convenience innovations—here's pure magic! There's a new Console-Key instrument panel, with push-button switches, and black-lighted Flite-Glo dials. There's push-button control for the new wrinkle-resistant RoboTop . . . the new Prest-O-justment front seat . . . and *all four* windows. There's new Comfort-aire ventilation, and many another great advancement.

So don't be content just to admire a picture in a magazine!

Your dream car awaits your inspection—now—at your Packard dealer's. Go see it—and hurry! *Today* is not a day too early to do something about making it your own!

ASK THE MAN WHO OWNS ONE

THE NEW PACKARD *CONVERTIBLE*

HONORABLE HORACE WHITE OF NEW YORK

is the owner of the Pierce-Arrow in the photograph . . . a car which has been in the constant service of the former Governor and his family since 1917

The Convertible Sedan of Group B . . . $3650 at Buffalo

SURVIVAL VALUE • A PIERCE-ARROW FUNDAMENTAL

What community today is without its ten- or twelve- or fifteen-year-old Pierce-Arrows . . . still superbly patrician, still rendering distinguished service to the original owners? Therein lies the deepest-rooted, most foundational, of all Pierce-Arrow characteristics —a quality that has been called *survival value.*

Because an essential part of its beauty is in its character . . . a part that is unchanging . . . the Pierce-Arrow of yesterday, or of a decade ago, finds complement in the smartest of today's models. And thus a great Pierce-Arrow fundamental becomes also a fine safeguard for each Pierce-Arrow owner's investment.

Twenty-nine New Models . . . *with Free Wheeling* . . . from $2685 to $6400 at Buffalo. (Other Custom-built Models up to $10,000.)

ENDLESS ARE THE EXAMPLES OF PIERCE-ARROW SURVIVAL VALUE

A sidelight on Pierce-Arrow character is the almost affectionate regard in which this car is held by so many of America's most representative families. Some of the most enviable Pierce-Arrow service records have been made within these distinguished circles. . . . Neither great dependability, nor exceptional performance, could alone win preference for the same Pierce-Arrow year after year. But both qualities combined, and enhanced by real patrician character, have won a great unchanging loyalty to America's finest motor car . . . To the graceful beauty, the luxuriousness of appointment and courtly conveyance which have always been Pierce-Arrow, is now added the new luxury of Free Wheeling . . . the most important automotive development of the past decade.

TWENTY-NINE NEW MODELS . . . WITH FREE WHEELING . . . from $2685 to $6400 at Buffalo. (Custom-built Models up to $10,000)

MR. JOSEPH E. WIDENER, *nationally known financier and sportsman, has owned the Pierce-Arrow shown in the photograph since 1926.*

PIERCE-ARROW

"I bought that PIERCE-ARROW *because it's the* Safest Car in the World"

PIERCE ARROW

YOU'LL BE PROUD TO OWN A PONTIAC

PONTIAC DE LUXE EIGHT BUSINESS COUPE

Exceptionally spacious luggage space in rear deck. Additional space behind split, three-passenger seat. Mohair or Bedford cord upholstery. Running boards optional.

PONTIAC DE LUXE EIGHT TWO-DOOR TOURING SEDAN

Split, sedan-type front seat. Recessed ash trays in rear seat arm rests. Adjustable driver's seat. Combination arm rests and door handles. Mohair or Bedford cord upholstery. Running boards optional.

The New 1949 PONTIAC

The Most Beautiful Thing on Wheels!

PONTIAC MOTOR DIVISION of GENERAL MOTORS CORPORATION

THE
Reo-Royale
EIGHT

THE urge to own the new Reo-Royale Eight is sweeping America. From coast to coast the verdict of crowded showrooms is everywhere the same—"A car of character and distinction."

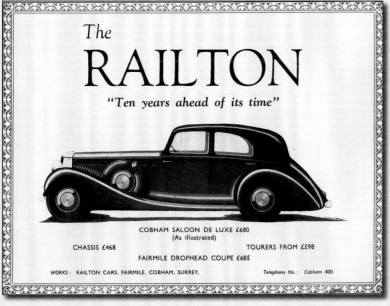

The RAILTON

"Ten years ahead of its time"

COBHAM SALOON DE LUXE £680
(As illustrated)

CHASSIS £468   TOURERS FROM £598

FAIRMILE DROPHEAD COUPE £685

WORKS : RAILTON CARS, FAIRMILE, COBHAM, SURREY.   Telephone No. : Cobham 400.

Finer than the finest
STUDEBAKERS
ever built

THESE lowest priced Studebakers in history are also the finest cars that ever bore their honored name. Superbly streamlined bodies of seamless steel reinforced by steel sheath spacious interiors of extraordinary luxuriousness. High-powered, economical, flawlessly functioning engines stem straight from years of triumphs in stock car and speedway racing. Comfort, new in motoring, results from Quadripoise Suspension, the dramatic Studebaker discovery which scientifically cradles the action of all four wheels. Uncanny "mechanical brains" make driving so automatic there is little to do but steer. Prove to yourself in a convincing trial drive that these skyway style Studebakers of 1934 definitely and substantially add brilliant new lustre to a record of achievement unique in motordom.

$685 and up, at factory

FROM THE SPEEDWAY COMES THEIR STAMINA   FROM THE SKYWAY COMES THEIR STYLE

STUDEBAKER

+ DICTATOR + COMMANDER + PRESIDENT +

$645 $845 $1045

AND UP, AT THE FACTORY   AND UP, AT THE FACTORY   AND UP, AT THE FACTORY

From the speedway comes their stamina + *From the skyway comes their style*

From the
SPEEDWAY
comes their *Stamina*
From the
SKYWAY
comes their *Style*

Startling New
**STUDEBAKERS
OF 1934**

NO OTHER CARS HAVE THESE ADVANTAGES

"NOBACK"
for better driving

"Noback!" The sensation of the Automobile Shows! Automatically prevents undesirable and dangerous backward-rolling of car on hills and inclines, without the use of brakes. "Noback!" A most tremendous aid to safe and comfortable driving.

DE-CELERATION
for more perfect control

De-celeration! The most modern braking control known. Giant four-wheel hydraulics—with vacuum booster on Stutz. This new de-celeration gives perfect mastery of speed, protects lives and saves valuable minutes in traffic. A Stutz safety feature.

LOW-WEIGHT
for greater safety

Low-weight! The worm-drive permits lowered center of gravity for greatest ease of riding and driving, road-adhesiveness, safety. Eliminates side sway, "toppiness," and overturning danger.

WEYMANN BODIES
for supreme elegance

Weymann bodies! These modish, flexible type, European body creations are to be had exclusively in America on Stutz and Blackhawk. Strong, extremely quiet, ultra comfortable and unusually distinctive.

And, of course, there's safety-glass all around—four quiet forward speeds—double adjustable seats, both front and back—a special new gas pump for constant flow—"side-bumper" running boards, integral with frame—bodies by Le Baron and Fleetwood—and other advantages. See these two specialty cars—Stutz $3395 to $6895—Blackhawk $2345 to $2955—f. o. b. Indianapolis.

S T U T Z
and
B L A C K H A W K

THE ultra-low chassis of the New Safety Stutz, achieved without lessening road-clearance, is the triumph of a different and advanced engineering.

This chassis allows the custom-body designer to attain a heretofore denied smartness and symmetry in his creations.

And, with this new beauty, the New Safety Stutz engineering provides a new and altogether surpassing degree of safety, performance, road-tenacity, and luxurious carriage.

The complete line of standard, de luxe and custom-built bodies offers the choice of 60 body styles and appointments, with unlimited choice in many of the models.

Stutz Motor Car Co. of America, Inc. · · · Indianapolis

The Symbol of Safety

Included in recently displayed custom examples are Weymann Flexible Bodies, one of which is shown here. This type of body, widely adopted in Europe, was introduced to America on the New Safety Stutz Chassis.

The Improved New
SAFETY STUTZ

EDMUND DAVENPORT

GLOSSARY OF TERMS AND ABBREVIATIONS

BHP The abbreviation for brake horse power, the measure for the (usually maximum) power an engine produces.

BALL BEARING A ball bearing is a form of bearing where the space between the stationary and rotating elements is filled by a series of balls usually restrained within a cage

BHP/LITRE This is a measure of specific output from an engine, which relates the power produced to the size of the engine (see also kW/litre).

BIG END The 'big end' is the end of the connecting rod, the rod which connects the piston to the crankshaft, attached at the crankshaft end.

BORE The bore is the diameter of the engine's cylinders.

BORE:STROKE RATIO This ratio reflects the shape of the cylinders. When the stroke is greater than the bore the engine is said to be 'under-square'; when the bore is greater than the stroke the engine is said to be 'over-square'. Over-square engines are usually able to run faster, whereas under-square engines tend to deliver good low speed torque.

CC (OR C.C.) The abbreviation for cubic centimetre, a measure of cylinder volume.

COMPOUND CARBURETTOR This was a feature which enjoyed brief popularity in the 1930s. Basically it comprised two separate carburettors, but only one of which was directly linked to the accelerator. The second, remote, carburettor was only brought 'on stream' when the maximum acceleration was required. It was not a success.

COMPRESSION RATIO The ratio between the space above the piston when it is at its lowest, and that when it is at its highest. Generally speaking a high ratio translates into more power.

CONNECTING ROD (OR CON ROD) The component in an engine which connects a piston to the crankshaft.

CU IN (OR CU.IN.) A measure of the total volume the pistons in an engine sweep with each complete turn of the crankshaft. The cubic inch measure is mainly used in the Americas. One cubic inch equates to 16.39 cubic centimetres.

CV An abbreviation of 'chevaux vapeur' (or steam horses), this was a crude measure used for car taxation in France. The original formula was:

$$CV = n \times D \times D \times L \times w \times K$$

Where n is the number of cylinders, D is the bore, L is the stroke, w is the maximum engine speed in rpm, and K was a coefficient depending on the number of cylinders. The value is therefore directly related to the size of the engine. The formula has evolved over time but only recently has included a factor for engine power.

CYL Abbreviation for cylinder.

DOHC (OR D.O.H.C.) An abbreviation for dual overhead cam, where the valves are operated by two separate camshafts in the cylinder head. This allows all the valves to be operated directly without the need for rocker arms, which allows the engine to run faster.

DE DION AXLE The simplest form of rear suspension for a car is a beam axle where the beam incorporates the differential gear and the drive shafts. A de Dion axle is also a beam axle, but one where the differential is attached to the car's chassis and the drive is taken from that to the wheels which are supported by the separate 'dumb' beam. The de Dion axle has the advantage that the heavy differential is not part of the suspended weight.

DESMODROMIC VALVES In the majority of automobile engines the valves are opened by levers and cams, but closed by the pressure of a spring. Desmodromic valves differ in that both the opening and closing is positively done by cams and levers.

DISPLACEMENT This is the total volume swept by all the cylinders in an engine, measured either as cubic centimetres (cc) or cubic inches (cu in). Displacement is given by the formula:

$$\text{displacement} = B \times B \times S \times N \times 0.785$$

Where B is the bore, S is the stroke and N is the number of cylinders.

DOWNDRAFT CARBURETTOR A carburettor, usually of the fixed choke type, where the flow of air and fuel is vertically downwards so that gravity assists injection to the inlet manifold.

DRY SUMP A lubrication system where a scavenger pump is used to pump oil from the sump through a cooler to a reservoir, from which the oil is fed under pressure to the moving parts of the engine. In a wet sump engine the sump is always full of oil.

EXHAUST MANIFOLD A robust casing, usually cast iron or steel, attached to the cylinder head to collect exhaust gases from each exhaust port and direct them to the exhaust pipe.

F HEAD This is an American term for an IOE (inlet over exhaust) engine where the inlet valve is in the cylinder head, and the exhaust valve is within the engine block.

FIRING ORDER The order in which the sparking plugs ignite the mixture in the cylinders. In the case of a straight eight engine the firing order is particularly important to deliver smoothness and minimise torsional vibration.

FLATHEAD An American term for a side valve engine, one where both inlet and exhaust valves are in the cylinder block.

FT LBS Abbreviation or foot pounds, a measure of the torque produced by an engine.

FWD (OR F.W.D.) An abbreviation for front wheel drive, where the engine drives the front wheels of the vehicle.

HP (OR H.P.) An abbreviation for horse power, which variously can mean brake horsepower (bhp) or the horsepower used for tax purposes, such as CV in France and RAC hp in the UK.

IOE (OR I.O.E.) An abbreviation for inlet over exhaust. This is where the inlet valve is in the cylinder head, and the exhaust valve is within the engine block. In the US this is often referred to as an F-head.

IN-LINE ENGINE An alternative term for a straight engine.

INLET MANIFOLD A manifold or duct along the side of the engine which distributes the fuel/air mixture to all the cylinders.

KM/HR Abbreviation for kilometres per hour, a measure of velocity.

KW Abbreviation for kilo-Watts, an alternative to bhp as a measure for power output.

KW/LITRE Kilo-Watts per litre, a measure of the power output in relation to engine size.

L HEAD An American term for a side valve engine, where all the valves are contained within the cylinder block.

LITTLE END The end of the connecting rod where the piston is. The little end bearing is significantly smaller than that at the big end.

LITRES A litre is 1,000 cubic centimetres (cc), and engine sizes are often quoted as a number and fraction of litres, for example 3.5-litres (3,500 cc).

MAIN BEARING The bearing at the base of the connecting rod which links the connecting rod to the crankshaft.

MPG (OR M.P.G.) Abbreviation for miles per gallon.

MPH (OR M.P.H.) Abbreviation for miles per hour.

NATURALLY ASPIRATED An engine which does not have forced induction through a supercharger or turbocharger.

OHV (OR O.H.V.) Abbreviation for overhead valve, where the valves are in the cylinder had rather than the block, as in a side valve engine.

OHC (OR O.H.C.) Abbreviation for overhead camshaft, usually implying a single camshaft as opposed to dual overhead camshafts.

OVER-SLUNG CHASSIS A chassis where the sprung axle is below the chassis frame.

OVER-SQUARE ENGINE Where the bore is greater than the stroke.

PLAIN BEARING Unlike a ball or roller bearing, a plain bearing is where the rotating shaft is supported just by a ring of soft metal. This is by far the most common form of bearing.

PUSHROD A pushrod is a long rod, driven by a camshaft set low in the engine, which actuates the valves at the top of the engine.

RPM (OR R.P.M.) Abbreviation for revolutions per minute, a measure of the rotational speed of the engine.

RAC HP An early taxation measurement in the UK, first used in 1910 by the RAC at the invitation of the British Government. The RAC hp is given by the formula:

$$\text{RAC hp} = D \times D \times n/2.5$$

Where D is the engine bore, and n is the number of cylinders. The 2.5 was derived from typical cylinder pressure and piston speeds.

ROLLER BEARING Similar to a ball bearing, but where the balls are replaced by small rollers.

ROOTS SUPERCHARGER A form of supercharger where the compression is achieved via two figure-of-eight rotors rotating in close contact.

S8 An abbreviation for straight eight.

SIDE VALVE Valves which are wholly contained within the cylinder block not the cylinder head. Side valves stopped being commonly used shortly after the Second World War when overhead valves became popular.

SLEEVE VALVE in a sleeve valve engine, there are no normal poppet valves. Instead inlet and exhaust are governed by sleeves concentric with the cylinder, and these either oscillate up and down or rotate to open and close valve openings.

SQUARE ENGINE an engine where the bore is the same as the stroke.

STROKE the total distance the piston travels within its cylinder as the crankshaft rotates.

SUPERCHARGED an engine where the fuel/air mixture is forced under pressure into the inlet manifold, offering very significant increases in power.

TANDEM ENGINE this refers to an engine which is, in effect, two separate engines linked together, often on a shared sump. Two tandem four cylinder engines were frequently used in the early days to create a straight eight.

TORQUE The twisting power an engine can produce. It is different from horsepower. Horsepower is a measure of the rate at which torque can be delivered.

TORSIONAL VIBRATION A regular twisting oscillation on the crankshaft or camshaft, common on long engines such as straight eights, caused by each cylinder firing at separate times.

TWIN CAM Another term for dohc, or dual overhead camshafts (see dohc).

TWIN SPARK Where an engine has two sparking plugs in each cylinder. This improves the evenness and speed of combustion.

TWO STAGE SUPERCHARGING A setup where the air or fuel/air mixture passes through two superchargers in tandem, enabling much higher pressurisation than is possible with a single supercharger.

UNDER-SLUNG CHASSIS This is where the axles on a car are suspended above the chassis frame. This allows the vehicle to have a lower profile.

UNDER-SQUARE ENGINE Where the stroke is greater than the bore.

UPDRAFT CARBURETTOR This is where the fuel/air mixture enters the inlet manifold from below. This arrangement can help give the engine a lower profile, but often it is necessary to provide some sort of drip-tray to collect leaked fuel.

V8 An engine where the cylinders are arranged as two blocks of four in a V shape.

VOITURETTE A French term for a small light automobile.

WET LINER This is where the piston runs in a (usually) steel tube which inserted is into the cylinder block but maintaining a gap in which the cooling water circulates. This gives very efficient cooling for the cylinder and pistons.

PHOTO CREDITS

Design:	Jodi Ellis Graphics
Printer:	Interpress Ltd, Hungary
Page Size:	219 mm x 290 mm
Text paper:	130 gsm Garda Matte
End paper:	170 gsm Woodfree Offset
Dust jacket:	150 gsm Glossy Artpaper
Casing:	Foil stamping on front and spine, on black Wibalin, over 3 mm board
Chapter Heads:	38 pt. Notable
Body Text:	9.5 pt. Montserrat Light
Captions:	9.5 pt. Montserrat Medium